MEETING NEEDS

STUDIES IN MORAL, POLITICAL,
AND LEGAL PHILOSOPHY

General Editor: Marshall Cohen

MEETING
NEEDS

David Braybrooke

PRINCETON UNIVERSITY PRESS
PRINCETON, NEW JERSEY

Library of Congress Cataloging in Publication Data
will be found on the last printed page of this book

ISBN 0-691-07727-4 (cloth) 0-691-02259-3 (pbk.)

Publication of this book has been aided by a grant from
the Whitney Darrow Fund of Princeton University Press

This book has been composed in Linotron Palatino

To my children:
May their needs be met
without prejudice to meeting
the needs of others

CONTENTS

vii

CONTENTS

ADVICE TO READERS

With an argument restoring the credit due the concept of needs this book combines a compendium of philosophical reflections on various aspects of the concept. These are, of course, not independent features. Passages present chiefly to fill gaps in the compendium reinforce the argument by helping to lay to rest various particular objections to the use of the concept. However, to follow the main argument on a first reading readers will find the going easier if they skip the starred passages. Starred or unstarred, first reading or last, no passage leaves anything important to the argument, even nuances, in the notes. These have little or nothing to offer besides filling out the documentation for sources named in the text and adding some peripheral bibliographical information. The notes have therefore been relegated to the end of the book, where they will be found keyed to chapters and sections of chapters.

MEETING NEEDS

"What do you think George was doing in the passage?"

"Something we shall soon know," said Emilia.

"Helping himself to the pudding from the table. There was a sight to meet my eyes."

"The sight of a great human need," said Mortimer. "What a dignified experience!" . . .

"Perhaps the wages of a man would dispose of the need for such conduct."

"Do not be foolish, Charlotte. The pudding was not his. . . . Some people might prosecute."

"No, not for a slice of pudding," said Emilia.

"They would hardly like it to be known that he needed it," said Charlotte.

"He did not need it; he merely wanted it," said her husband.

—Ivy Compton-Burnett,
Manservant and Maidservant

"Should further cutbacks in government expenditures be deemed necessary to balance the operating statement, government resources should be relocated [reallocated?] on the basis of needs, not wants."

—John C. Crosbie, M.P.,
Minister of Finance in
the Government of Canada,
1979–80, writing in *The
Financial Post*, 2 October 1982

O N E

THE CHARGES AGAINST THE CONCEPT OF NEEDS

This book aims to show how the concept of needs operates when it is working well and giving firm guidance in the choice of social policies. I shall also examine connections in which the concept breaks down and its guidance lapses. To describe how it operates when it does work well, I shall have continually in view a schema filled out in part by a specific list of basic needs. I shall treat the schema with this list in place as a model, in the sense of a paradigm. The list is, I think, as convincing as any. It will not be part of my purpose, however, to perfect this list. I shall rather be concerned to show how the schema, with any such list, basic or amplified, in place, supplies all the means required to make the concept of needs intelligible and effective, with a distinctive job to do. I shall discuss, with the schema in hand, the place of the concept of needs in reasoning about justice and in utilitarianism, and explain how far the use of the concept can be reconciled with a concern for liberty. I shall outline the dimensions over which the concept expands, running ever greater risks of skepticism and controversy the further it expands beyond some such basic list; and demonstrate how firm ground for the concept can always be restored by moving back from disputed uses toward the list.

The concept of needs differs top and bottom from the concept of preferences. Yet I shall have to show how the two concepts work together. Only in rare limiting cases

5

would social policy ever be directed at meeting needs without any regard for heeding preferences; and everywhere emphasis on needs tends to make social policy heavy-handed. When people's preferences run contrary to their needs, perhaps the project of meeting their needs will have to be suspended. If the project did no more than circulate information about the discrepancy, this itself is liable to be heavy-handed, and unwelcome. When the preferences are compatible with the needs, social policy will try to meet the needs with forms of provision suited to the preferences. Social policy may be in a position, not only to do this, but also to keep some resources free for use according to preferences in matters that do not have to do with needs at all. Assertions of needs, however, always threaten in some degree the carefree gratification of preferences.

I shall have to remove the discredit and confusion into which the concept of needs has fallen with sophisticated thinkers, in particular, on its normative side, with orthodox non-Marxist economists. This discredit and confusion arise in part from philosophical mistakes about what is at issue in the relevant applications of the concept. Among those mistakes are mistaken inferences from observations relating to abuses of the concept. However, the abuses are real, and some of the discredit attaching to the concept comes from legitimate reactions to the abuses. Some discredit comes, with some of the confusion, from perceptions of real limitations in the concept.

I shall postpone discussion of those limitations until the very end of the book, for treatment after my main argument has been completed. It will, I expect, astonish some readers that I shall have found so much to say meanwhile. Yet the connections in which the limitations are most obtrusive—in which the guidance of the concept of needs lapses—do not imply ruin for the concept elsewhere. Elsewhere it has a large and important field of operation. There is, moreover, a great deal to distinguish and notice about the use of the concept in this field—among other things, its use in a simple but trenchant technique for advancing toward unanimous consent for certain policies, thus in effect avoiding the difficulties that social choice theory has found in aggregating preferences.

My original point of departure in this work was the thought that advanced Liberal theory—by which I meant the theory of orthodox non-Marxist economists—had relied on the concept of preferences and neglected (even repudiated) the concept of needs, while Marxist theory had done just the opposite—relied on the concept of needs and neglected the concept of preferences. Was not each tradition thus one-sided and in a position to learn from the other? And if each learned what the other had to teach, would not the two traditions come together on common ground?

I now think that my original formula expressed the complementarity of the two traditions too glibly: The place of needs in Marxist theory is less central and secure than the formula implies. Indeed, Marxism, taking one subtendency with another, may have given less attention to needs than other currents of socialism. On the other hand, Liberalism in practice—Liberalism in office—has inevitably given a good deal of attention to needs.

Nevertheless, the suggestion of complementarity is one that I stand by. The most fundamental issues of politics arise as aspects of the general social task of reconciling attention to needs with attention to preferences. On these issues, Liberalism and Marxism will turn out to be more agreed than opposed. Liberalism reaches that common ground once it abandons any inconsistent and adventitious tolerance of class privileges and acknowledges that due weight must be given to needs. Marxism arrives there, too, once it recognizes the scope for politics even in a classless society and acknowledges that due care must be taken in politics to heed preferences, letting them vary freely from person to person.

My inquiries will thus, I hope, throw light simultaneously on the most fundamental issues of politics and on the present significance of Liberalism and Marxism. They will also, I trust, throw some light on elementary considerations in ethics. What consideration in ethics could be more elementary than the response of human beings to one another's needs? We are certainly not licensed to disregard one another's preferences; but needs make a claim on us more compelling than mere preferences do. An altruism that responds to the claim is a more plausible ingredient of ethics than an altruism generalized over other people's preferences. Needs are more strongly linked to hardship and suffering, which it is surely part of the first business of ethical theory to understand, as it is the first business of ethics to prevent.

Because of this linkage the concept of needs lends itself to formulating a surrogate for utilitarianism more cogent than Bentham's doctrine, which was unwisely precipitate in its emphasis on net pleasure, and more cogent than successor-doctrines based on preferences. The surrogate is more easily reconciled with the concepts of rights and of justice, since in received moral discourse the concept of needs has been intimately associated with these concepts. Part of its cogency, however, arises just from the more decisive impact of the concept of needs on motivation: Even an ethics circumscribed by contractarian principles having to do with rational preferences must grant the importance of attending to needs; and insofar as ethics must appeal to concern for others, needs are more suited than preferences to bringing the appeal home. Historically, utilitarianism has exercised its practical influence through the surrogate of needs and hence has had in practice the advantages of the surrogate.

In spite of the importance to ethics that these observations attest to, the concept of needs has been neglected by philosophers. The neglect is the more astonishing, since the concept is both familiar and controversial. It must be as frequent in everyday use and in discussions of social policy as the concepts of rights and justice; more frequent than the concept of obligations. Psychologists and anthropologists have vigorously contested its value as an explanatory category, however; and, more to my present purposes, economists have vehemently condemned the concept as a category for evaluating policies. The condemnation has, I think, been arrived at without a trial, at any rate, without due process. Let us see what the charges against the concept amount to, and how far the concept of needs escapes them. To characterize the charges, I shall rely, for the moment, on an intuitive understanding of the concept. To answer the charges, I shall develop, in chapters to come, a systematic account.

1.1 Charges against the Explanatory Use of "Needs"

The most abundant and persistent sources of charges against the concept of needs are economists. Their charges fall in the main upon what preoccupies me in this book, the normative use of the concept to assess social policies. There are also charges, pressed by psychologists and anthropologists, against its use in explanations. Perhaps the most sustained attack on this side can be found in the writings of the anthropologist Mary Douglas, who holds that

> The history of anthropology has been one of continual disengagement of theoretical fields from the intrusive assumptions from common sense. In each case enlightenment has followed a decision to ignore the physiological levels of existence which sustain the behavior in question . . . [Let us] therefore rule out, as an unnecessary distraction, the physical uses of goods . . . We can suspend our knowledge that goods serve bodily needs . . . Forget that commodities are good for eating, clothing, and shelter; forget their usefulness . . . Treat them as a nonverbal medium for the human creative faculty . . . Focus on the classifying project to which

9

they are recruited, [where they are used to communicate and stabilize] the categories of culture.

My project with the concept of needs does not require me to quarrel with anything in this position. To be sure, it would be paradoxical indeed for the concept of needs to have no commonplace explanatory use and yet to have the commonplace normative use that I shall be preoccupied with and trying to explicate. But the concept surely does have commonplace explanatory uses. If people realize that their lives depend on providing for certain needs, we may expect them to take steps to provide for them; we explain the steps taken by citing the need. Thus in every climate in which people need shelter, whether it is from cold and snow, from rain, or from the sun, they make provisions for shelter. Furthermore, it is hard to see how people could invoke the concept of needs to evaluate alternative policies before them as persons or groups without our sometimes being able to explain that they chose a certain policy in order to meet a need. Thus, numbers of times, we might have been able to say that the elders of one Iroquois village or another agreed to forego an exciting warparty in order to repair their collapsing longhouse before winter set in.

Strictly read, Douglas does not gainsay such explanations. She herself resorts to the concept of needs for commonplace explanations, and on occasion to the equally commonplace distinction between needs and luxuries (though she holds that the distinction between "physical goods" and "spiritual goods" is a false one). What she is concerned with is getting beyond the commonplace to explain variations in forms of consumption. It is perhaps extravagant of her to declare, "Consumption is a ritual process whose primary function is to make sense of the inchoate flux of events." Yet she may well be correct in thinking that an interesting, comprehensive theory of consumption will come about only through a break of some sort away from commonplace explanations—more of a break than has been made hitherto either in anthropology or in economics. One might even entertain the possibility that such a theory, once arrived at, would invite superseding the concept of needs in its normative use. The attractions of doing so could hardly be assessed, however, unless we first knew what that use amounts to, and how effective it is. To make that out, we need assume at most, on the explanatory side, a commonplace use.

1.2 Charges against the Normative Use: Too Fluid

I shall have only incidental remarks to make hereafter about the explanatory use of the concept of needs and the charges under which it labors there. So it is the attack by economists upon the concept in its normative use that chiefly concerns me. When they have in mind a professional commitment to orthodox, non-Marxist theory, economists react to attempts to use the concept in their presence with the same sort of instantaneous conditioned reflex that champions of sanitation manifest, swatters in hand, when swarms of houseflies invade their kitchens. Or so an unqualified partisan of the concept of needs, which I am not, would be inclined to say. Robert R. Alford cites a study of hospitals by one economist that notes with satisfaction how an earlier study by another economist "took hospital utilization out of the ambiguous category of 'need' and placed it within a demand model." With this precedent in mind, the later study was emboldened to contend that in hospitals which it considered there is "a reasonably satisfactory allocation of resources in terms of the implicit social welfare function," that is to say, a social welfare function established in the market by demands for resources, without any questions raised about the distribution of income between rich and poor.

Ambiguity would threaten the intelligibility of the concept; it is threatened further, in the view of economists, by subjectivity and indeterminacy. Conveying the wisdom of orthodox American economists to a French audience, Jean-Jacques Rosa finds occasion to say,

> The very widespread idea that the consumer is alienated, that false needs are imposed on him, contrary to his true interest, by advertising and distorted information, has an obvious weakness: How does one distinguish true needs from false ones? Where is one to draw the line between them? And who is going to draw it? There cannot be any absolute or objective hierarchy, because everybody makes different choices. There can only be desires and personal preferences.

In this passage, Rosa does more, of course, than question the objectivity and determinacy of the concept. He suggests, as orthodox economists characteristically do, that one will find enormous variation between persons in what they conceive to be their needs. He intimates, again characteristically for his profession and school, that to identify some needs as true ones would be arbitrary and officious.

Economists do not lack support on these points. The variability of needs, everyone will agree, is a theme readily amplified. Not only do needs, as people conceive of their needs, vary from person to person: One person cannot do without a garden; another needs a view. Needs vary enormously, it will be said, between cultures, so much so that the differences in acceptable forms of provision overshadow any verbal gestures at there being common, universal needs. A Masai drinks the blood of cattle; an Eskimo eats blubber; a Buddhist monk needs a bowl of rice with some vegetables. Even in respect to food the differences seem much more important than the abstractly postulated common basis; in respect to clothing, which is as much ornament as necessity anyway, and other matters, the differences are even more striking.

Within a culture, to be sure, people may not be free to choose between the differences; they may (without feeling any loss of freedom) be strictly governed by convention.

But if anyone is ever in a position to choose between conventions, is not the choice just a matter of preference? Needs are so largely determined either by conventions or by preferences that it is misleading, some will charge, to pretend they have a natural footing and idle to try to give them one.

Given the chance, needs may seem ready to expand indefinitely, just like wants or desires, which is one more sign that they are not usefully distinguished from them. Jean Fourastié, who may have wants as much in mind as needs, gives the most elaborate picture of expansion:

The quantity and variety of growing needs, and the marginal position that turn by turn they take among the concerns of a man whose standard of living is rising, may be represented by the image of a series of spheres of increasing radius. The volume of the sphere represents satisfied needs, hence the standard of living; the surface, the needs unmet. In proportion to the increase in the radius of the sphere, the volume of satisfied needs increases, but the needs unmet, far from being reduced simultaneously, grow without stopping . . . Moreover, these marginal needs, represented by an ever increasing spherical surface, become more varied as they grow in number.

However, this picture seems too systematic; and hence, one would think, too comfortable to suit most economists. Fourastié himself does not attack the concept of needs for its expansiveness. The concept of needs may expand indefinitely; but other economists, and not only economists, would hold that it is too fluid and too unstructured to expand in any orderly way. It expands amid continual confusion. Has not every appliance with which a North American household is equipped been argued to meet a need? But what sense can a person make of needing an electric toothbrush or a color TV as well as needing a furnace? Some confusion may have crept in already, when one moved on from needing a furnace to needing an air conditioner. Too fluid, the concept of needs can evidently be adapted without much argument to calling anything whatever that a person very much wants a need; or even wants enough to make a point of pressing for. Too unstructured, it seems, in spite of being conventional in conception, to have no limiting conventions within which a principled resistance to such abuses could be organized.

If there were any grounds for interfering with people's preferences, or even for criticizing them, which economists aroused to full professional frenzy are almost equally loath to concede, needs might serve as such a ground. To try to make use of the concept of needs in this way, however, would, according to economists and others, be officious and paternalistic. Not only may the people whose preferences are interfered with, or criticized, by citing needs that those preferences contravene, be ready to dispute the needs; they may claim the liberty to make their own decisions about the relative weights that they are going to give the needs, disputed or not, as against their preferences. It is paternalism to interfere; it is a step toward paternalism to criticize. Given the weaknesses just surveyed, it looks worse than paternalism; it looks like paternalism hand in hand with fraud.

1.3 Charges against the Normative Use: Too Easily Satisfied

Reeling from this barrage of objections, one may find it difficult to think of anything to say on behalf of the concept of needs. Suppose, however, that, suspecting the barrage may not have hit everything in the field on which it has descended, one catches at the commonplace idea that human beings, wherever they find themselves, in whatever culture, have a need for food; a need for exercise; and other needs universally shared. Suppose one is so naive and stubborn as to insist that there are such needs and that meeting them can be imposed as a perfectly definite condition on social policies. Then the economists and their allies may shift to another line of attack entirely. They may concede that there is firm footing for such needs, and that the concept can be used pretty well free of the objections laid down in the previous barrage if the concept is confined to such matters. Confined to them, it will be suggested, the concept does not amount to much. It does not discriminate between social systems enough to go more than a short distance toward determining the allocation of resources. C. E. Lindblom remarks,

> Even at today's prices, in the United States an adult can meet his physical nutritional requirements for an expenditure of not more than 75 cents a day. What he spends beyond that is for variety, palatability, and other intangibles; and even the poorest persons in the society insist on the intangibles rather than a cheap synthetic diet for nutrition alone.

Lindblom here is chiefly concerned to make the point that the motivations of economic activity go far beyond needs. In several later passages of the same book, he makes what is in effect telling normative use of the concept of needs to remark defects in the performance of the American economic and political system. Yet in those passages, though particular instances of needs figure (medical care, nutrition, bodily safety), the concept itself is not invoked explicitly. Lindblom does not see these instances as occasions for disavowing the suggestion that many will take from the passage quoted, namely, that insofar as needs can be firmly established as such, they can be met quite cheaply; or for disavowing the implication of short distance to be found in that suggestion. When anything like a comprehensive list of basic needs is taken into account, the suggestion becomes manifestly false, and the implications are forestalled. Safety does not come cheap; nor does sanitation.

The suggestion nevertheless has wide appeal. Socialists,

as well as orthodox Liberal economists, may be tempted to adopt it: For does not socialism look forward to abundance, and may not abundance be conceived of as circumstances in which needs are met so easily that meeting them goes without saying? Or at any rate without pondering? Socialists and others might also be persuaded that most societies which men have known even outside socialism or latter-day capitalism have been societies in which needs could be met—or could have been met—well within the bounds of the resources available. Certainly, with warrant in the texts of Marx, socialists would apprehend that stress on meeting needs is a device for drastically limiting the horizon of social policy. The concept of needs would thus seem to offer not only a very undiscriminating test of the productivity and potential benefits of social systems but a test that is ideologically pernicious as well.

In reply, one might say that where the concept does discriminate between the benefits attainable in different social systems, it offers an all-important service; and where it does not, it can still furnish a heart-rending test of actual performance. Cheap as nutrition (by itself) may be, there are still old ladies starving to death in Washington, D.C.; and tens of thousands of people homeless through the winter in New York and Chicago. It will turn out, however, that the main point to seize for a theoretical understanding of the concept of needs is the way the suggestion that it goes only a short distance reflects, distortedly, the technique with which the concept of needs is used as a device for guiding social policies. The technique depends on keeping the task of meeting needs well within the scope of available resources. Success in doing so is a virtue that the suggestion about short distance gets upside down.

1.4 Charges against the Normative Use: Too Clumsy

There is still a third line of attack that economists may pursue against the concept of needs. Everything that is salvageable in the concept as making good sense about issues important or unimportant, they may contend, can be captured by the concept of preferences and the analytical treatment that economics gives to preferences; hence the concept of needs is a superfluous concept. Moreover, it is unnecessarily and misleadingly rigid. In particular, it apparently claims something like lexicographical priority, which would imply that at least until needs have been met at accepted minimum standards, the tiniest increment of provision for needs is to be preferred to any quantity of provision for anything else. The minimum standards are so far conventional that this sort of priority is not plausible; it will break down whenever a sufficiently dramatic choice is presented. But, waiving lexicographical priority, everything that is done with the concept of needs can be done by mapping preferences by conventional (indifference-curve) analysis, so as to show the very high value placed on the initial increments of provision under certain heads.

If some of these heads concern the means—the conditions—of getting any other preferences heeded, one would expect the preferences of informed people to reflect such facts. In the required quantities, the means will have a high value; the demand directed upon them will be inelastic. They may even be spoken of, and thought of, as objects of needs; but the needs here are entirely subordinate to preferences, and statements about them can, in principle, be entirely replaced by statements about what informed people prefer. To the extent that informed people have, out of prudence, the same preferences, the description of their preferences will show it; and the difficulties about variations from person to person, variations from culture to culture, and indefinite possibilities of expansion become no difficulties at all, since there are no difficulties about supposing that preferences vary in all these ways.

This objection, too, can be refuted; and in due course I shall proceed to refute it. I shall point out that the idea of preferences for the conditions of getting any other preferences heeded serves to take the place of the concept of needs only insofar as it trades on an unreduced allusion to that concept. I shall also argue that we cannot make sense of the relation of a person's preferences to her interests without invoking a thorough-going distinction between preferences and needs. Moreover, attempting to suppress the distinction makes the notion of a common interest paradoxically relative to the contingent set of policies that have actually been proposed.

1.5 Foundations for Charges in Real Abuses

Nevertheless, refutable or not, there is much to learn from this objection, just as there was much to learn from the objections and charges brought forward on the two previous lines of attack. In the face of the first line of attack in particular, with its bundle of charges about indeterminacy, no one can deny that in some respects—for example, in what provisions are familiar—there are variations in needs between persons and between cultures. The variations between cultures imply that needs are affected by conventions and suggest that truly general—universalized—arguments for meeting any specific need with specific forms of provision may be hard to find. The normative force of the concept, which is also undeniable, thus becomes suspect; and suspicion may turn into outrage when one reflects on the abuses to which the concept lends itself.

Indeed, the concept attracts abuse. Much hangs on abusing it; for, wary as sophisticated people may be about demands put forward under it, to get something accepted as a need still makes a substantial difference to getting it attended to as an object of policy. That it should be attended to (if it is not automatically met) ceases to be a political issue; the issue becomes, how. But acceptance as a need may have been arrived at through unscrupulous stretching; and even when it is at bottom a genuine need, organized political causes and coherent class interests may stretch the conventions to sanction dubious forms of provision—private cars rather than public transportation, perhaps.

Abuses are perhaps easiest to see on the international scene, where people in the rich countries take themselves to need so many things that after all there is little to spare for people in the poor countries. Even in domestic politics, however, what middle-class people conceive that they need (music programs in the schools) can become highly controversial when the urgent problems of the poor are brought into the picture. The needs of the less prosperous classes may occasionally be inflated in turn, by politicians and bureaucrats seeking larger funds for bigger agencies. Perhaps in this connection abuse of the concept of needs facilitates abuse of the concept of social justice, leading people to claim under the heading of justice things that the poor or their friends just happen to fancy for them. Certainly thinkers who fear abuse of the concept of social justice (some of them to the point of wishing the concept away altogether) have reason to fear along with it, or in lieu of it, abuse of the concept of needs. Marxists, it is true, would contend that the abuse runs more often in the other direction, contracting the claims of needs and with it the relief of poverty to a minimum far below what would make a full human life possible. Not all abuses of the concept are expansive ones.

Not only does the concept attract abuse, which it would do, given its significance, even if it were relatively hard to abuse. It is spectacularly easy to abuse. All that variability and conventionality prepare people to accept more, or at least to find nothing incongruous when more is forthcoming. Moreover, inevitably, some of the variations observed and some of the conventions concern relatively peripheral matters, or relatively unfamiliar ones, and perhaps very specific forms of provisions for these; so that people are prepared to find nothing incongruous in having the concept of needs stretched to cover all these things. At the very heart of the concept, as close to a firm footing for it as it ever gets in ordinary use, conventionality takes the place, with out renouncing the claims of biological necessity: What people are held to need for subsistence is always considerably more than the biological minimum required to sustain life. Is there pretense here that establishes a precedent for pretense wherever the concept stretches?

The pretenses—the abuses—aggravate the paternalism that haunts the concept. Yet the paternalism might well have been thought an intolerable danger even were the concept of needs used with utmost sobriety. It is not only with economists that the concept has fallen into disrepute. Clients of the professions and of the bureaucracies have organized under the banner of "rights" to contest the rhetoric of liberal reformists, who have relied on the concept of needs, and relied on the good will of active, paternalistic professionals, in bureaucracies and out of them, to improve the condition of the dependent disadvantaged. Reliance on the concept, as well as reliance on the professionals who were to act under the concept, it is now widely felt, was misplaced; the needs do not get met. Accordingly, arrangements that embody paternalism are suspect, on practical grounds as well as the moral ground of threatening personal liberty; and so must be a concept that can so easily lead to such arrangements.

1.6 Mixed Prospects of Vindication

Various and densely arrayed though these charges and cries of abuse may be, they do not represent all the currents of contemporary thought that have moved one way or another upon the concept of needs. Besides the currents moving against the concept of needs, there have been some notable movements in its favor. It has, of course, never fallen out of use in discussions engaging the general public. Lately, it has received renewed attention from social scientists under the banner of "social indicators," including life expectancy, level of education, employment, crime rates, which they are going to invoke in the course of drawing up "social accounts" of the performance of social and political systems. Economists, taking some liberties with their commitments to orthodox theory, have contributed substantially to the development of social indicators. They have proposed a Basic Necessities Index as a means of monitoring the condition of the poor. They have adopted "a Basic Needs Approach" to international aid for "Southern" countries struggling with economic difficulties. Long before these ventures started up, moreover, economists had ways of their own of getting some of the work done that people seek to do with the concept of needs. Richard Musgrave's concept of "merit goods"—goods the consumption of which social policy is to encourage, for example, school luncheons, low-cost housing, education—is the most important example.

Whether the concept deserves more favor or more disfavor is not, however, something that one can determine without a careful account of it. The number and force of the charges against the concept imply, or come near to implying, that even if after such an account the judgment upon the concept is favorable, the favor will be qualified: It will be favor conditional upon the observance of certain precautions in the use of the concept; and those precautions may include renouncing any attempt to use it in some connections—allocation of resources to medical care; triage— where it has been specially looked to for guidance. Foreseeing such results, one would be unwise to be an unqualified partisan of the concept of needs beforehand; and even more unwise to be one afterward, with such results in hand. Indeed, it is best to keep open the possibility that when as much has been done as one can think of to make the concept intelligible and its use convincing it will still be beset by so many difficulties that it should be discarded.

Yet, meanwhile, it is only reasonable to see what can be said for the concept. The objections that I have taken from economists and others furnish a program for clarifying it, and for identifying precautions that might be attached to it.

21

The account of the concept of needs that I shall offer in the following chapters will aim to remove, by drawing distinctions between uses or senses, any ambiguity or appearance of ambiguity ascribed to the concept. It will thus (if it succeeds) remove one cause of indeterminacy. To arrive at a fully determinate concept, however, the account must go on to deal with the apparent variation in respect to needs between persons and likewise with the apparent variation between cultures. If these variations are accepted (to some extent) as genuine, can they be accommodated in a list of universal needs, ascribed to all human beings in all cultures? Or will a determinate concept require many lists, at the limit one for each person, though perhaps the lists for different cultures will throughout exhibit some similarities?

The account will deal with the suggestion that the concept of needs goes too short a distance in its demands on resources to amount to much as a guide to policy. Some delicate balancing may be required on this point. The account will predictably find that the concept of needs in fact makes considerable demands on resources, even when it is firmly and soberly used. Will there not then be some difficulty in asserting that it is part of the technique of using the concept to confine the demands within the limits of the resources? There are, nevertheless, as will appear, good reasons for making this assertion.

Equally sensitive footwork will be required in the discussion of conventionality. It may be easy enough, in the account, to distinguish the surprisingly many different ways in which needs are conventional; and their number may not itself be an embarrassment. However, will it be easy to make out an honest—a defensible—relation between conventions as to the minimum standards for meeting needs and natural necessities as established by biology (and possibly psychology)? I have already alluded to pretense. Do people, in the use of the concept of needs, allow themselves to pretend that what is merely conventional should have the credit of natural necessity? Should they get away with such a pretense if it occurs? That the pretense might be rather the result of sloppy thinking than of deliberate fraud would not vindicate the concept.

Rescued, if it can be rescued, from any appearance of fraud, the concept of needs might still turn out to be less suited, even for its designated jobs, than alternative concepts, in particular, the concept of preferences, which might seem ready to do much more work besides. I shall try in my account to demonstrate that the concept of needs cannot be reduced to the concept of preferences, or easily superseded by it. Nevertheless, the account should explain how far the concept of needs is adapted to work in conjunction with the concept of preferences. What sort of priority is to be given needs if it is not to be lexicographical priority? It will have to be a sort of priority that allows a good deal of room for heeding people's preferences in some degree.

It will also have to be a sort of priority that allows for reconciling the concept of needs with several other general standards for social policy. Due allowance for heeding people's preferences should block any possibility of gathering much credit for paternalism from the concept of needs. This will go a long way toward reconciling the use of the concept with the pursuit of liberty; and it may well improve the chances of meeting needs effectively—of not only making provisions for needs, but also of getting people to take up the provisions. Liberty, along with preferences, can be served substantially here and elsewhere even while needs are accorded what I shall call "strict final priority." So can justice; I shall show how needs with such priority inevitably figure in reasoning about justice under several different conceptions of it. I shall also devote a chapter to seizing upon certain conceptual relations between needs, preferences, liberty, and justice to recast, at least in outline, the theory of utilitarianism.

In all of these discussions, strict final priority for needs will be presupposed. A looser sort of priority—what I shall call "role-relative precautionary priority"—must be recognized, however, as matching more closely in upshot the actual use of the concept of needs in real-world politics. It is closer at the same time to making as full an allowance for liberty as some people would require, even at some cost to strict justice, or to strict utilitarianism. I shall complete my discussion of how attention to needs is to be reconciled with attention to preferences with a chapter in which this looser sort of priority will be defined.

I shall discuss all these matters holding in check—at least for the duration of the chapters concerned—the tendency for the needs to expand in number and variety. This expansion brings some good with it; for one thing, it enables the concept of needs to make a better match with the requirements of a full human life. On the other hand, expansion threatens the determinacy of the concept; jeopardizes its moral force; and tends to restrict unduly the variety of human life-plans. Often, it is best to retreat from expansion. I shall try to give a balanced treatment of expansion in the next to last chapter.

Expansion may bring about breakdown more quickly; but even without expansion the concept of needs breaks down in a number of connections. It breaks down if morally embarrassing needs have to be acknowledged. More important, it breaks down—imminently if not currently—in application to the prolongation of human life and in application to the relief of poverty in the world at large. In my final chapter, I shall deal frankly with these points of collapse. They are very serious; but they do not discredit the concept of needs in other applications. This is fortunate, since we have nothing to take its place.

DIALOGUE

CRITICAL READER: *Nothing to take its place! Why not utility, which has been so beautifully refined by the economists and lends itself to such subtle mathematical theories?*

NOT-YET-REPENTANT AUTHOR: *Refined, beautiful, an instrument for subtle theories, yes. But what use is it in practical politics? What use will it ever have? There are no individual maps. There's no calculus. There's not even a census comparing the effects on people's utilities of different policies. When is there going to be?*

READER: *But there are approximations to utility. We can look at the prices that people are willing to pay for various policies; or at the effects of policies on incomes.*

AUTHOR: *Very bad approximations. If you brought back the older, Benthamite conception of utility, you'd find that these approximations just beg the questions that utility then had the virtue of keeping people in mind of. The prices that people are willing to pay depend on the money they have in hand, which varies enormously. It's the same with the effects of given gains or losses on their incomes. Though we don't need utility to make the point, and utility can even be mishandled to obscure it, it's clear that taking $1000 away from a part-time secretary who has an income of $6000 can be expected to make a great deal more impact on her than taking that amount away from a movie star with an income of $600,000. With the newer concep-*

25

tion of utility, a construction from preferences precluding interpersonal comparisons, utility itself leaves out of account differences in personal holdings along with anything like practical evidence. Preoccupation with utility is a fantastically gross distortion of theory away from practice. If anything is an ideological distortion, isn't this? It evades all the hard questions about current systems.

READER: *And you propose to face those hard questions with the concept of needs? But it's so slippery; so untidy; so boring to boot.*

AUTHOR: *Slippery, yes, as I've already admitted; untidy, too. I shall be reducing the impression of untidiness and taking steps to get the slipperiness under control. Is the concept of needs boring? Sophisticated people think it's boring. But I think that it's boring—commonplace—because it works. Nowhere in philosophy do we need more patience with the commonplace if we are to see things clear.*

READER: *But commonplace concepts are likely to break down under the demands of comprehensive theories. That's why sophisticated people are interested in utility.*

AUTHOR: *Sophisticated people are not going to make anything practical of utility. But I agree; that's one reason why sophisticated people fly from the concept of needs. Because that concept, though it works lots of the time in practical politics, doesn't always work even there, and because it works rather cumbersomely even when it does work, sophisticated people choose instead to give their regard to a concept that doesn't work at all outside their theories (and maybe an occasional laboratory exercise).*

READER: *So it's too bad it's boring?*

AUTHOR: *"Boring"? I'll say a word more about "boring." Suppose you find your impressions exiting from the subject very different from your impressions entering. In the end, a clear view of the concept of needs will turn upside down the ideas currently prevailing in philosophy and social thought about a lot of things. Consider them: altruism; the reduction of interests to preferences; the prospects of escape from the impasses of social choice theory; the prospects of consensus about social policy; the effectiveness of utilitarianism. Is it boring to turn all these ideas upside down?*

READER: *Revolutionary sentiments! And yet you say you're not an unqualified partisan of the concept of needs?*

AUTHOR: *I'm an unqualified partisan of examining the concept of needs patiently.*

THE CONCEPT OF NEEDS
IN NORMATIVE USE
APPLIED TO SOCIAL POLICY:
BASIC ACCOUNT

The confusion about the concept of needs arises in part from the complication that the term "need" is used for adventitious needs, like a need for a spinnaker, or for a typewriter, which come and go with particular projects, as well as for course-of-life needs, like a need for exercise, or for a mate, which every human being may be expected to have at least at some stage of life. In both these connections, there is the further complication that the term is sometimes used to refer to a need that is not being met, and to call attention to the deficiency; but sometimes used also to refer to a need that has been met all along, and that is going to go on being met. In the latter cases, the persistent cases, there is an implication about deficiency; but it is not one that, as in the episodic cases, concerns an actual deficiency. The implication is rather that should the need cease to be met, a deficiency of some importance would appear, which anyone interested in having the need met might be expected to call attention to.

2.1 The Relational Formula: Illuminating but Not the Last Word

Importance—how much importance? And who should be interested in having it met? A number of people who have

thought about the concept of needs have come to the conclusion that the key to answering these questions is to apply to any need the relational formula "N needs x in order
to y." Once this formula has been filled in, one can judge
the importance of the need by the importance of the end y,
or, more exactly, by the importance of N's attaining that
end, both to N and to other people who are concerned
about him or who will be affected. At least, one can make
such a judgment if the relational formula does not come up
again, through a question pressed about N's need for y and
demanding that this need, too, be considered within the
formula.

Unfortunately, the formula often does come up again,
over and over, which leads some people to found a sort of
skepticism about needs on the formula. Thus it is all very
well to learn that N needs fresh bat's urine to finish his experiment on biological clocks; but does he need to finish his
experiment on biological clocks? And if he needs to do that
to keep his job as an experimental zoologist, does he need
to keep his job? Perhaps he is growing stale in it. All along
the line, the ends, and with them the needs, seem arguable.
Nevertheless, skeptical effect or no, the application and
reapplication of the formula can be illuminating, because in
a rich context of ends, projects, and activities it maps the
place of the need encountered in the first instance.

I agree that questions insisting on the relational formula
often uncover illuminating information. I am even ready to
agree that nothing that cannot be fitted into the relational
formula can be regarded as a need. However, not all the
champions of the relational formula have seen that it gives
disappointingly unilluminating results when it is applied to
certain course-of-life needs, to wit, the most obvious and
basic ones. Consider, for example, the assertion that N
needs food and water, or that he needs exercise. How is the
relational formula to be filled out in these cases? "N needs
food and water in order to live"? "N needs exercise in order
to function normally (or, robustly)"? These expressions

30

make good enough sense; but they are hardly illuminating; they are perfectly banal.

Yet they have a certain importance; they stand at the limits of the use of the relational formula. No further information bearing on the justification of N's need for food or water or exercise is to be got from applying the formula to a supposed need to live. It is true, whether people go on living or, living, function normally or robustly depends in part on whether they want to, a contingent matter. Sometimes they will not want to, and sometimes this fact will deserve respect; sometimes they will want to take great risks with their lives, even though they want to live, and this fact will deserve respect, too. They may in these connections or elsewhere disregard their own needs. At times we may have to disregard their needs, or at least decide that we cannot meet them.

Nevertheless, one cannot sensibly ask, using the language of needs, "Does N need to live?" or "Does N need to function normally (robustly)?" N does not have to explain or justify aiming to live, or aiming to function normally. It is not the only end that he might be expected to have as a moral agent; for one thing it notoriously does not automatically harmonize even with the same end pursued by other agents. However, there is no more fundamental end that he could invoke to explain or justify this one. Being essential to living or to functioning normally may be taken as a criterion of being a basic need. Questions about whether needs are genuine, or well-founded, come to the end of the line when the needs have been connected with life or health.

Indeed, they may already have come to the end of the line when the needs have been connected with keeping important parts of the body. We can put "a need to keep important parts of one's body" in one version or another of the relational formula: "N needs to keep important parts of his body in order to live normally (or well)." The effect, however, if it is not banal, is forced. It seems at least equally

31

consonant with the language of needs to treat keeping important parts of the body not as a need subordinate to living or normal functioning but as an ultimate end on the same footing. To show that a person will lose an arm unless she has x (a shield on her machine, say) suffices to establish that she needs x (even though she still has another arm, and could cope with life without this one).

2.2 At the Limits of the Relational Formula, a List of Course-of-Life Needs

At these limits, where the relational formula finally touches ground in basic course-of-life needs, some questions about the importance of needs reach firm answers at last. One virtue of pressing questions with the relational formula is just to trace needs ultimately derivable from course-of-life needs back to such firm ground. Otherwise, the formula goes on coming up as long as ingenuity can keep it going; and, when ingenuity finally lapses, runs out of space with the assertion that N simply finds pleasure or enjoyment in pursuing a certain project. That may not be a bad reason; but it is not a reason that falls within the bounds of course-of-life needs. Even if a number of people share the project— so that there are, for example, lots of people curious about the outcome of experiments on biological clocks—and the project gains some importance thereby, it is not in the end a matter of need. All the needs involved turn out to be adventitious ones. They depend on preferences. By contrast, course-of-life needs do not depend on preferences: People have a need for exercise regardless of what they wish, prefer, want otherwise, or choose. They have the need even if they do not much care to live or be healthy.

Will there be more agreement on course-of-life needs than on adventitious needs? It is course-of-life needs that are crucial to assessing social policy. The more skeptical champions of the relational formula find it easy to picture people as hopelessly at odds about needs because of having different ends; and it is certainly true that people differ a good deal in the projects that give rise to their adventitious needs. In principle, however, there is no reason why people could not agree in observing which projects are to be ascribed to which people, and what adventitious needs derive from the different projects. Putting aside for the moment the question of agreeing that the needs ought to be met, fiddlers need fiddles; photographers need cameras. In principle, people should be able to do at least this much in determining course-of-life needs. Can they do more? Will they ascribe the same course-of-life needs to everyone? Or supposing that the lists of needs which they would independently offer to be ascribed to everyone differ in some items, especially if the lists are carried to great lengths, is there not still some minimal list on which they would all agree?

2.21 A Family of Lists

I shall argue that there is; in fact, that there is a family of such minimal lists. The main business of this chapter will be to show how such a List of Matters of Need is associated with Minimum Standards of Provision for each such matter; to supply a Criterion by which the List and the Standards can be generated; and to set forth a Principle of Precedence that gives course-of-life needs thus accounted for priority over preferences. In the course of giving this account, I shall systematically distinguish between the population—the linguistic community—that has the concept of needs and the reference population to which the needs are ascribed; the two populations may not always coincide, or even intersect. I shall also (in the discussion of the Criterion) try to explain systematically how the needs on the List are identified. For the moment, however, I shall proceed more informally, taking up some lists publicly suggested as lists of needs ascribable to all human beings and asking how these lists might be revised and supplemented. What would be a reasonably rich, nonredundant list of course-of-life needs, which people generally would agree have as a matter of fact to be met in order for life and normal functioning to continue?

Two lists of human needs, given respectively by the economist Jan F. Drewnowski, writing under the auspices of the United Nations, and by the Marxist writer Ernest Mandel can serve as examples. I juxtapose two lists of "social indicators" given by Nestor E. Terleckyj of the National Planning Association, Washington, and by the OECD.

These lists furnish useful evidence respecting convergence on content. They are not, as they stand, very satisfactory lists of needs, however. They may serve well enough as lists of "social concerns" without falling in with the grammar of "needs," but some of the headings do not seem, strictly speaking, to name needs at all. They are headings that could not without anomaly be substituted in

Course-of-Life Needs

Drewnowski (UN)	Mandel	Terleckyj	OECD
Nutrition	Food	Health and	Health
Shelter	Clothing	safety	Individual develop-
Health	and shelter	Education,	ment through
Education	(and warmth in	skills, and	learning
Leisure	some climates)	income	Employment and
Security	Protection against	Human	quality of work-
(personal	animals, climate	habitat	ing life
safety,	Desire to decorate	Finer things	Time and leisure
economic	Sex	Freedom,	Command over
security)	Reproduction	justice,	goods and
Environment	Hygiene	and har-	services
(cultural, social,	Health care	mony	Physical environ-
and physical)	To increase one's		ment
	knowledge (ex-		Personal safety and
	tending into		the administra-
	enriching one's		tion of justice
	leisure)		Social opportunity
			and participation

a form of words like "People have a need for x." Thus "desire to decorate" (Mandel), "physical environment" (OECD), and "environment (cultural, social and physical)" (Drewnowski) all fail the test of substitution. Perhaps "health" might pass the test as naming a cluster of needs; but if this is so, one of the lists seems confused about genus and species, for it gives both health and specific needs falling under health: "nutrition" and "shelter."

In respect to the concept of needs, there is another sort of redundancy on three of the lists. Drewnowski gives "economic security"; Terleckyj, "education, skills, and income"; the OECD, "employment and quality of working life" and "command over goods and services." These all represent efforts to make sure that people have the income required to meet the terms on which the forms of provision for their needs—as specified under other headings—are available. (I give the phrase "forms of provision" a technical twist, by extending it to cover every direct means of meeting a need, whether freely available in nature or obtained only by elaborate and costly efforts. If a person has such a means in hand, then the need in question has been provided for and met, though in some cases the person may still waste the means.) There may be important needs that having jobs directly satisfy; there may also be important needs that having an income, or more exactly, the discretion which comes with an income, satisfies. I shall not take them up here. Here I wish to do no more than maintain that both jobs and incomes, so far as they are required to obtain forms of provisions for other needs, are already embraced by lists of those needs; if one says those needs are to be met, one says already that whatever is required to obtain the forms of provision must itself be present (provided, in the technically extended sense). Thus for the reason cited it is redundant to put jobs or incomes on the lists.

2.22 A List to Represent the Family

Freely consolidating the lists in the table, eliminating redundancies, and asking what else would be of comparable importance to life and functioning, one may arrive at the following List of course-of-life needs, taken, abstracting from specific forms of provision, as generalized Matters of Need. The List of Matters of Need has two parts.

The first part is strongly colored by notions about physical functioning. It includes

1. *The need to have a life-supporting relation to the environment*
2. *The need for food and water*
3. *The need to excrete*
4. *The need for exercise*
5. *The need for periodic rest, including sleep*
6. *The need (beyond what is covered under the preceding needs) for whatever is indispensable to preserving the body intact in important respects*

The second part, though it has connections with physical functioning that make it impossible to draw a hard and fast line between the two parts, has to do more with functioning as a social being. The second part includes

7. *The need for companionship*
8. *The need for education*
9. *The need for social acceptance and recognition*
10. *The need for sexual activity*
11. *The need to be free from harassment, including not being continually frightened*
12. *The need for recreation*

The List may be kept free of redundancy by taking due care about such dangers as having the third need included under the first, or having the seventh and the ninth needs merge. Suitable definitions and suitable rulings about borderline cases will suffice.

Is the List complete? That is a much harder question to deal with. Though the List does not have to be complete to be effective in assessing policies, traditional thinking about needs calls for a complete list, and is inclined to treat such a list as the one just given as a complete list, or tantamount to one. Many needs, among them important ones like the need for safety, the need for medical care, and maybe the need for psychotherapy, can be derived from the needs that are on the List; so their absence is no argument against its completeness. On the other hand, it is quite easy to think of further matters of need that could not easily be derived from the List as it stands: for example, the need for some stress; the need to have at least some of one's preferences heeded; the need for meaningful work; the need for social orientation; perhaps the need to be sure, in the popular psychological sense, of one's identity.

Moreover, cogent philosophical reasons argue against holding that any such List could ever be completed. For how could it be completed without setting a limit to the categories that are to be used and the distinctions drawn in describing human beings, their environment, and the relations between them and their environment? It would be unjustifiable to set such a limit; and without it, even if one thinks the possibility of making new discoveries with present concepts might someday fade out, one will always confront the possibility of making them with categories newly invented. Given that human beings have certain features, never distinguished before, then the environment must have certain others, which themselves might have been previously uncategorized, or else those beings will not live or function well. Before the work of Selye and others, the features that have interested them in the human beings undergoing stress and equally the features of the environment that supply the stress may not have been categorized, at least not defined, in the ways that led not only to findings about the causes of too much stress (Selye's main interest), but also to findings about the unsettling effects of too little. So stress may perhaps furnish an example of a need discovered in the course of categorial innovation. In Alvin Gouldner's claim that a fatal collapse of personal morale may ensue from the absence of struggle, of "agonic" factors in life, the category evidently can find an innovating name.

As it stands, complete or incomplete, without further elaboration, the List of Matters of Need is full enough to refute dismissive suggestions that the concept of needs goes too short a distance in allocating resources to make much difference to policy. Even if people's nutritive requirements can be met for 75 cents a day per capita, their clothing, shelter, and fuel will still have to be paid for; in populous societies, the need to excrete calls for enormous outlays on sanitary engineering works. The dismissive suggestions do not take into account the expense of furnishing the full range of provisions, physical and social, indicated by the List. Nor do they take into account the hardship or suffering entailed by not furnishing the provisions. In some cases these effects are not easily expressed in money: What value is to be put on a man's legs, or his life? Sometimes, too, the effects are not easily prevented by any means within the reach of inexpensive provisions. Safety precautions in industry are forms of provision required both by the need for a life-supporting relation to the environment and by the need to preserve the body intact. They are often both expensive and insufficient. In the asbestos industry, and perhaps in others, nobody knows how to make them sufficient within socially tolerable limits of expense.

2.3 *Minimum Standards of Provision*

People who, having the concept of needs, agree that the matters on the List are course-of-life needs, will also agree that with each of them are associated Minimum Standards of Provision.

2.31 Linguistic Community with Concept: Reference Population with Needs

I shall begin at this point to make use of the distinction between the people who have the concept, and with it a consensus upon the List and the Minimum Standards, and the people to whom the needs are ascribed. The latter set of people form the Reference Population, which may differ in membership from the set of people who have the concept. Whether the needs of the Reference Population have been met or not is to be determined by observing the condition of its members. What their needs are, met or unmet, is to be determined by inquiring what the concept of needs means to the people who have the concept, and this inquiry must embrace the Minimum Standards of Provision as well as the Matters of Need. According to the concept, people need provisions in some forms and quantities or other answering to the Matters of Need; and need specifically to have provisions in forms and quantities that are called for by the Minimum Standards of Provision.

In the first instance, the people who have the concept may be thought of as all the fully competent native speakers of English. They, of course, share the concept of needs (or cousin concepts that make discourse about needs translatable) with the speakers of many other languages, to whose thinking I expect the findings of the present study to extend. So far as the concept works well, represented in the linguistic practices of speakers of English, it will work well, given parallel representation, in other languages. Whether, given the terms and nuances of those other languages, one had best think of parallel representation as representation of the same concept by different locutions or of different concepts particular to the locutions in the different languages, I shall not try to decide. So far as I can see, other languages—other linguistic communities—could be embraced either way.

To begin with, however, my findings are arrived at as hypotheses about how speakers of English use the term "needs." Their linguistic practice in using this term to debate social issues, with the nuances of their practice, serves as the focus of my thinking about the concept. I am ready to formalize—to idealize—to a degree my account of the practice, but I present the account with specific tests of it always in mind. It is as hypotheses contributing to a perspicuous account of a specific practice in English that I put my findings up for immediate test by philosophical disputation (dialectic). If the findings survive this test, by all means let the hypotheses be extended to embrace the terms and nuances—the practices—of other languages. They would then confront a further test; it would be nice to assume that, coming second, it would be an easier one.

Just what reference population are speakers of English, in their practice of using the term "needs," to be supposed to have in mind? Not, I think, a very exactly circumscribed reference population. The List of needs has been generated by considering what "human beings" must have if they are to continue to live and function. However, though the people with the concept may, far from excluding any members of the human race, intend their assertions about needs to embrace all human beings, they are likely to have centrally in view themselves and other people—kith and kin and fellow citizens in similar, familiar circumstances. So I shall impute for the time being to the population that has the concept the assumption of a Reference Population with the following character: It is determinately bounded so as to include all the people living in the English-speaking parts of the world; it is not determinately bounded so as to exclude anyone else. When I asked, what matters of need would the people who have the concept of needs agree to have on the List, I was asking, what needs would they ascribe to the members of that Reference Population, with the determinately included members (themselves) centrally in view. And when I ask, as I now ask, what Minimum Standards of Provision do the people who have the concept associate with the needs on the List, I am asking a question similarly relativized to the assumed Reference Population, with the same members of that population centrally in view.

To proceed in this way begs a number of questions, which I am deliberately postponing. The procedure will let views of needs pass that are ethnocentric. Worse, it will not discriminate between the natural aspects of needs and the conventional aspects. Once differences in culture and conventions are taken into account, how many of the Minimum Standards of Provision that it seems sensible to ascribe to people in the English-speaking parts of the world will apply to people in other parts, in Africa or Asia, especially in less Westernized regions? Will even the List of Matters of Need apply to human beings everywhere, in every culture, and under all existing conventions? I postpone these questions; I shall not fail to deal with them.

2.32 Variation (Other than Conventional) in Standards

If variations in the conventional aspects of needs are disregarded, as I am for the moment only disregarding them, a good deal of variation must still be allowed for under Minimum Standards of Provision, given natural differences between members of the Reference Population in respect to physique, temperament, and circumstances (e.g., climate, physical demands of work). They may in this sense have very different needs, though the existence of natural maxima (e.g., for eating without eating too much) as well as natural minima helps make the allowances for variation manageable.

Could even the needs of one person, in the sense of the Minimum Standards of Provision applying to her, be fixed very exactly? No one who would agree that the person in question needs eight hours of rest every day could sensibly hold out against agreeing to seven hours and fifty minutes or to eight hours and ten. Moreover, the provisions for some needs are much harder to quantify than the provisions for others. A great variety of provisions for recreation might be minimally adequate without being reducible to any common measure: How does one compare the provision of music and a dance floor with the provision of a book of poetry? The amount of time available for using either

41

would not do as a measure, at least alone; for it is not just having free time that counts, but having suitable facilities for use during the free time. One should hesitate to resort to utility, in the economists' sense and the sense used in decision theory, even if one were satisfied by any method of arriving at utility from preferences; for what counts here is meeting the need, not the subjective value anyone puts on meeting it. Provisions short of the standard are, in the opinion of the people who have the concept and agree on the standard, less than suffice to meet the need. (Provisions beyond may be useful or desirable, if such provisions do not exceed natural maxima like having too much food, or too much fatty food, but they are not accepted as strictly needed.)

The case of food, in which one imagines (not quite correctly) that the elements of nutrition have all been identified (proteins, carbohydrates, fat, minerals, vitamins) and minimum daily requirements of each specified, is thus misleading. It gives an impression that measurement is easy. It even offers more than one means of measurement, by calories as well as by elements of nutrition. On the other hand, the case of food helps make the point that provisions for needs (and hence deficiencies in respect to those provisions) can often be measured, in ways characteristic of the provisions, without resort to sophisticated notions like utility. Moreover, the less quantifiable needs, like recreation, at least admit of the specification (though in terms less than maximally specific) of a disjunction of provisions, in the absence of which, or falling grossly short of which, the need will be considered unmet. The need for recreation can be met only if a person has (at least) several hours a week free for it; some facilities, beyond a cell, a bench, a table: facilities, such as they may be, that support fairly continuous activity during his recreational time. Standing for the whole time of a game or inning, along with ten other extra fielders, waiting for balls that are never hit in his direction, is not enough softball, not enough recreation, certainly not enough exercise.

The variation from person to person, given differences in physique, temperament, and circumstances, in respect to the minimum provisions required under given needs might be accommodated (insofar as the provisions can be readily quantified) by associating a set of Minimum Standards with each need, and associating each person in the Reference Population with one of the standards in each set. For certain purposes—discussions of global policy—one might use the notion of the mean or the median of the minima in each set. For other purposes, the maximum of the minima in a given set would invite attention. That figure might be inflated by a pretense of need on the part of the person for whom it has been granted to be the Minimum Standard of Provision; and any widespread expectation that provisions would be supplied up to that standard, as a matter of social policy, might lead to further pretense by other people. However, the maximum of the minima would show how far in one sense the concept of needs currently carried respecting provisions: It would show the amount of variation that people with the concept were prepared to accept.

A diagram may help to make clear the possibilities of variation just discussed. To make the forms of provision for different needs roughly comparable on a quantitative basis, I postulate a measure on the horizontal axis of the expense of supplying them for given numbers of people in the Reference Population.

With some people, the variation in the sets of minimum standards may rise higher than anything accepted as falling within the normal range of variation. Disabilities of one sort or another may have this effect: Some people cannot survive except in a specially constructed dust-free or germ-free environment; others cannot meet the need to excrete unless special machines are brought in to assist or supplement the functioning of their kidneys. Addictions, too, push the variation beyond the normal range of standards. I set ad-

43

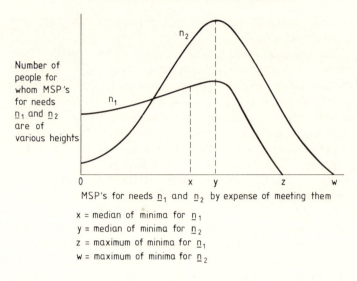

MSP's for needs $\underline{n}_1$ and $\underline{n}_2$ by expense of meeting them

x = median of minima for $\underline{n}_1$
y = median of minima for $\underline{n}_2$
z = maximum of minima for $\underline{n}_1$
w = maximum of minima for $\underline{n}_2$

dictions and disabilities aside for later treatment, in the chapter on breakdowns in the use of the concept of needs. To try to accommodate them here would cripple the chances of showing, in my basic account, how the concept of needs works when it is working well.

2.33 A Rebuttable Presumption of Universality

The sets of standards associated with some needs range no lower, in reaching the minima of the Minimum Standards, than some substantial provisions: For example, every human being needs some food, some water, and (in cold climates) some clothing, some shelter, some heat. With other needs on the List, however, the range goes to zero. There are people who get along with no sleep (overlooking for the moment that they must notwithstanding have some form of rest); or with no companionship; or with no sex. The fact that the range goes to zero does not hinder us from using the concept of needs and the associated concept of Minimum Standards of Provision to determine whether or not the needs of people have been met throughout the range of

44

Minimum Standards for any given Matter of Need. The fact does, however, create a certain logical difficulty, given that all the Matters of Need on the List are such that people using the concept of needs are ready to ascribe them to every member of the Reference Population and indeed to every human being. Should we say that the needs are to be ascribed even to people for whom the Minimum Standards of Provision are zero? That would save their claim to be considered universal, at the rather high cost in paradox of jumping over the differences between a very small provision and no provision at all.

The paradox is factitious. If it were real, one might try to escape it by theorizing that in every zero case some displacement and sublimation could be found, which might be taken as evidence of universality. Or one might edit and reformulate the List so that no zero cases could be found in the Minimum Standards of Provision associated with the remaining Matters of Need. These maneuvers, however, seem to me to be unnecessary, and even false to the concept of needs. I do not think that people with the concept of needs think of them as having to be strictly universal. They are ready to find them so, and hence ready to ascribe them to everybody, sight unseen, in the present Reference Population. They will be ready to ascribe some needs across cultures, to any Reference Population that comes up. The ascription, however, is made in either case as a rebuttable presumption: It will not be discredited, and the standing of the corresponding needs on the List will not be shaken, by the discovery of some exceptions, so long as the exceptions in any Reference Population are relatively infrequent.

Another logical difficulty arises from the possibility of interaction among the Minimum Standards of Provision. For example, if the standard for exercise is set higher, the standards for food and rest will have to be higher, too. There seems little reason to apprehend strategic abuse of this possibility, say, by people who, wishing to claim more food, try to establish the claim by feigning a need for more exer-

45

cise. However, one might be uncomfortable logically about not being able to find a unique bottom on which to rest the Standards: For which should one set first, the Standards for food and rest, or the Standard for exercise?

To some extent, however, the question is sensibly settled in the same way as I have been supposing Minimum Standards of Provision may be fixed when interaction does not affect them, namely, by falling back upon the status quo in the part of the Reference Population that is centrally in view. Given with the status quo is a certain distribution of strenuous "exercisers" and nonstrenuous "resters," and a corresponding range of Minimum Standards of Provision for food, rest, and exercise. If, as time goes on, the exercisers redouble their efforts, the status quo will change, and higher standards for food and rest may be accepted. This effect may renew misgivings about conventionality, since the amount of exercise that people choose to do is culturally determined by a social practice at least like a convention in this, that apart from their choices neither would exist. However, though the misgivings about conventionality are still to be treated, they will not create any special problem here.

Were one free to set Minimum Standards to meet various reasonable constraints of principle, one might find principles that suggested setting them in a certain order, e.g., beginning with a level of exercise beyond which there is no causal evidence of a gain in fitness. The Minimum Standards for food and rest could then be set relatively to this level. It would, however, be a rash hypothesis to suppose that the present use of the concept of needs systematically reflects such principles. As we shall see, the notions about hierarchizing needs that do exist have their sources elsewhere. The hierarchizing notion most firmly established in received usage applies only to the urgencies of a short-term emergency: rescue from fire, wrap up, give food, worry about recreation later. The causal evidence and the causal beliefs on which the present use of the concept of needs rests may be assumed to be less sophisticated than systematic constraints on the interaction of Minimum Standards would require.

2.4 A Criterion for Inclusion in the List and for Height of Standards

The belief that people who exercise more frequently and more strenuously need more food and more rest is one causal belief of many on which the current application of the concept of needs depends. Causal beliefs support in multiple ways the variations in provisions needed by people differing in physique, temperament, and circumstances. One of them is the belief that such differences imply variations in Minimum Standards. Others bear upon having the List include various matters as needs in the first instance, and the understanding that as needs they are to be ascribed, in the way of rebuttable presumptions, to every human being, with some associated Minimum Standards of Provision. The import of these beliefs can be captured, and the present account of the concept of needs further filled out, by stating a Criterion for inclusion among the Matters of Need that are to be on the List. The same Criterion can be invoked to determine the height of the associated Minimum Standards of Provision.

2.41 A Family of Criteria

In fact, more than one Criterion could be found. I have presented the List as generated by asking what people with the concept would agree were course-of-life needs that have to be met in order for life and normal functioning to continue. However, the relational formula could have been applied to other ends: to taking care of oneself in a normally independent way; or to avoiding hardship and suffering; or, as I shall now apply it, without entirely renouncing other criteria, to functioning envisaged more narrowly, as functioning without derangement in carrying out the tasks assigned a person in a certain combination of basic social roles. Used

47

to generate the List, these notions would give similar results, though the notion of hardship and suffering might
have a significant tendency to deviate from the rest, if it
were allowed to extend to such things as suffering from unrequited love. The notion of hardship and suffering also
more surely attaches the concept of needs to the deepest
places in our moral feelings. With the List in being, presented without a generating notion—and none may have
been invoked—any of these ideas, however, might reasonably be inducted as the principle on which Matters of Need
had been included in it and Minimum Standards of Provision fixed at the heights accorded them.

2.42 A Criterion to Represent the Family

The Criterion that I shall settle upon is being indispensable
to mind or body in performing the tasks assigned a given
person under a combination of basic social roles, namely,
the roles of parent, householder, worker, and citizen. If
what is thus indispensable is not supplied, the person's
functioning in those tasks is deranged. I include sheer incapacity (for want, say, of strength or skill) under derangement. I also attach the proviso that being indispensable
amounts, in the case of Matters of Need (always implying
some Minimum Standard of Provision or other), to being
indispensable, at least in the way of a rebuttable presumption, to every member of the Reference Population at some
time in the course of life. This proviso of presumptive universality suffices to rule out tools and facilities required in
tasks assigned to some people and not to others at any time
in their lives; and so makes the phrase "to mind or body"
redundant if there are no tasks that everybody performs
and must have the same tools to perform. Later, furthermore, the Criterion will be relaxed to allow for members of
the Reference Population, young, old, and certain others,
who do not perform all the roles, much less all the tasks that
people in their prime are expected to be able to perform. For

the time being, however, I have in view people who are performing the four roles of parent, householder, worker, and citizen, or who, if they are not parents, are of an age at which they are expected to be able to function as parents. The phrase "to mind or body" makes explicit the implication that the provisions or deficiencies in question come home to the people in question in physical or psychological effects that they manifest in themselves.

Like the other criteria in the family from which it is drawn, this Criterion is firmly placed at the limits of the relational formula. No more justification is required for people's aiming to function without derangement in the tasks and roles mentioned than is required for their aiming at health or at living. No justification, referring to some more ultimate and compelling end, could be supplied. Could we pretend to justify aiming to perform those roles and tasks by a more fundamental aim, living, or having a life of minimum normal scope? But having a life of minimum normal scope consists just in having an opportunity to perform those roles and tasks, and derangement to a degree that prevents normal functioning in those connections implies derangement in living itself.

To decide by the Criterion whether something is a need is to decide a question of fact. Something is a Matter of Need, by the Criterion, if there are good grounds in causal evidence for presuming that any member of the Reference Population would be unable to carry out the tasks assigned her by one or more of the roles mentioned if the matter in question were not provided for at the Minimum Standard appropriate to that person's physique, temperament, and circumstances. She would be unable to carry out the tasks because of physical weakness—fatigue, faintness, dizziness, shivering, actual collapse; or from not knowing how to go about them; or because of depression or inability to concentrate; and similar handicaps. A Minimum Standard of Provision has been correctly established, by this Criterion, when provision at less than the given Standard could reasonably be expected to lead to incapacity or derangement.

The Matters of Need on the List are course-of-life needs. Hence provisions according to the Minimum Standards must be offered in every lifetime—every day, if provisions are required that frequently (as they are for shelter, clothing, and perhaps food); or during appropriate periods, with appropriate frequency during those periods (as with the need for sex). Accordingly, the Criterion will certify something to be a Matter of Need, and some Minimum Standard of Provision to be appropriate, if without provisions under that head and by that standard, it may be universally presumed that people will suffer during their lives from a derangement of function in one or another of the four basic social roles.

2.43 Length of Life to Be Provided for

How long is life to go on? What is assumed under the Criterion about the length of life, that is to say, the length of time during which the matters of need are to be provided for? Something is assumed: One could hardly say that a person's needs were provided for if for want of provisions for them functioning was going to stop substantially short of any arguably normal life span: tomorrow, next week, next month, next year, for a person now just twenty-five. I think a minimum bound for the length of life assumed might be found in the mean life expectancy over all occupations; but if occupations varied greatly (as in fact they do) in hazards to life, one would do better to take as the minimum bound the mean life expectancy of people in the most favored occupations—say, all those occupations in which the mean life expectancy was greater than the median life expectancy over all occupations. The Criterion would imply that something was a need if failing to provide for it with appropriate frequency led to so drastic a derangement of function as to amount to a life shorter than the minimum bound.

It is harder to specify a maximum bound. One might stipulate, however, that the Criterion be understood to support providing for course-of-life needs at least as long as people remain capable (as my father does in his ninety-fourth year) of performing some complete assignment of tasks under all four basic social roles, whether or not the people concerned actually choose to perform all of them. A complete assignment would include the work of some recognized full-time occupation, though it might not be a strenuous one. In fact, even this allowance, as we shall see in a moment, does not relax the Criterion sufficiently to accord with its natural generalization to people who, because of age or otherwise, are incapable of performing a complete assignment. In issues about social policy that can take the maximum bound as given by the current facts about mortality, neither the present allowance nor this further relaxation causes any trouble. They do cause trouble when medical care and medical research are at issue, but I postpone discussion of this trouble to the chapter, at the end of the book, about breakdowns in the use of the concept of needs.

2.44 Causal Beliefs Implied by the Criterion

The causal beliefs brought forward under the Criterion are most firmly founded when they relate to the alternative of providing nothing at all or substantially less than the asserted Minimum Standard of Provision than when they have to do with providing only a little less. These beliefs might, furthermore, turn out to be false with regard to any item on the List of needs. It might be discovered, for example, that most people do not need to sleep at all; a book was published a few years ago purporting to convey just this discovery. Or, contrary to the powerful impression that people have had since the middle of the last century of the disastrous effects of solitary confinement, and lots of other evidence, further inquiry may show that it is an exaggeration to speak of a need for companionship, in the sense of having other people bodily present: Having a radio, or even a book, will suffice to forestall derangement almost always; and perhaps, if they are otherwise comfortable, most people might turn out not to require even those things.

Could all the Matters of Need purporting to have places on the List be discredited by further causal inquiry, rigorously scientific or otherwise? I think the answer is "Yes." If the whole present list were discredited, our beliefs about human beings and the terms on which lives are carried on, together with those commonplace explanations of their actions that invoked basic needs themselves, not merely beliefs about them, would be just about as thoroughly unsettled as they would if it proved impossible to find anything (whether it is an item on the present List or not) that could keep a place on such a list. But I think that possibility, too, which amounts to discovering that there are no needs which have to be met to sustain life and functioning, is conceivable. The immortal gods of the Greeks had passions and pleasures. They even suffered occasional vexations, especially from the interferences and obstructions practiced by their fellow gods. However, they did not have to meet any conditions to go on living and acting; and were consistently conceived as not having to. If there were no course-of-life needs, the concept of needs would still have application to adventitious ones. So one could say there were instances of needs, but none of them, as a contingent and causal matter, happened to be instances that satisfied the Criterion and fitted into the present List, or any other. That many matters do actually fit into such a List is an empirical truth. However, it is a very basic and obvious one, as things stand, as is the assertion that a good part of the present List is in no real danger of being discredited. We have no reason to expect that science is going to discover that human beings do not need food, or exercise, or to keep their bodies intact. Human beings are not, like the gods, immune to bodily impairment; and there is no prospect of their becoming so.

2.45 Generalizing the Criterion to the Elderly, to Those without Roles, to Children

The Criterion relating functioning to a combination of basic social roles, firm as may be the place that can be found for it at the limits of the relational formula, is not something that I put forward as the most natural way of arriving at the needs on the List. In some cases, it is quite an unnatural way: No one would suggest, I think, that the chief ground on which human beings were ascribed a need for companionship was that without companionship they would not be able to function smoothly, effectively—without derangement—in their tasks as parents, householders, workers, and citizens. The depression that people without companionship are liable to fall into would be cited much more readily, and cited not as a handicap to carrying out tasks, but as an instance of hardship and suffering. The Criterion founded on basic social roles, however, does supply a feasible route that people with the concept might follow to agreement on the whole List of needs. It is, moreover, a route that has the advantages of avoiding or at least minimizing emotional complications and of making as specific as possible the connections of the needs with causal beliefs.

At the same time, the needs established by the Criterion are easily generalized, along with the Criterion. The Criterion focuses attention on adults in the prime of life, indeed, upon a subset of them who are actively carrying out the tasks of all four roles as parents, householders, workers, and citizens. However, the needs established for people in this subset are in fact ascribed also to people who as they have grown older have retired from activity in one or more of these roles. The ascription is readily justified: Not only would it be inhumane to fail to acknowledge retired people's needs; they commonly are still carrying out some of the tasks that are assigned under the combination of basic social roles. The combination may have shrunk in their cases; it may go on shrinking; but it will remain, pretty much to the end, a shrunken version of the same combination envisaged in the Criterion. So the Criterion approximately applies to most people even in retirement, and continues to apply, with asymptotically diminishing foundation, as tasks are given up.

Similarly, the Criterion applies approximately to younger people who, from disaffection with their society, renounce tasks or even entire roles. We may find cases in which people, young or old, have renounced all four roles though still fit to perform them and all the tasks. These are hardly to be taken as normal cases. On the other hand, cases in which people are prevented from having one or another of the basic social roles are all too common. They may live under an oppressive regime, which denies them any substantial role as citizens; or in a poor country, where they cannot become parents or householders because they do not fall among the small number of people allowed to marry; or in a country that is rich, but has no work to offer many of its inhabitants. Yet the Criterion applies to all these cases, to people who are denied roles as well as to people who renounce them. If such people are to carry out the roles and tasks, the needs on the basic List must be met for them. They may be met without the roles and tasks being carried out; but they are necessary conditions of carrying them out.

Just what roles and tasks are the people concerned to be made fit to carry out? Even in the case of people who will be assigned all the roles anyway, some allowance must be made for variation in the Minimum Standards of Provision with variation in assignments; and some allowance for variation in the assignments pertaining to any given person must be made if any variation in life-plans for that person is to be possible. Is he to be a clerk or an acrobat? With people who will be assigned all the roles anyway, we may fall back again on the status quo with respect to that part of the Reference Population which is in view. The Criterion presupposes the assignments for them that exist in the status quo, and, with those assignments, a given pattern of Minimum Standards of Provision. The Criterion allows, however, that the pattern may change with changes in the assignments. For people who in the status quo lack assignments to one or another of the basic social roles, we may stipulate that the Criterion ascribes to them in each case Minimum Standards of Provision midway between the lowest and highest of the Standards, Matter of Need by Matter of Need, associated with the assignments—for example, the kinds of work—which the person in question is currently mature enough and skillful enough to undertake. Should the person acquire new skills or further maturity, the Minimum Standards of Provision (and hence the overall pattern of Minimum Standards for the Reference Population) would shift, under the Criterion, accordingly.

The Criterion, on this understanding, can be generalized far enough to support calling many of the requisites of various life-plans "needs." It does not cover all life-plans or all such requisites. Some requisites will be needs only in the sense of adventitious needs. Were given people to adopt the life-plans for which they are requisites, they would need to have them met. Nothing in the Criterion, however—nothing in my basic account—guarantees that people will be able to adopt any life-plan that they wish to among the life-plans currently being followed by some members or other of their society, much less any life-plan that they might fancy. People are not even guaranteed that they can choose the assignments, among those that they are qualified to undertake, with the highest Minimum Standards for one or another Matter of Need. To give people in the Reference Population opportunities to make such choices, a surplus may have to be made available to them that goes beyond meeting current needs.

The most obvious, and the most compelling rationales for ascribing the needs on the List to children would again take some directer and more natural route than that offered by the Criterion. The most obvious, and probably the most compelling rationale that does go by way of the Criterion would take up the question how children are to be prepared for adult life. Children have yet to assume the basic adult roles, but whether they will be able to do so, when their time comes, and carry out the tasks assigned them, depends on meeting their needs under each head of the List of Matters of Need while they are growing up. For them, and in accordance with the rationale of preparing them for adult roles, the need for education is especially prominent and calls for elaborate provisions; other needs, too, may be more demanding in the case of children—the need for companionship, for example, evidently enlarges into a need to be loved, especially in young children. If those needs do not receive timely provision, the whole course-of-life of the children, and of the adults that they become, may go awry.

In the larger perspective created by the rationales extending the Criterion to old people and children, and to the disaffected and socially handicapped as well, the needs established by the Criterion are manifestly course-of-life needs for everyone. In that perspective, if one expected agreement on Matters of Need and Minimum Standards of Provision to come easily, one might wish to cast loose from the present Criterion and, where the Criterion relies on functioning without derangement in the tasks assigned under a combination of basic social roles, simply cite normal functioning as a human being. The present Criterion would still, however, provide a more effective basis for identifying, through the roles that it refers to, specific tests of functioning, not only in those cases to which it squarely applies. It would help get agreement for this reason. It would also help get agreement because of its concern with useful, productive roles, likely to be respected by people who would receive other criteria less charitably.

2.46 Cultural Variations in Provisions and Roles

The needs established by the Criterion are not only easily generalized to children and old people—as they should be to keep in step with the usage and beliefs of the people with the concept of needs. They are also easily generalized over the variations of physique, temperament, and circumstances found among adults in the more visible part of the Reference Population, in particular over the variations of circumstances that have to do with different sorts of work. To mention just one such variation: Some people in the Reference Population have exceptionally enjoyable, indeed engrossing jobs, and their needs will reflect this fact, often by a drastically diminished need for recreation (implying a much lower Minimum Standard of Provision) and in other ways. However, no obstacle arises to fitting these differences under the needs in the same List and within the scheme of associated Minimum Standards of Provision. Such differences have already been allowed for.

The allowance made for them is a good part of the answer to the question whether the List of Needs and the scheme of Minimum Standards of Provision can be generalized over the differences in culture, some of them very profound differences, that separate the less visible parts or possible parts of the Reference Population (in that direction indeterminately bounded) from the more visible part. It can be seen already that the present account allows for a great deal of variation in Minimum Standards of Provision, and in forms of provisions as well, where these actually will serve to stave off derangement of function. In principle, widening the allowance, if doing so is required to embrace other cultures, should not create any insuperable difficulties, or threaten to distort the concept of needs as so far described. The same Matter of Need remains through the variations in provisions.

It may be suggested as notice of a limitation of the Criterion that in some cultures roles corresponding to parent, householder, worker, and citizen, as these are known in the English-speaking parts of the world, will be difficult to find. I expect there is most to say for this suggestion in respect of the roles of parent (at least, of male parent apart from insemination) and householder. But are there not everywhere analogues of such roles, even in matrilineal societies, in communal lodges, or among peoples that do not have permanent dwellings? Uncles may have to play the role that a male parent does with us; it may be difficult to distinguish the lodge dweller's role as sharing householder from his role as citizen of the commune; it may be difficult to distinguish in the leadership of the Bushman group the roles of parent and householder. However, the Criterion would lead almost as surely in these cases to identifying tasks the performance of which depended on meeting needs as it does in the English-speaking part of the world; and I suggest that the Matters of Need would be the same, though the forms of provision would in many ways be very different.

2.47 Roles with Intolerable Tasks

It may also be suggested, not just as notice of a limitation in the Criterion but as an exposé of an insidious implication in it, that it in effect endorses whatever tasks are currently assigned under the four roles. But some of those tasks may be intolerable. Some people in the Reference Population may have exceptionally enjoyable jobs; others may have exceptionally disagreeable ones, which cannot be made tolerable and should therefore be eliminated.

Nothing in the Criterion stands in the way of denouncing such jobs, however. At worst, the Criterion leaves open, to be settled before it is invoked, the question of what tasks shall be assigned under the four roles.

It may do more. The Criterion may engender arguments for eliminating certain tasks, and this in at least two ways. First, it invites us to consider whether performing those tasks does not so much interfere with meeting needs in respect to performing other tasks, under other roles, as to jeopardize functioning there. Second, it invites us to consider whether there is any way of meeting needs that would enable a person to go on performing those tasks throughout the length of the working lives enjoyed by other people (on the average, or in the most fortunate occupations), with a normal period of retirement beyond. No doubt the Criterion cannot be consistently used unless tasks and needs are consistent with one another. If an inconsistency crops up, it may be removed sometimes by adjusting the needs (most likely, by raising the Minimum Standards of Provision). Sometimes, however, the way to remove the inconsistency may be to adjust the tasks (making them less onerous).

It remains true that tasks and needs may be made consistent while the lives in which they figure remain mean and circumscribed (even if duly prolonged). I shall have to return to this topic. Either much that is morally urgent is left to do when needs have been met or the full moral urgency of needs requires a use of the concept expanded far beyond my present deliberately narrow account.

2.5* Consistency of the List and Standards; Completeness of the List

It is desirable to have the List and the Standards consistent; and were it not impossible, for reasons already mentioned, it would be desirable to have the List complete. I shall say that the List and the Standards are consistent if and only if resources can be specified in kinds and amounts that would suffice to meet at the same time for every member of any set of persons [P], all the needs n_i on the List at the Minimum Standards agreed on, together with any needs conceptually derived from the needs n_i and any needs derived from them through laws of nature. (Derivation in various senses, including these, will be discussed in the next chapter.) I shall say a list $n_1, n_2, \ldots n_n$ of matters of need would be complete if and only if there were no matter of need n_x that satisfied the Criterion but that is not on the List or not such that it can be derived from those which are. Further, a List may be defined as minimal if and only if it is complete and no Matter of Need n_x can be omitted without completeness failing. Then we could say that agreement on the List of Matters of Need could be thought of as agreement on a family of consistent minimal lists, each calling for overall resources that are available if and only if the overall resources called for by every other list in the family are available, too. (I thus allow for the possibility that agreement on the List of Matters of Need may vary with the level of resources available, a topic to be discussed more closely later.)

However, the impossibility of actually completing any list compels us to think rather of agreement on incomplete lists that so far make the same demands on resources, taking the needs on the lists and the derived needs together. No doubt we could not infer from people's being agreed on incomplete lists that they would agree on items to be added to these lists. We could not realistically expect the agreement to be exact even for the incomplete lists; the concept of needs does not in this sense have exactly the same content for all the people who have the concept. Yet the notion of agreement on incomplete lists does not seem to þe a very great idealization respecting sameness of content; and something may be salvaged later even from the notion of completeness, in answer to certain traditional views to be discussed under normativity.

2.6 Given List, Standards, and Criterion, a Principle of Precedence

The normative force of the concept of needs, in its use for evaluating and choosing social policies, finds concentrated expression in a Principle of Precedence. This Principle prescribes that the needs of a certain human population, the Reference Population, as the List, the Standards, and the Criterion define the needs of the members of that population, take priority over their preferences or anybody else's. Just what this priority may be held to amount to, along with the moral significance of the Principle, will come to light stage by stage with the argument in the rest of this book. It is obvious at once, however, that the Principle does something to order and harmonize different ends and the ends of different people, though it may not do everything that ethics requires.

In this chapter, I shall define a sense of priority stricter than the one that best matches the way in which the Principle of Precedence operates in current politics. The stricter sense will carry me through the chapters in which I relate the Principle and the concept of needs to justice and to utilitarianism. Moreover, the less strict sense introduced later, in the interest of simultaneously matching current politics more realistically and showing what full reconciliation of needs with liberty requires, will not derogate from the primacy in principle of the strict sense to be defined here. The strict sense is required to express the full normative force of the concept of needs.

2.61 Making the Principle Determinate as to Reference Population

If we are to have a determinate notion, strict or unstrict, of priority, the Reference Population can no longer be left in the partly indeterminate condition that sufficed, I assumed, to generate some sort of theoretical agreement on the List, on Minimum Standards of Provision, and the Criterion— sufficed, one might well believe, only because no commitment to do anything about the needs of everyone in the population was prescribed. With a determinate Principle of Precedence, such a commitment becomes inescapable. Anyone who accepts the Principle defined for a certain Reference Population accepts responsibility for meeting the needs of that population. In the face of that implication, people are likely to insist on proceeding with a good deal of caution in defining the Reference Population.

I shall treat the definition of the Reference Population as relative to particular self-governing subsets of the linguistic community that has the concept of needs in just the form which I have outlined. That linguistic community as a whole may agree on what are Matters of Need, on the Criterion, even, in the absence of a commitment to a determinate Principle of Precedence, on what are currently Minimum Standards of Provision. It may agree that a full account of the concept of needs must incorporate something like a Principle of Precedence. However, the linguistic community is not by any means always the main locus for the power and responsibility to adopt social policies that answer to such a principle; and adding other linguistic communities that approximate to having the same concept of needs moves even further away from any principal locus. The presence of the same concept, or of cousin concepts, in many different linguistic communities offers a foundation for international cooperation in meeting needs—a foundation that we should cherish and reinforce. But I take it that the decisions to cooperate are, at bottom, national decisions by national governments on which the responsibility of meeting needs at home has already been imposed. Insofar as they fulfill that responsibility, they are already conforming de facto to some determinate Principle of Precedence; and it is to them in the first instance that their citizens look when they argue for expanding or contracting the Reference Population to be served. To treat the Reference Population as relative to self-governing linguistic subsets gains for the Principle of Precedence the realism of recognizing national governments as the instruments for the application of the Principle.

At the same time it retains the link, on the side of the people who have the concept of needs, manifested in a shared linguistic practice, with a whole linguistic community. I may be making too much of this link; and the abbreviation of "self-governing linguistic subset" that I shall use to mark the link—"Selfgovliset"—is ugly and obtrusive enough, though usefully transparent, to designate a newly organized agency of the Soviet Union. Greater differences in policies about needs may crop up between two self-governing subsets of a given linguistic community than between either of them and self-governing subsets of other linguistic communities. May not New Zealand under a Labour government run closer in this respect to Sweden than to Britain under a government like Thatcher's? Moreover, I am ready to treat the United States, with a substantial and growing minority of people who speak only Spanish, and even Canada, in which English is only one of two official languages, as self-governing linguistic subsets of one—the English-speaking—linguistic community. Nevertheless, I want to go on insisting, in methodological punctilio, that my account of needs consists of hypotheses in the first instance about the use of the term "needs" by speakers of one linguistic community, welcome and expectable as further scope for the hypotheses may be. So I insist on considering how the Reference Population, and with it the Principle of Precedence, becomes determinate as something agreed on within some Selfgovliset, specifically a Selfgovliset of the English-speaking world.

Having identified such a Selfgovliset, one would next have to assume, and I do assume in this account, that there is one largest non-empty population P_g on which all members of the Selfgovliset are agreed in subscribing to the Principle of Precedence. This does not go without saying: For one member of the Selfgovliset might have one reference population in mind, while other members had other populations; and though pair by pair those populations might overlap, the intersection of all those populations—families and friends, perhaps, in the largest cases—might be empty. The assumption that there is at least one population P_g forestalls such a result, without this time departing very far or very abruptly from reality; for all the Selfgovlisets or approximations therefore mentioned a moment ago follow policies designed to make sure of meeting the needs of broad populations, and these policies (in spite of grumbling about their costs) enjoy widespread support of long standing. Realism in fact supports extending the assumption to having P_g embrace the whole membership of the Selfgovliset itself.

How many more people besides the members of the Selfgovliset would it include? Earlier, when the List of Matters of Need and the Minimum Standards of Provision were thought of as being compiled in abstraction from particular social policies and in abstraction, too, from taxes and other obligations incurred with such policies, it was suitable enough to think of the Reference Population as indeterminately open to including perhaps every human being. Here, while we work out the bearing of the Principle of Precedence in actual policy-making, it may be best (thought artificial to a degree) to think of the Reference Population as sharply limited, reflecting caution within the Selfgovliset about keeping obligations and costs within bounds.

In a particular case, having fixed upon a particular Selfgovliset, we might proceed in this way: Assume that everyone in the Selfgovliset has some notion of how the List and the Standards (together with the Criterion) will operate in combination with the Principle of Precedence, applying them all to some reference population (say, to the partly indeterminate Reference Population earlier supposed to be in view). Without inquiring of anyone just what population she feels responsible for under the Principle, we proceed to discover who uses the concept of needs most strictly and thus has the least rich List and the lowest Minimum Standards of Provision (the lowest mean minima or median minima, or the lowest maxima of minima). If we wish to rule out extreme and bizarre views, we might disregard ten per cent of the Selfgovliset and fasten upon the person with the strictest views of the ninety per cent who remain. The point in either case is to fix the empirical content of the concept of needs in a way that enjoys very widespread normative commitment.

To proceed thus would, one might hope, reduce the chances of having the content of the List and the amplitude of the Standards fixed directly with a view to keeping costs and obligations within bounds. The caution about these things is to fall, as much as possible, not upon understanding what human beings need, but upon accepting which human beings it is whose needs one is to meet. I assume away the complications that one person might be strictest and lowest on one need, another on another; or that two people might have equally short Lists, differing as to the items included (even when derived needs are taken into account). It will be the List and the Standards accepted by one strictest, least generous, person that we take as the List and Standards agreed upon by the whole of the Selfgovliset for policy-making purposes.

Now we ask this very person, once identified, to specify the largest reference population, including the Selfgovliset itself, for which he accepts some responsibility under the Principle of Precedence. This population may be expected to be identical with P_g, by previous assumption the largest population for which all members of the Selfgovliset agree to take responsibility. It could not, logically, be smaller. If it were larger, including P_g as a proper subset, there would be some member of the Selfgovliset who, though ready to agree to a more generous List and more generous Standards, would apply them to P_g as a smaller population than the one to which the least generous person would apply his List and Standards. This is not an impossible position; but at least given favorable circumstances regarding resources (which I am continually assuming), it could be reduced by persuading the person who holds it to accept first the larger population and the less generous List and Standards, then work to treat the smaller population more generously. Alternatively, the least generous person could be persuaded to accept a more generous List and Standards with the smaller population. In either case, P_g and the least generous person's Reference Population end up matching.

We would now have fixed the List, the Standards, and the Reference Population, together with the reach (in persons covered) for the given Selfgovliset of the Principle. (The Criterion may be thought of as fixed, too, by being adjusted so as to be consistent with the fixed List and fixed Standards.)

Thus, with only the relevant notion of priority itself to be defined, we move into a position to invoke the Principle of Precedence in a fully determinate way. In later chapters, when I amplify my account of the concept of needs in its basic normative use to embrace such matters as the impact of increases or decreases in the resources available to the Selfgovliset and the possible tendency for Minimum Standards to vary inversely with the size of the Reference Population, the present fixity will be reconsidered. For now, however, I wish the main features of the account to be thought of as fixed, in application to actual policy-making, in some such way as just outlined. If the assumptions made earlier hold, P_g will include at least all the members of the Selfgovliset. It may include a substantial number of other people (citizens of friendly countries; inhabitants of colonies).

Fixing upon a Reference Population by associating it with a specific Selfgovliset clearly makes fixing upon it a matter of political significance. A Selfgovliset is by definition a political entity. This is as it should be; it would be quite unrealistic to seek determinacy on some other basis. But the concept of needs is inevitably political in other respects, too. What is included among Matters of Need on the List becomes a political decision, as does the amplitude of the Minimum Standards of Provision, as soon as any prospect arises of political responsibility for a Reference Population. In turn, the determination of the List and Standards may be expected to affect any explicit political decisions that the associated Selfgovliset might take to meet the needs of a Reference Population. So I have properly portrayed the Reference Population as fixed for a Selfgovliset that has before it a given List with given Minimum Standards. All these things are fixed with a political significance that attaches to each in the presence of the others.

I have portrayed this combined determination as resting on something like a consensus; indeed, I have been willing to contract the List or, at least, to scale down the Minimum Standards of Provision in order to be able to assert a consensus. When it comes to making political decisions about the actual arrangements for meeting one or another need, the Selfgovliset concerned may by majority vote or otherwise choose arrangements that do not suffice for provisions at the Minimum Standards. I am supposing, however, that this occurs, for the points on which consensus is asserted, because, correctly or incorrectly, people believe that those arrangements will suffice or will be adequately supplemented by other measures. This amounts to assuming that the tendency to give needs a certain priority is carried to the end in the Principle of Precedence. With that priority, another aspect of the politics of needs is realized. Once matters have been classified as needs, with Minimum Standards of Provision, the tendency is to put them beyond politics, as matters that have been decided by consensus. What remains for politics are questions about efficient arrangements.

People may, of course, dispute so much about efficient arrangements that the advantage offered by the consensus on the List and the Standards will count for disappointingly little in reducing political conflict. One may anxiously seek means of resolving such disputes. Should I brush them aside? Should I not instead direct my account of the concept of needs so as to resolve them? But to make what the concept of needs signifies, in its use assessing social policies, depend on resolving conflicts about efficient arrangements or about other points, however desirable it may be to have means of resolving those conflicts, will inevitably overshadow, and maybe cast into doubt, what can be accomplished with the concept when the conflicts are avoided. That is, surprisingly, a good deal. Sometimes the conflicts do not arise; sometimes, if the concept operates with certain simple precautions, as in the present account, it can make a substantial contribution to settling upon policies without having to descend into the mêlée.

2.62 Making the Principle Determinate as to the Priority Relation: Strict Final Priority

Just how is the priority that the Principle of Precedence gives needs to be conceived? This question, too, has to be answered before the Principle becomes fully determinate; and there is a good deal to be said about this question. I shall say only part of it in this chapter, where I shall define what I call "strict final priority." Later—but not until, in intervening chapters, I have discussed complications surrounding the basic account, the relation of needs to justice and a needs-oriented surrogate for utilitarianism—I shall replace this conception with one that is more relaxed, which I call "role-relative precautionary priority." The demands of realism and of liberty coincide in motivating this replacement, though it may cost something important by putting justice in jeopardy. Meantime, however, I shall work with strict final priority, which suffices for the intervening discussion—indeed, facilitates it—and will retain a place in the more relaxed conception.

Strict final priority is not so strict as lexicographical priority. It is not even so strict, need by need, as lexicographical priority with satiation limits, another notion explored by economists. A good G is lexicographically ordered above a good H, $\mathcal{L}$ [G,H), (G',H')] (where (G',H') is some other combination of the same goods), if and only if (G > G') or (G = G' and H > H'). Assume that H is a positive good with which the agent or agency that confers the priority is not and will not be satiated. Then G has lexicographical priority over H when, given the quantity of G, combinations of that quantity with amounts of H will be chosen when the combinations contain more H, but a combination with a finite increment of G, however small, will be chosen rather than any of those. Applied to a matter of need, say food, as against a matter of preference only (dance lessons, repairs to the State Opera), lexicographical ordering with priority for food would imply that the tiniest increment in food, however much food the Reference Population has already, outweighs having a year's course of dance lessons for everybody with the most agreeable teachers one could imagine, or a complete restoration of the opera house.

Lexicographical priority with satiation limits is more plausible. We already have, in the Minimum Standards of Provisions, the means of defining the limit for each Matter of Need. One might imagine first ordering Matters of Need; and then, below all such matters, matters of preference only. The Selfgovliset, in choosing social policies, would order a policy offering a combination x_{hg} of goods ahead of another policy offering another combination x'_{hg} whenever x_{hg} does more to meet the highest-ranked need on which a discrepancy between the combinations is encountered. However, the Selfgovliset would do this only so long as there is someone in the Reference Population for whom that need has not yet been met at the Minimum Standard of Provision ascribed to her. Once the Minimum Standards of Provision have been met for everybody in the Reference Population, the Matter of Need in question drops out. The active alternatives in the choice field for social policy will henceforth be confined to policies offering combinations all of which, for everybody in the Reference Population, meet that standard or surpass it. The Selfgovliset moves on to looking among the policies that are left for policies that meet, for everybody in the Reference Population, at the appropriate Minimum Standard of Provision, the next-ranked need.

Sooner or later, if provisions for all matters of need have been assured, without exhausting the resources available to the Selfgovliset for use with respect to the Reference Population, the choice field will be reduced to a number of policies equally effective in meeting needs. Then the turn will come for matters that are matters of preference only. These will be invoked to sort out the remaining policy alternatives. The sorting may not come easy. We can imagine a Selfgovliset agreeing about what matters of preference are to be attended to, and even about the lexicographical ordering for attending to them. However, this is a much less plausible thing to imagine than agreement in the same connections for matters of need. People will have different orderings of preference for matters of preference. Combining these orderings in a social ordering will be beset by all the difficulties of social choice theory. I shall not, since I need not, assume any one way of coping with these difficulties here. I simply suppose, for the purpose of discussing lexicographical priority with satiation limits, that if the Selfgovliset does agree on a complete lexicographical ordering of matters of preference, they will all be ordered below matters of need; and that if it does not agree, some way of giving matters of preference effect in social policy will be found, and its drawbacks put up with, all the while leaving matters of need priority over matters of preference.

May we suppose that some of these matters of preference only will have to do with preferences among forms of provision for needs? I think that without any great difficulty we may: Evaluating a combination x for the degree to which it meets a certain need is a task that can be firmly distinguished from the task of evaluating it for the degree to which the provisions that it offers to meet the need are agreeable ones. Think of a nutritious diet composed chiefly of dried soy beans, as compared with one largely composed of such things as a nice white Burgundy, chicken Marengo, buttered asparagus, and black raspberry ice cream. In fact, of course, with a lexicographical ordering of the sort here in view, preferences among forms of provision will count only when all the alternatives are minimally nutritious; but on this point, too, the distinction goes through between attending to these preferences and looking for degrees to which the need is met. The procedure might be to settle tentatively on the cheapest alternatives that meet the Minimum Standards of Provision for given needs, and then go back, revising the alternatives in an overall solution for matters of preference only.

A literature of long standing, extending from Karl Menger and before to Abraham Maslow, has theorized about hierarchies of needs or wants, in which a higher need or want is attended to only after more basic needs have been met. It is just such a notion of hierarchy that the economists who have been lately exploring the notion of lexicographical ordering with satiation limits are trying to capture. Some hierarchies are more ambitious and more controversial than others. Some, like Maslow's, may be conceptual innovations for describing levels at which human life may be lived more or less fully rather than results of considering received thinking and present agreements on wants or needs. I shall discuss such innovations in a later chapter. A hierarchy of a less ambitious sort, more surely founded in present agreements, can be found by considering how long people can survive unharmed without meeting various needs—a good deal longer without meeting the need for companionship than without meeting the need for food; longer without meeting the need for water than without meeting a need to escape the threat of fire. We can imagine ranking the needs on the List on that basis.

Would it normally be appropriate to do so, however? If each need is essential to full capacity and smooth functioning, bodily and mental, as all the needs on the basic list supposedly are, they all would seem to have an equal claim to being met in a sufficiently long period of consumption. It would not for most of them be a very long period, perhaps a month. Even during that month needs falling due for any given person at longer intervals—for example, the need for terminal care—would be represented statistically as requiring meeting for a proportion of the population. From the point of view of social policy, which operates over periods years in length, it would seem only sensible to accept them all as having an equal claim. It would be highly advantageous, too, since any attempt to rank them (for such periods) is bound to start up controversies, perhaps interminable ones.

These considerations lead me to reject, for the use of the concept of needs that is the subject of this book, the notion of a hierarchy of needs and with it priority interpreted as lexicographical ordering with satiation limits. Suppose we take the Principle of Precedence as requiring that combinations not be ordered by preferences answering to other wants until on the agenda of social policy only combinations remain all of which meet all the needs on the List at Minimum Standards of Provision. Strict final priority for needs, so conceived, implies among needs themselves neither lexicographical priority nor lexicographical priority with satiation limits. It does not say which is to be preferred, a policy that meets need n_1 but not n_2 or one that meets n_2 but not n_1. (As I shall make clear, this omission does not even then inevitably bring the policy-making process to a standstill.) Strict final priority, so conceived, may, nevertheless, be said to rest on lexicographical priority for needs with a satiation limit consisting of the conjunction of the Minimum Standards of Provision for everybody in the Reference Population for every Matter of Need on the basic List. Matters of preference only, whether or not they are ordered among themselves, are ordered all together below needs.

Is strict final priority feasible? If a great number of needs are brought up, each demanding a comparative examination of policies, discussions in which the application of the Principle of Precedence is sought might be interminable. Perhaps it would be doubtful whether any of the policies actually proposed, or to be proposed, could survive protracted discussion: sooner or later, for any policy, some need from that great number would turn up that it failed to meet. A strong incentive thus arises to keep the List of needs from proliferating freely.

Even if the number of needs given attention is kept manageably few, however, meeting them might sometimes be more than the resources available to the Selfgovliset sufficed for. The Principle of Precedence, with strict final priority, offers no help in such desperate circumstances. Some ordering by urgency of matters of needs among themselves might help if the circumstances were going to persist only for a short time—an emergency. I shall, however, set aside such circumstances. I assume that, normally, the resources available suffice for strict final priority; for one thing, because we are dealing with a Selfgovliset that is itself a going society capable of surviving. The List and the Minimum Standards of Provisions may also be supposed to have been adapted, in ways to be discussed later, to the resources normally available to the Selfgovliset for meeting the needs of the corresponding accepted Reference Population and thus to fall well within the limits of those resources. (The Reference Population, it is to be remembered, may in some cases not extend far beyond the Selfgovliset itself.)

Keeping the tests for meeting the needs on the List as simple as possible assists in making strict final priority a manageable consideration in policy-making. Subtler tests, aiming to establish the degrees to which policies fall short of meeting needs, will generate problems of measurement that can be avoided by asking simply whether or not the Minimum Standards of Provision have been met. As I have allowed, these vary, for any given need, from person to person. People of the same size and in the same circumstances vary widely in the amount of food that they need; and this amount varies, too, if their circumstances are not the same—if one person is doing very much heavier work than another, for example. Having established that a given policy meets one person's need for food, but falls short in this respect of the Minimum Standard of Provision for another, are we to decide which to weigh more? How are we to weigh meeting one need against failing to meet another, especially when more than one person is involved? Strict final priority avoids all such problems by requiring a policy to meet the Minimum Standard of Provision for every need of every person being considered. Given a favorable relation between needs and resources, this requirement will not be heroic.

Not heroic. It may seem disgracefully the reverse of heroic. Here again my basic account may seem to shirk a sort of conflict that cries out for resolution. However, we can in fact get along well enough in many real circumstances without resolving it—a point not to be missed. Moreover, once again I maintain that it is conceptually confusing to allow anxiety about resolving conflicts hurry us past seeing how much can be accomplished with the concept of needs when the conflicts are avoided. I think it is a characteristic failing in philosophy and social science (in particular, economics) to neglect, in the search for sophisticated universal principles of conflict resolution, the limited but real efficacy of less sophisticated concepts, and to assume that those concepts were somehow wholly discredited before the search for sophisticated principles began. They were not; nor are they proper targets for any of the frustration experienced during that search. Moreover, I shall show in due course (in Chapter 5 below) how conflicts between needs are in practice often resolved by revising the set of proposals.

Is the cost of carrying out the Principle of Precedence with strict final priority going to fit whatever the least generous member of the Selfgovliset had in mind in accepting "some responsibility" for meeting the needs of the Reference Population determined on the basis of this acceptance? Would he not have second thoughts after the Principle of Precedence has become determinate in this way? Perhaps. However, the responsibility of each member of the Selfgovliset, even when the needs of the Reference Population are accorded strict final priority, might consistently extend no further than taking some part in meeting those needs, and this part would be a division of a task shared with other members of the Selfgovliset in almost every case.

Moreover, social and psychological theory might teach that it would be best not to offer provisions to those members of the Reference Population who lacked them: Laissez faire would work better; or self-help under some other arrangements (e.g., national autonomy and socialist planning). Then what the Principle would require would be support of laissez faire or of the other arrangements for self-help.

Of course, even if social theory and psychological theory do not sanction laissez faire or other forms of self-help as the best arrangements for remedying deficiencies in respect to needs when deficiencies appear, the members of the Selfgovliset may be lucky. They may be spared any costs (beyond what they are doing each to take care of their own needs), because there are in fact no deficiencies; all members of the Reference Population are in a position to meet their needs. When unmet needs do appear in the accepted Reference Population P_g, the limits of P_g itself as the people included and the associated agreement at the least-generous level on the List and the Standards of Provisions set limits to the help that the Principle calls upon the Selfgovliset to mobilize. Even then, a record of waste and frivolity on the part of the people in need, and the prospect of their wasting any new provisions given them, may justify the Selfgovliset in suspending action on the Principle. Such a record with such a prospect is a genuine possibility, though I suspect it is, as a talking point, most often raised without evidence as a means of subverting humane treatment of people genuinely in need.

DIALOGUE

CRITICAL READER: *With all that lengthy account, please tell me—have you anywhere been straightforward enough to give a definition of needs?*

NOT-YET-REPENTANT AUTHOR: *But I don't want to give a definition of needs. I take up a concept that is in common use and I offer an account of its use in certain connections—specifically, in the evaluation of social policies. I depend on people's recognizing that this account makes explicit features of their own thinking about needs in these connections. If this recognition is forthcoming, to set forth a definition in solemn formality would be superfluous; and very likely, misleading.*

READER: *But couldn't you say that whatever fits the account—satisfies the Criterion, figures on the List or among the Minimum Standards of Provisions, and has the backing of the Principle of Precedence—is a need? Can't you make a definition out of that, and if so, haven't you supplied a definition in spite of yourself?*

AUTHOR: *If you like, that could give some rough service as a definition of "needs-in-their-socially-evaluative use." But note—it's not just my way of using "needs" or the way that I've decided upon for present purposes. It's the way that the concept is commonly used that's in question. Note, further, the Criterion is one of a family. As I pointed out in the text, it doesn't cover the whole range of the socially evaluative use of the concept of needs as well, in*

77

places, as alternative criteria. That's an impediment to the Criterion's being a definition on its own. Nor will bringing in the List and the Minimum Standards of Provision suffice for a complete definition. The List is—it must be—incomplete.

READER: *You disturb me. What else have you left out?*

AUTHOR: *I've by-passed various questions about what the concept of needs signifies to a person making discoveries and decisions about the scope of her own needs. She might recognize matters of need like those on my List, with similar implications for Minimum Standards of Provision. But in applying the concept to her own case, she would not be primarily concerned with how her needs fit into the social use that I concentrate on—the use in which public issues about shared needs take the stage. She would feel free to count some things as basic needs for her that weren't needs at all for other people. That may not make any trouble for a comprehensive definition of needs . . .*

READER: *It would make trouble for you?*

AUTHOR: *It's trouble I mean to be avoiding. The socially evaluative use, which I mean to be describing, insists upon comparisons with other people—on shared needs (even if they are needs with varying Minimum Standards of Provision). Hence the concept won't do the work assigned it unless it offers an intelligible foundation for statistics. Furthermore . . .*

READER: *What! More furthermores?*

AUTHOR: *Excuse me. I have to make a number of points to explain how selective my focus is. Even within the range of socially evaluative uses, I'm setting aside adventitious needs, which are sufficiently defined by the relational for-*

mula. I'm also setting aside those special needs that cannot be regarded as extraordinary variations in Minimum Standards of Provision. These may sometimes make a difference to choices of social policy, and sometimes should. Other things being equal, wouldn't we try to spare people distress who are terribly upset by certain colors or noises? I expect that special needs like this aren't, in most people's eyes, so steadily important morally as presumptively universal needs. But whether that is so or not, it's on the presumptively universal needs that I focus.

THREE

COMPLICATIONS SURROUNDING THE BASIC ACCOUNT: DERIVATION, CONVENTIONALITY, NORMATIVITY

To give as clear an initial picture as possible of the chief features of the concept of needs in its use assessing social policies, I postponed treating a number of complications. Several of these complications arise so quickly, on every hand, that they resist easy postponement. Unless they are accommodated, it will be hard to see how, in complex current societies, the concept of needs could be used very often, or maybe even at all, in accordance with the basic account that I have given. I shall deal with derivation and conventionality, two such complications, in this chapter and also, under "normativity," with certain normative presuppositions, not yet treated, that come with the concept of needs in the use that concerns me. I shall show how the concept of needs and my basic account, free of any false pretensions and preserving a commitment to empirical testing, can bear the weight of these complications. I shall then, in the two chapters following, show how the concept of needs, understood as in my basic account and vindicated in respect to the complications, may be held to figure in justice and in a surrogate for utilitarianism. Only after doing this shall I consider modifying any of the central features of my basic account. Three chapters hence, I shall modify it by shifting away from strict final priority. Four chapters hence, I shall consider more expansive use, with a richer List of Matters of Need, some of them possibly not supported by the present Criterion.

The normative force expressed in the Principle of Precedence extends to needs derived from the List and incorporated in the Minimum Standards of Provision, even when the derivations depend, as inevitably many of them will, on conventions. Moreover, in spite of this conventionality, and in spite of further aspects of normativity affecting the List itself, firm judgments of need in accordance with the Criterion will still be forthcoming, founded on causal evidence—evidence that not meeting the need in question will lead to deranged functioning in the combination of basic social roles.

3.1 Derived Needs

3.11 Needs Derived from Conceptual Connections and from Discoveries in Natural Science

Besides the Matters of Need—basic needs—mentioned in the List, Matters of Need derived from these have claims to precedence. The subject of derived needs leads quickly to the subject, with which it is intimately connected, of the conventionality of needs. Nevertheless, it will be useful to treat the two subjects under separate heads.

The derivations on which derived needs depend may rest on conceptual connections, or on scientific laws and empirical generalizations. A derivation resting on a conceptual connection runs from the need to preserve the body intact to the need to keep one's arm unbroken. A derivation resting on a scientific law runs from the need for food to the need for vitamin C as an essential ingredient of the diet. If we add the law that sauerkraut is (as Captain Cook discovered) a good source of vitamin C, and the empirical generalization (which might apply in certain circumstances, as it did on one of Cook's voyages, while his ships were at sea) that sauerkraut is the only source available, a need for sauerkraut might be derived, too.

Needs for medical care might be derived in either way—conceptually, taking (for example) the need to preserve the body intact to include a need to restore it so far as repairs can restore it; or through empirical science, when a physical failing has been identified as one that can be remedied to some degree by a known means. For maladies now incurable, both ways work together in deriving a need to find some such means, or better means, which it is thought lie within the reach of scientific discovery and technological advance. A need for some sort of remedy is derived conceptually from the debilitation threatened by the malady. Science is called in to certify whether the search for one is more than wishful thinking.

Some of the scientific laws and empirical generalizations on which the derivations rest may, as in the dietary examples just given, fall within the sphere of natural science—biology or physics or psychology. Others have to do with social arrangements, some of which may perhaps be found in all human societies, but others of which are found only in some or in subcultures of these (though perhaps they could not be found there or anywhere else without certain conditions regularly holding). Such generalizations include the following: Provisions to meet most of the needs on the List, or derived therefrom, have to be bought, and the money to buy them must come from rents or profits or wages.

3.12 Needs Derived from Social Arrangements

Generalizations like these might as well have been said to depend on conventions as to depend on social arrangements; but I mean different things by these two terms. I use "convention" in a very broad sense. The clearest kind of convention is an explicit formal rule—a statute, for example, about collecting income taxes, which is generally known and generally conformed to in the behavior of the members of the Reference Population to which it is ascribed. However, I also include under conventions rules that are known and conformed to without ever having been legislated, like the rule, current among European peoples until at least recently, according to which women marry only men their own age or older. I include, further, coordinating schemes that, unlike rules proper, have no prescribed sanctions attaching to them, but which members of the group keep up because of mutual advantage. An example is the practice whereby the first car to arrive at an intersection controlled by four stop signs moves through the intersection first. Finally, I include various approximations to rules (and to coordinating schemes) in respect to which conformity of behavior is found, though the people conforming do not fully recognize this fact, and have nothing like a rule in mind to which, on the relevant points, they intend to conform. Passing dishes with vegetables and meats around the dinner table clockwise rather than counterclockwise might be an example.

In every case, I take it as implied that there is an alternative to having the rule or coordinating scheme, which the members of the group might have chosen, supposing them or whoever acts with authority for them to be confronted by the choice. The alternative might be doing nothing—letting nature take its course (e.g., people's letting their ears go uncropped). Almost always, there are in fact alternative conventions, which amount to more than this and which would accomplish much the same purposes, as the convention of eating rice accomplishes in some cultures what the convention of eating bread does in others.

With "convention" defined, I can readily say that I include under "social arrangements" conventions, and, besides conventions, both the actual behavior conforming to the conventions and the man-made physical settings reflecting the conventions and adapted to them. I also include man-made physical settings that are now reflected in behavior and conventions, though they developed not so much because conventions required them to take the forms that they did but because of the absence of conventions precluding those forms.

Derived Matters of Need that depend on such arrangements, and hence on conventions, create some uneasiness, even if empirical generalizations—laws of social science—can be invoked to establish them. It is otherwise with needs conceptually derived from needs on the List, or derived from those needs through laws of nature, that is to say, through laws within the purview of natural science. They are not subject to social options in the same way. I shall set them aside during the discussion to follow.

The social arrangements currently prevailing in Canada and the United States about buying provisions and obtaining money to buy them might be invoked in an argument deriving a need for transportation (for the moment waiving the point whether by public or by private means). Suppose that only a few people, who can be disregarded, have enough income from profits or rents so as not to need wages; or suppose that even those few have to travel to do the business from which their profits and rents flow. Then three further generalizations about social arrangements will take us almost all the way to a derived need for transportation. First, that the places of employment are dispersed and will remain so. Second, that people's dwelling-places are dispersed. Third, that the two dispersions are so far nonmatching that almost everybody lives more than two hours' walking distance from his or her place of employment or business. Two hours' walking distance would mean four hours going to work and back every day. With a workday of 8 1/2 hours, allowing half an hour for lunch, 11 1/2 hours would be left in the day for rest, companionship, and recreation. Assume that leaving any fewer hours would imply inadequate provisions for these needs. Then transportation is needed to reduce the walking time at least to two hours each way.

Whether needs purporting to be derived needs get the backing of the Principle of Precedence depends on whether clear and cogent derivations run to them from the needs on the basic List. Sometimes I conjecture, very often it is easy, as in the illustration just given, to produce such a derivation. Even when it is, however, the claim of the needs so derived may be brought into question by questioning the social arrangements. Why should these arrangements be taken for granted? Might not alternative arrangements eliminate the need?

Under other arrangements the need for transportation might so much diminish as virtually to disappear, not only for getting to work, but in other connections too. The places of employment and the dwelling-places do not have to remain dispersed, or at any rate dispersed in nonmatching ways. It is by convention that people do not live on the premises where they work. Grocers and physicians might come to the door, from neighborhood headquarters. Recreation of sorts requiring massive, concentrated facilities could be renounced. People might stop trying to start up or to keep up friendships beyond walking distance from their homes. Indeed, one can imagine much more drastic alternatives. Going back to the needs on the List and considering alternative social arrangements in full generality, one might imagine reverting to a hunting culture, with people scattered so thin on the ground and moving so frequently that they would not have any use for permanent shelters or for transportation connecting settled dwelling-places with fixed places of employment. They would have no need, either, for septic tanks or sewers and treatment plants or any of the other public works indispensable under present social arrangements.

Some of these flights of imagination can be checked by considering the catastrophic consequences for the social product of making the changes in arrangements. There are now too many people in the world—certainly too many on the territories of Canada and the United States and other

86

Selfgovlisets that might be foremost in our minds—to be supported by a hunting culture. In general, social arrangements that would so adversely affect the relation between social product and provision for the needs on the List as to leave some needs of some people in the Reference Population unprovided for can be ruled out by direct application of the List, the Minimum Standards of Provision, and the Principle of Precedence.

There seem to be all too many alternative arrangements remaining, however. Some of them may be ruled out by other principles—liberty or justice. Will not some have to be ruled out, however, if they are ruled out at all, by appealing, explicitly or implicitly, to people's preferences? It would, perhaps, be a very strenuous undertaking to move places of employment and dwelling-places about so that everyone ended up living within easy walking distance of his place of employment. It would be expensive, too. But suppose the expense was not so great as to jeopardize, even during the changeover, meeting the needs actually on the List, plus derived needs, other than the need for transportation or needs that derive from it. The need for transportation then seems, far from being inescapable, to depend on having some social arrangements that people simply prefer not to take the trouble of changing.

3.13 The Inexorability of Social Arrangements

An individual member of the Reference Population cannot, however, change the arrangements by herself. Suppose she has the support of others willing to have the arrangements changed to ones that would eliminate the need for transportation. Meeting the need for transportation is still something that they must attend to, as a fact imposed upon them, so long as the change is blocked—say, by opposition from a majority of the voting members of the Selfgovliset. Is the need, for those other people, who belong to that majority, something which they impose (on themselves, if they, too, belong to the Reference Population), and hence in the end not so much a need as an option depending on their preferences?

So matters might stand if the issue were actually drawn and a vote were taken; but in reality the issue would be decided, and the change blocked, only rarely by an explicit negative vote. We must not lightly assume that every society has procedures for calling up social arrangements of the sort involved and putting them to a vote. When a society does not, change—at least change deliberately sought by the mass of members—is not just blocked; it can hardly be proposed. Moreover, where there are procedures for broaching issues and voting upon them, it will often not be an easy or straightforward matter to bring them to bear on standing social arrangements.

The issue about transportation is likely to be lost from sight amid dozens of other possible issues. There would be indefinitely many other equally drastic ways in which social arrangements could be changed. Would the change that would eliminate the need for transportation have the highest priority for attention among them, or any special priority at all? Even if we imagine the members of the Selfgovli- set searching among such alternative arrangements, we must consider that they may not have taken sides on the issue about the change that would eliminate the need for transportation. While the issue remained dormant, the need for transportation would in effect be imposed on each of them.

Moreover, such fundamental issues are not only likely to be dormant, but quite disregarded. The alternative arrangements that are debated and put to a vote will ordinarily involve much less drastic changes. By comparison with the real exigencies of current arrangements, any decision that as an effect of consciously preferring certain fundamental social arrangements leads away from a need for transportation will often be remotely hypothetical. In practice these arrangements normally go unquestioned in the relevant respects.

The possibility of alternative arrangements the acceptance or rejection of which, should they be brought forward, would depend on the preferences of members of the Selfgovliset does somewhat weaken the claim of a derived need susceptible of being eliminated. Occasionally at least social arrangements are deliberately abandoned, or they wear away. Sometimes alternative arrangements exist that would be surer to meet most people's basic needs and to suit their preferences as well. Ignorance and confusion, cultivated by parties with a vested interest in the status quo, may stand in the way of changing to such arrangements. Were the alternative arrangements brought to the top of the agenda for the Selfgovliset, in public debate, in Parliament, one of them might be adopted; if they were all rejected, the dependence of the need on preferences (for some people at least) would be almost equally nakedly exposed.

Yet generally speaking, in current political practice, one does not get back to those preferences easily or straightaway. One has to have some reason for thinking that the relevant issue will in fact get to the top of the agenda rather than any of many others which might compete with it for attention; and, if it is an issue about drastic changes, some reason for thinking any issue of that kind will be given attention. Otherwise it is idle, both in speaking of any individual person in the Reference Population and in generalizing about social policy over all the persons in the Population, to reject the derived needs in question. They are genuine needs for the time being, firmly connected to the Criterion, and presumptively universal for the whole Reference Population. They will in any case have to be taken into account pending any social transformation. They will have to be examined in examining the costs—the disruption and suffering—caused by the transition to a new society should the transition ever get underway.

A continuum of derived Matters of Need, from less to

more cogent, spreads out over possible issues about alternative social arrangements. A derived need that depends on a social arrangement for which easily installed alternatives offer themselves, frequently undergo debate, and from time to time actually get tried out is in a weak position. As one moves toward more consequential arrangements less often (if at all) on the scene of political discussion the footing for the derivations becomes firmer. The situation is untidy. One will have to inspect particular derived needs and assess their footing case by case.

However, in a very large number of cases, considering the difficulty of getting arrangements changed even if they are debated, and the compounding difficulty that they are not debated, there being no prospect of changing them, will not the footing be firm enough? We may still wish to deplore the footing; radical social critics will and I shall often applaud. For any individual member of the Reference Population, however, the need, though derived, will be inescapable; for the time being it must be accepted as a datum for social policy. The contrast between meeting matters of need at Minimum Standards of Provision and supplying additional graces and comforts in accordance with preferences does not apply so trenchantly as it does when changing the assumed social arrangements would lead to a catastrophic reduction in the social product. The alternative arrangements cannot be excluded in any of the present cases without invoking some people's preferences, at least hypothetically. Something like the contrast survives, however, while current arrangements continue.

3.2 *Conventional Determinants of Needs*

Some social arrangements not ineluctably dictated by principles like justice or liberty or by basic needs are going to exist in any society. Every society will thus have, alongside needs derived conceptually or through laws of nature, some derived needs that depend on these arrangements and the conventions that the arrangements embrace. Derived needs, even derived needs of this kind, can therefore hardly be repudiated wholesale as a class of needs. But if this is so, needs are not to be repudiated just because of conventionality either. Yet is it not conventionality that does most to make derived needs vulnerable to skeptical challenges? Social arrangements are constituted by conventions; and the dependence of needs on social arrangements is reflected in the conventional aspects of needs, though not always directly or plainly. The conventionality of needs is a complicated subject in its own right, and worth treating as such. We shall come out in the end at much the same place as the discussion of derived needs brought us to, but we shall along the way come upon different points if we make a new beginning with conventionality.

3.21* Multiple Aspects of Conventionality

Some needs are not conventional, or even (we may presume, from past examples) hitherto conceptualized. Human beings need vitamins, and did so before they had any notion of vitamins. It is true, the needs that people consciously provide for are conceptualized. All such needs are so far conventional, since in being conceptualized they fall under linguistic conventions that might have been different—which were started up on human initiatives and continue subject to modification by changes, meditated or unmeditated, in conventions. "So far," however, is not far enough to make the truth of the propositions that people need food or need exercise dependent upon human initiatives or linguistic habits alone. If they needed both "food" and "drink" under one conceptualization, they would still need some of each under a conceptualization of "ingestible" that did not distinguish them.

Even so, to be conventional to the degree that just being conceptualized makes a need conventional is already something possibly far from innocuous. What men conceive of themselves as needing from women—indeed, from other people generally—varies with the conventions adopted to conceptualize the needs. To need services from other people may be argued to have the same natural foundations as to need their company and collaboration, but the implications are very different.

The prejudices that certain modes of conceptualization express and perpetuate resemble, in fact, and may sometimes be identical with, the prejudices embodied in certain conventional beliefs. People have such beliefs, for example, about variations in needs between social groups or social classes. Men, and women, too, have conventionally believed that women did not have the same need as men for education or for the status and recognition given some sorts of work outside the home. Privileged people, leading soft lives, find it easy to believe that people leading harder lives do not need comparable protection from the heat of the sun or the furious winter's rages.

There seem to be needs that are conventional without being conceptualized. North Americans, if they are not to feel uneasy in ordinary conversations, and are to speak with entire coherence and effectiveness, need to keep a greater distance from the people with whom they are talking than South Americans do. Some sort of comparative anthropological observation was required to bring this difference in conventions to light and bring it under concepts. Perhaps unimportant one by one, differences like this may cumulate to create culture shock, revealing a need for social orientation, which might claim a place on the List of basic needs if no satisfactory way of deriving it from the needs for companionship, education, and social acceptance could be found. The need, itself, however, would not be conventional in the sense that the need to keep a certain distance in conversation is. Human beings naturally live by conventions; so they must be said to have a natural need for some minimum familiarity with the conventions of the society in which they find themselves.

The class of needs created by convention has many members. Some of them are much more elaborate than the need to keep a certain distance, and equally exacting, or even more so, and even more directly derived from needs on the basic List, though we can trace the need to keep a certain distance pretty quickly through the need to have comfortable conversations to the need for companionship. Families cannot, for example, have social acceptance and recognition without fulfilling various conventions. They have to send their children to the right schools and outfit them appropriately. When an uncle of mine won a scholarship to Christ's Hospital in the second decade of this century everything was provided for him except tennis flannels; it was not easy for my hard-pressed grandmother to find the money for them. Among the Kwakiutl, a family, when its turn came, had to give a feast for the whole village and destroy all sorts of valuable goods publicly, lest it lose face forever. Fishing families in Cape Breton used to regard lobster as ineligible food from a dirty bottom-feeding scavenger. They were so desperate at times during the thirties, however, that they had to give their children lobster sandwiches to take to school. The children would throw the sandwiches away rather than have their schoolmates find them reduced to eating lobster.

In some of these cases, the social arrangements assumed are highly questionable. The elaborations may have gone, in our view, well beyond reason. They may differ markedly from the needs on the List in their claim for attention across cultures. I am not defending them or endorsing them. My present point is their exactingness, which may, taking one ineluctable demand with another, fall upon the lives of the people affected by these conventions with a weight differing little from that of the basic needs. Not only can individual persons and families do little to escape the weight; the societies concerned, as I have already noted, may have no devices under which their members can readily unite to consider whether they wish to carry the burden further.

This may be so even when the exactions exceed available resources, so that it is impossible to meet all the needs consistently.

Conventions do not create needs out of nothing. Typically, one must draw upon the natural basic needs on the List not only to derive proofs that (under given social arrangements) what the conventions have elaborated as demands figure among people's needs; one must also draw upon the basic needs to explain how the motivation to conform to the conventions is generated. The presence of a need for social acceptance and recognition in the second part of the List guarantees, with troublesome consequences that I shall discuss later, a footing in basic needs for all needs that are engendered by accepted conventions. However, the other basic needs may have to be at stake for the conventions to be followed. An important, comprehensive connection that in many societies has the effect of putting them at stake lies in the fact that the means to obtain provisions to meet the needs cannot be had without maintaining some sort of position in society, and heeding the conventions that surround the position.

If any needs are natural rather than merely conventional, the needs on the List are. So it may be said that the most conventional needs have by derivation or by motivation some footing in natural ones. It may equally be said that the most natural needs are attended and shaped by conventions, and not only by the conventions introduced by language with conceptualization. The content of the List, to some extent, and the amplitude of the Minimum Standards, to some extent, vary with conventions. I say "to some extent" because some items are going to be on the List (or items from which they can be derived will be) regardless of convention. Anyone who has the concept of needs at all will recognize that human beings have a need for food and water and a need for exercise. Similarly, anyone who has the concept of needs at all will grant that there is some minimum provision of (the minimum of the minima) food and water that cannot be renounced, or reduced by conventions, if the need is to be met at all. It is not easy to say exactly, since it has not been settled how small effects in derangement of function (to cite the Criterion set forth in the previous chapter) may be and still be counted as signifying deficiencies. It is easy enough, however, to specify provisions that fall short of the minimum of minima for every human being. Getting less than one pound of food per month falls short.

3.22* Changes in the List and in the Minimum Standards

The effects of conventions may also show up in changes in the items that figure on any version of the List. There may have been a time, for example, when there was no agreement among speakers of English that human beings have a need for education or a need for recreation. There may come a time, perhaps a time of great hardship, when either of these items, or one of the others, loses its place on the List.

Yet if we take the List together with the derived needs, we may expect the content of this body of needs to change mainly by adding or dropping derived needs. In the simplest cases, where the people who have the concept and the Reference Population that is at issue more or less coincide, that will happen as a consequence of accepting or rejecting various conventions and the social arrangements associated with them. They begin to be acknowledged as inexorable requirements of normal life; or, once acknowledged, they now cease to be. Thus both men and women may cease to need hats, regardless of the weather, on occasions formerly conventionally unavoidable, like going to church, when hats used to be conventionally required. On the other hand, sometime in the past, during the changeover from subsistence agriculture, there may have been a stage at which the derived need for a job earning money was added to the derived need to have money of one's own. The latter presupposes arrangements under which provisions have to be bought. The former presupposes such arrangements, and, besides, that money is not available for those who do not work for wages or do not have someone to earn money for them.

In more complicated cases, the Reference Population may diverge from the people whose conception of derived needs is at issue. I shall discuss this sort of case at the end of the book, when I consider what responsibility a Selfgovliset may accept for a Reference Population that may belong to a wholly different culture. Here, I shall just point out that the divergence may sometimes be helpful. When the derived needs of the Reference Population can be met with substantially fewer resources than the derived needs of the Selfgovliset, this would help to incline the Selfgovliset toward accepting responsibility. Were the derived needs more demanding in resources than the derived needs accepted as such under the conventions of the Selfgovliset, we might have expected the Selfgovliset to resist being assigned responsibility.

Sometimes it becomes difficult to distinguish between conventional effects on the content of the List, extended to include derived Matters of Need, and conventional effects on the amplitude of the Minimum Standards of Provision. How high—on the average or anywhere in the range—will the Minimum Standards for given needs rise above the standards (difficult to locate exactly) that must be conceded in recognizing any such needs at all? That will depend upon conventions. In part, the upper bounds reflect conventions about social arrangements that link meeting the basic needs with meeting derived ones. Under some arrangements, people live dispersed, in private houses, which, to satisfy Minimum Standards, must have indoor toilets, further plumbing, (in northern climates) a furnace, and a cooking stove. Is having a house that meets this standard a derived Matter of Need, and thus implied by the List in conjunction with the arrangement of dispersed dwelling-places? Or is it something that illustrates how a certain amplitude of provision may be conventionally accepted as Minimal? It seems best to say that it is both. To define Minimum Standards of Provision, given certain social arrangements, is to establish Matters of Need that are derived from the List and the same arrangements.

3.23* A Formal Analysis of Conventional Variations in Forms of Provision

The Minimum Standard of Provision for a Matter of Need n on the List or derived therefrom may be thought of as calling for a form of provision answering to a description D_i that figures with n in an ordered pair (D_i, n). (n may be thought of as standing either for the need itself or for its name.) D_i, and hence the form of provision that meets the need n may vary, as my basic account allows, from person to person in a given Reference Population. Conventions prevailing in that Reference Population combine with n (operating through the Criterion) to determine D_i, which may be so specific that just one combination of goods and services answer to it as a suitable form of provision for i. We shall be ready to say, however, both that a member of the Reference Population has a need n (something described as a Matter of Need on the basic List or derived therefrom— say, food)—and that she needs D_i (where she herself is the i in question)—say, rice or something equally suitable if more than one form of provision is suitable and only one is available. If, in either case, D_i varies from person to person, that will not threaten the presumptive universality of n, the Matter of Need, over the Reference Population. Indeed, sometimes the same n will figure across several Reference Populations or all Reference Populations in ordered pairs with D_i, which itself may vary greatly. Moreover, if in a given society there is only one combination of goods and services that will satisfy (D_i, n) for any D_i—only rice; or only rice combined with some other staple—the normative force of the need n is communicated in the need for D_i, diminished only to the degree that more attractive conventions, which would modify n or D_i, are options on the agenda of social policy.

Having in view only one combination of goods and services that will satisfy (D_i, n) may be the effect of having only one of many known suitable combinations of goods and services actually available; or it may be an implication of specifying D_i so exactly that only one combination, whether it is available or not, is suitable. It is hard to be as specific as that; perhaps impossible. Everyone needs, among the Minimum Provisions for food, a minimum amount of salt; so every combination answering to (D_i, n) in this case must include a minimum amount of salt. Not only, however, might (D_i, n) allow for alternative combinations varying in other respects; salt itself, it might be claimed, comes in alternative forms, differing in source, differing in packaging. One might reject the distinctions as trivial. However, even if one does not, the point remains that it is D_i that is needed, and not any particular combination, if more than one is acknowledged to be actually available; or, if more than one are equally suitable, when none are available. (There is a little delicate shifting in usage here, which I shall not do more than note.)

Sometimes, especially when a variety of provisions present themselves, a Minimum Standard of Provision may be regarded itself as a (derived) Matter of Need. Then, in turn, it will have associated with it a Minimum Standard of its own, which might figure, if the basic Matter of Need is kept in view, in an ordered triple, (D'_i, D_i, n), where now $D_i = n'$. Suppose for some i the Minimum Standard of Provision for transportation must be some form of public transportation; then the means and frequency of service may be determined as a further Minimum Standard of Provision D'_i. Thus the distinction between Matter of Need and Minimum Standard of Provision becomes a relative one, changing with changing perspectives, and transposing as often as the description D_i, D'_i, or D''_i etc., last arrived at seems to demand further specification and deliberation.

When specification has become as strict as it is desired to be, the need for n carries through a need for D_i and a need for D'_i to the last and most specific description D'''_i of a form of provision, so that everyone in the Reference Population will be said to need something answering to that specification, as well as to all the specifications preceding. If more than one form of provision answers, and more than one form is available, only some one or other of these particular forms is needed.

In some cases the distinction between effects of conventions on the content of the List and effects on the amplitude of the Standards goes through without faltering. Suppose, for example, that the need for food can be met by diets with the same proportions of nutritive elements but varying in amplitude from quantities that would just keep people alive and capable of performing their tasks without gross derangement to quantities that would make them—given simultaneously a moderate amount of exercise—robust and full of a sense of well-being, and free even of subtle derangements of function (like a low-grade depression or repeated distraction by thoughts of food). The need for food would have a place on the List all along, with the content of requiring a balanced diet. Moreover, we might surely assume that the same social arrangements could be maintained—as indeed has happened in countries during wartime—with the scantier diets. Similar examples could be drawn from housing, having in mind variations in space per inhabitant, or the amount of heat supplied to the rooms in most use. Conventional factors of some kind must operate to determine whether or not the Minimum Standards of Provision call for ampler diets or ampler housing.

3.24* Adaptations to Changes in the Resources Available for Social Policy

What are these factors? They are to a degree obscure because they have to do with the adaptation of the Standards to changes in resources and (a connected matter) in the expectations of the people who have the concept of needs. This adaptation is brought about in part by changes in the policies adopted in various jurisdictions—in various Selfgovlisets—to meet needs. However, there are grounds for thinking that the adaptation and the implied changes in the conception of needs do not come about chiefly through explicit debate. It would be awkward, indeed counterintuitive, for anyone to declare in debate, in so many words, that because resources had become more abundant the needs of people in the Reference Population had become greater, or even that what had not previously been considered a derangement of function was now suitably considered one. People would object, quite sensibly, that what were needs and derangements before the coming of abundance was something that could then be established as facts, and that the facts had not changed, though of course the abundance makes it less excusable to fail to deal with them effectively.

The adaptation goes on without deliberation and for the most part without being noticed. In some cases, where there is a middle class in the Selfgovliset, something like the following may happen: The proportion of people belonging to the middle class increases as that class becomes more affluent. Members of the class gradually acquire a feeling of security about the affluence that they enjoy. As an effect of these processes, opinion in the Selfgovliset shifts toward accepting ampler diets as constituting Minimum Standards of Provision for food in at least the more proximate and visible parts of the reference populations that it deals with.

Similar effects occur under the other heads of need on the List. More agreeable forms of provision are accepted as coming within the Minimum Standards, even if they are more costly. Ampler provisions for housing, heating, and hot water come to seem minimal. During the same processes more agreeable provisions that do not admit so readily of the distinction between changing the content of the

100

List and changing the amplitude of the Standards creep in, among them indoor plumbing.

3.25* Elaboration of Conventions of Decency

Moreover, greater affluence and security lead to support for a more elaborate—or at least more costly—body of conventions. It is possible for conventions—about dress, for example—to call for more costly minimal provisions than hitherto: complications in underwear; changes in clothes; different clothes for different occasions; fairly elaborate outfits just to be presentable on occasion; more occasions when being presentable matters.

Both Karl Marx and Adam Smith list shirts among what Marx calls objects of "prime necessity." Adam Smith explains:

> By necessaries I understand, not only the commodities which are indispensably necessary for the support of life, but whatever the custom of the country renders it indecent for creditable people, even of the lowest order, to be without. A linen shirt, for example, is, strictly speaking, not a necessary of life. The Greeks and Romans lived, I suppose, comfortably, though they had no linen. But in the present times, through the greater part of Europe, a creditable day-labourer would be ashamed to appear in public without a linen shirt. . . . Custom, in the same manner, has rendered leather shoes a necessary of life in England. . . . Under necessaries, therefore, I comprehend, not only those things which nature, but those things which the established rules of decency have rendered necessary to the lowest rank of people.

By comparison with the comforts that affluent members of the middle class reserve for themselves, of course, these ampler Standards, with their concessions to shared feelings about decency, may still not be very generous. Their generosity may be affected, too, by certain statistical facts, the influence of which may be felt even if the facts themselves remain obscure. For example, the maxima of the minima among the Minimum Standards of Provision may reach a higher level, being accepted as such in more decisions about policies, if only relatively few members of the reference populations cluster at or near such extremes.

3.26 Conventional Ceilings on Minimum Standards of Provision

In some respects, conventions may have the effect of making the standards less ample than even a strict application of the Criterion would seem to call for. Such needs as the need for a life-supporting relation to the environment and the need to preserve the body intact are invoked at least implicitly in attempts to eliminate or minimize the unsought risks that come with current activities. However, attempts to reduce risks fall far short of what they could accomplish in meeting the needs mentioned if we accustomed ourselves to leading very cautious lives. Leading such lives, we might refuse to swim in deep water, to ride in automobiles, or even to cross the street, to say nothing of going out to sea in sailboats or engaging in football or hockey. However, in current North American society, all these things are (given normal precautions, which do not eliminate the risks) conventionally accepted as normal activities with normal risks. We would not consider that the needs of the people who engaged in them had gone unmet just because the dangers involved could have been avoided entirely by not engaging in them.

3.27 Conventional Limits to Variety in Forms of Provision

My earlier discussion implies that equal amplitude in the Minimum Standards of Provision is consistent with different forms of provision, derived from different conventions. Among forms of provision for a given need (say, the need for food, or the need for shelter, which in some climates is part of the need for a life-supporting relation to the environment), some will appear equally ample to an observer comparing different cultures. Suppose his impression can be justified by the contributions that the provisions make to capacity and smooth functioning in basic social tasks. In one society, with one culture, however, the form of provision relied on in the other is regarded as intolerable, and vice versa. People in one abhor eating beef; people in the other, pork. Or one society insists upon single-family dwellings, simple ones maybe, but single; whereas the other insists upon living in communal lodges.

The stringency with which some forms of provision are excluded and others, no ampler, conformed to, may vary. People who deviate from the rule may inspire, depending on the rule and the culture, anything from light-hearted derision to moral outrage. This variation itself, however, lies within the realm of social conventions; for what sanctions attach to a given convention is itself a matter of convention. Sometimes, the conventions are so exacting and (not quite the same thing, though intimately connected) sometimes people's attachment to the conventions is so deep-seated that one can hardly distinguish between the need for some form or other of provision and the preference for one form. It diminishes the facts to speak of devout Jews or Muslims preferring to eat lamb to eating pork.

The more stringent the convention under which something is required, the more inexorable that requirement will be, and hence the stronger the case for treating the requirement as a need, both in individual persons' cases and in general social policy. Whether the conventions that enter into defining needs are stringent or not, however, the needs can retain normative force in spite of this dependency; and once a need has been defined, the question whether or not it has been met is a question of fact. The conventions make it a need by establishing, through connections with the List, connections with the Criterion. If it is not met by a form of provision conventionally acceptable, it

103

will not be met, and if it is not met, some observable derangement of function will ensue.

3.3 *The Surviving Normative Force of Needs*
Derived and Conventional

Neither being derived nor being conventional, I have maintained, takes away the normative force of needs or their factuality once the needs at issue have been arrived at. However, have I perhaps made more of the factuality, without
which the normative force could lapse, than I should have?
Operating together, derivation and conventionality certainly open room for abuses, though they are rather abuses
that people make in concert through upholding received
conventions and social arrangements, than abuses made
individually by free-wheeling propagandists. At best, it
might seem that the factuality of needs that derive from
conventions is residual. I have defended the factuality as
connected through basic needs with the Criterion of functioning without derangement in a combination of basic social roles. However, is not this connection at best a connection in which something that was (at least in our language)
unarguably a need might remain visible after conventional
commitments are waived? And what would this residuum
be but a matter of basic need or a need derived without reference to conventions (other than linguistic ones)? We may
in favorable cases be able thus to slide back from D_i to n.
But, whether we can do so or not, does not conventionality
threaten to dissolve the connection with the Criterion? Is it
plausible after all to hold that all the needs that are determined to be such by convention are such that derangement
of functioning ensues from not meeting them as described?
Conventionality would appear to strike at the basic needs
themselves: For if the upper bounds of the Minimum
Standards of Provision are conventional, will falling short
of those bounds lead to incapacity or derangement?

3.31 Does Conventionality Loosen the Connection with the Criterion?

Certainly, wherever the upper bounds are set, there is a pretty convincing case for thinking that incapacity or derangement of function will ensue for people whose provisions for given needs are entirely done away with. Who can get along with no food or (in northern climates) no clothing or no shelter? And some reductions, short of elimination, in the provisions going to given people would be substantial enough, allowing for the variations in the Minimum Standards that take into account their physique, temperament, and circumstances, to have observable adverse effects of the kind specified by the Criterion. Moreover, the conventional allowance for normal risks creates no problem about the causal connection. It is accepted with the allowance that everyone stands in some danger of injury; and, though the Criterion does not fix the allowance for risks, the injury, if it is realized, will cause effects of the sort envisaged in the Criterion.

Yet it seems reductions in significant, even substantial, amounts could nevertheless occur without such effects, if the amplitude of the Standards is at all great. Would a stockbroker in Scarsdale literally starve on a diet that would keep an Indian porter in good health? Or, cut out the fruit and fresh vegetables, cut out the hamburger from the diet of a family on relief. Would it not remain healthy and capable of performing basic tasks if it had to subsist on the famous seventy-five-cent-a-day regimen, largely beans? And surely, at least in sparsely populated areas, people could still get along without indoor plumbing. They do when camping.

I might have argued a moment ago that to reduce provisions so that they fell significantly short of minimal decency and humanity would have a causal effect, operating through the need for social acceptance and recognition, if not otherwise. For in those cases where the provisions actually have to be supplied—in relief to people out of work, for example—provisions too flagrantly different from those obtained by most respectable, self-supporting people will be felt by the recipients to be degrading. They will engender frustration, resentment, and depression. Moreover, there may be self-supporting people who do no better for themselves than something far short of the provisions most respectable people obtain. They will not think that they have succeeded in attaining respectability. Unless they are remarkably patient and deferential, they will feel frustration, resentment, and depression, too.

There is a good deal of truth in these reflections. However, the need for social acceptance and recognition is treacherous ground, on which I wish to tread as little as possible. That there is such a need, which would be present and important under just about all social arrangements, seems certain. Consider the effects on children of refusing them an acknowledged place, alongside the others, at meals or in other family activities; or the effects on adults of refusing them any marks of respect. Unfortunately, the need for social acceptance and recognition is peculiarly subject to abuse.

While the status quo persists, the conventions of the status quo are sometimes stringent in their impact on individual persons, and the needs associated with them inexorable. However, there is always some pretense, or at least some unwitting covering-up, involved in holding or presupposing that the conventions cannot be changed by social policy; and the opportunities for change reach a maximum with conventions that connect with basic needs solely through the need for social acceptance and recognition. There is no limit to the number or character of the conventions conformity to which may be demanded in some culture or another as the sine qua non of acceptance and recognition. They may be grotesquely artificial, as in hairdressing in some cultures or in tattooing in others.

It is true that the objection that observed incapacity or derangement is frequently an artificial effect of not being able to conform to questionable conventions does not rest on skepticism about the need for social acceptance and recognition alone, since conventions defining acceptable forms of provision for other needs may raise the same difficulty. People may starve when edible insects are available. However, the objection has most scope, and the richest material to draw on from the need for social acceptance and recognition, which more often than not affects the accepted provisions for other needs anyway.

Some mitigation of this threat to the concept of needs can be found in the fact that the pressure of conventions is very variable, so that often, especially in societies with mixed and changing cultures, people can defy conventions prevailing in their own culture and not suffer any penalty severe enough to cause incapacity or derangement of function. Perhaps the prospects of successful defiance will sometimes depend on how many other prevailing conventions the person concerned has defied already. In any case, it is indispensable to consider the evidence that any significant loss of social acceptance and recognition will actually occur, with incapacity or derangement following. No ground for using, or for overusing, the concept of needs can be found in an effect that will not come about.

This is perhaps enough mitigation to restore to the need for social acceptance and recognition the possibility of having some sharply delimited invocations. It may not be enough to safeguard this need against being invoked promiscuously. Nor does it make this need or any other a sufficient answer to the charge that derivation and conventionality afflict the concept of needs with abuses beginning perhaps in unwitting covering-up and ending in reckless fraud. Some such abuse seems to come in when the Minimum Standards of Provision for any of the needs on the List are treated as passing the causal tests implied in the Criterion, given Standards brought by convention and derivation to upper bounds as ample as those familiarly accepted in affluent societies. If this is a pretense, or something like pretense, is it not, furthermore, a pretense that quickly breaks down into double-talk? On the one hand, relying on the Criterion (or at least on the considerations expressed in the Criterion), one claims that even provisions rising to this amplitude are needed for functioning without derangement; on the other hand, one must admit, exposed to the least questioning, that this claim is an obvious exaggeration.

3.32 With the Connection Loosened, Is It Pretense to Invoke the Criterion?

Are the people who have the concept of needs and use it in the ordinary way really guilty of the pretense and double-talk, however? One might well consider that both the pretense and the double-talk are hypothetical. That is to say, in describing them, I am describing how people who have the concept might react when, confronted with the Criterion and explicit Minimum Standards of Provision, they try to go on somehow applying the concept of needs as they are used to applying it. In fact, the Criterion and the Minimum Standards of Provision are devices that I have introduced to make my account of the concept of needs in its basic normative use simultaneously as succinct and as manageable as possible. They do not radically idealize the concept or its use, but they bring with them enough idealization and formalization to cause some factitious trouble.

The question about the extent to which assertions of need turn on observational evidence is not factitious trouble. It is a merit of introducing an explicit Criterion and explicit Minimum Standards of Provision (as well as a definite illustrative List of needs) that it makes this question inescapable. The suggestions about pretense and double-talk, however, are factitious. The people who have the concept of needs and use it in the ordinary way are not in reality guilty of pretense and double-talk. They have only a loose causal connection in mind when they think of course-of-life needs in relation to any sort of incapacity or observable derangement. It is loose, in a respect that I have tried to capture with the notion of "rebuttable presumption," by not being categorically universal. Moreover, no exact rule could be given for how far short of being fully universal a need might be and still be accepted among those to be assigned to the List. The connection is loose, too, in respect to the upper bounds of the Minimum Standards of Provision. In the ordinary way, no one would really think that the Standards had been discredited, much less the assertion of the basic need, by observing that people could get along with provisions short of them. The causal effects of the provisions are not, in the ordinary way, insisted upon with such exactness.

Nevertheless, they come into the defense of the provisions, as they do into the criticism. Is not the ordinary way of looking upon these matters something like this? Provisions in effect meeting Minimum Standards of Provision are assigned in packets that have, taken as wholes, the causal properties required and, besides, answer to conventional notions about minimal decency and humanity. The packets are filled out in the latter respect because it would be uncomfortably mean or unreasonable to begrudge the filling out. However, they do not thereby get put beyond criticism. The filling out is checked by the possibility, frequently realized, of arguing that a less ample packet would do as well causally. Now, to be persuasive, the argument must cite an alternative packet that also satisfied conventional notions about minimal decency and humanity. In North America, it would be absurd to suggest, nowadays, doing without indoor plumbing; or, anywhere, without clothing presentable under the conventions holding for the Reference Population (Adam Smith's linen shirt). I conjecture, however, that keeping within the range of alternatives that satisfy conventional notions about minimal decency and humanity is something that most often goes without saying. Discussion is directed rather toward showing the causal adequacy of the alternative packet, sometimes, perhaps most often, by showing that is accomplishes the same things as the packet under attack, but more cheaply: the same housing space per capita; or the same range of special uses for clothing.

Two ways in which people who have the concept might react to the Criterion and the Minimum Standards of Provision, made explicit, are now visible. One way would be to match these things to their usage by incorporating in the Criterion references to conventional notions about minimal decency and humanity. Alternatively, short of such incorporation, they might say that the Criterion was to be understood in the light of the allowances that I have just been making. I shall take the latter course myself. Leaving the Criterion as it is no doubt unduly sharpens the causal issues. However, just for this reason, it serves, so formulated, as a rallying point for observations, and for discussion of assertions about needs on their causal side. It does not misrepresent the facts to maintain with the Criterion that the concept of needs is continually checked and influenced by causal considerations of the kind that the Criterion embraces. Not only are alternative packets—alternative forms of provision—challenged by questions about their causal adequacy. Conventions that interfere with meeting needs that the Criterion would endorse are liable to be resisted for that reason, though the Chinese practice of foot-binding and other grotesque conventions shows that the resistance sometimes lies dormant for centuries on end. We should recollect, too, that from the possibility of dispensing with the conventions, and eliminating the needs, if society as a whole gave the conventions up, it by no means follows that individual members of society can escape the conventions while society maintains them. For individual persons the needs are for the time being irreducible facts. So they must be for general social policy, too, in the absence of any immediate prospect of changing the conventions, and, when there is such a prospect, as a locus of costs to be faced during radical social change.

3.4* Further Aspects of Normativity

Whenever a need is derived from a social arrangement, and thus has a conventional aspect, whenever, indeed, it has a conventional aspect of any sort—for example, in the variety and amplitude of the Minimum Standards of Provision associated with it—its assertion and recognition imply a normative commitment to the conventions presupposed. The commitment may not go very far. It may go no further than to acknowledge that the convention, good or bad, must be conformed to for the time being. Enthusiasm for the convention would make the commitment robuster; but even the most limited commitment will impress the need with some normativity. The normativity is not something conferred on the need from the outside by the Principle of Precedence; it is there already. But this is true of every need, basic or derived, however little or great its dependence on conventions. Just by being asserted and recognized as a need it has normative force. The concept always wears normative vestments as well as factual ones; the passage from "is" to "ought" occurs within the office that it performs. Were the need only an adventitious one, it would have normative force, at least until application of the relational formula brought to light an end that ethics allowed us, or required us, to repudiate as indifferent or unworthy. When, basic or derived, the need is a course-of-life one, the relational formula is not likely to discover an indifferent or unworthy end.

There are further aspects of normativity that are even less happily thought of as imposed from outside on particular needs by the Principle of Precedence; and not happily thought of, either, as collected from particular needs taken one by one, though there is perhaps no harm in putting them, with their force, under the Principle, once they and their sources have been recognized. These are aspects not of needs taken one by one, but of needs taken together, in each other's company. They are two properties of the basic List of Matters of Need, which I shall treat as preserved through the whole body of derived needs and of conventionally required Minimum Standards of Provision.

3.41* The List Looked upon as Normatively Complete

In the first place, the List is open to challenge normatively unless it is complete in the sense that meeting the needs on it suffices to enable a person to lead, perhaps not a happy life, but at least a normally full one. This demand for completeness is very problematical. Even if the List in two parts as hitherto given were complete, meeting the needs on it would not suffice for a normally full life. One would have to open a third part of the List, as I shall consider doing in a later chapter, and make room for things even so elementary as the need to travel out of the house and around the block, if no further, and the need to have a variety of friends. But, as I have pointed out, the two parts are not complete; they cannot be completed without bringing conceptual innovation to an arbitrary stop. Yet the demand for completeness has deep traditional roots, for example, in the contrast between meeting needs (in accordance with God's and Nature's plan) and indulging in luxuries (the downfall of civilization). Can no sense be made of it?

Considering a possible need for psychotherapy will give us a clue to making some sense of it. I shall not differentiate between theories or techniques of psychotherapy, just as in considering a need for medical care I would not differentiate between various procedures or remedies. Let us just assume that some potentially effective kind of psychotherapy is available—perhaps only a palliative treatment, as is often the case with medical care in other connections.

After some vacillation, I decided, subject to later review, not to include a need for medical care on the List of Matters of Need that I have been working with. It is common enough, certainly, to be reckoned a presumptively universal course-of-life need; it is undeniably important. However, to add it would create some redundancy in the List. Medical care is needed to prevent or repair deficiencies in respect to other needs on the List: bodily injury, in spite of precautions against injury; infection, leading to damage to the body or impairing its relation to the environment; ingestion or inhalation of poisonous substances, with like effects. Genetic failures in organs or failures because of aging are in a somewhat different position, but even these may be brought in through the failures to meet needs that they lead to (e.g., through difficulties in digestion, deficiency in meeting the need for food). Asserting the needs thus put at risk already entails asserting a need for medical care.

Psychotherapy may seem to be in a similar position. If it is needed, some deficiency must have occurred, in respect to some need or needs, in either part of the List. The body has been poisoned; or the person has had too little rest, perhaps; or lacks companionship, social acceptance, and sexual satisfaction. If we could assume that sometime or other in their lives people would be as commonly afflicted with these miseries as with nonpsychological maladies, we would have an argument for thinking psychotherapy entailed, like medical care, by the needs already on the List.

However, the argument is not the only one that leads to need for psychotherapy. Another argument can be furnished, which also makes it a derived need, but takes a different route. This argument reveals something about how the idea of a complete List operates.

Suppose all the needs on the List are met for some person; yet, notwithstanding, he manifests conspicuous and persistent derangement of function.

One possibility is that a further need (other than a need for psychotherapy), not on the List but so widely shared as to be presumptively universal, can be identified—perhaps the need for some stress, perhaps the need for social orientation, perhaps a need for working out the characterological consequences of upbringing. (I am putting aside addictions, however widespread, for separate treatment later.) When this further need, now unmet, has been properly provided for, the derangement disappears. This need is therefore added to the List as something scheduled for provision hereafter. The need for psychotherapy is not. There is no more of a case for adding it than there is when the derangement is due to not meeting a need already on the List, though there, too, psychotherapy may sometimes prove useful as a stopgap.

A second possibility, however, is that the derangement arises from other causes—from personal characteristics that are idiosyncratic or shared with few other people: The person in question is extraordinarily timid; or extraordinarily quick to take offense; or extraordinarily and continually anxious. These characteristics may foster special needs— for example, a need for systematic reassurance—and the observed derangement may be attributed to deficiencies with respect to these special needs. But these needs will not be added to the List since they fail to be presumptively universal. Yet they will call for psychotherapy. A need for psychotherapy may thus emerge and even find its way onto the List. For although the special needs may vary from person to person, it may be assumed that everyone will have some such needs, unmet, at some time of life, and so stand in need of psychotherapy.

In effect, when psychotherapy is resorted to, successfully or not, in dealing with such special needs, it is, I think, commonly taken for granted that the List is complete without them. Or, more exactly, people turn to psychotherapy as if they were assuming that all needs which could be looked upon as presumptively universal, whether or not they have all been identified, have been met. The position then is that if the person is not functioning without derangement, though all those needs have been met, he ought to be. This "ought" no doubt often reflects received notions about

God's and Nature's plan; but it also expresses a conviction about what may be expected to suffice in normal cases. If normal provisions do not suffice here, something has gone wrong; therefore, measures of therapy should be taken to remedy the troubles, like neuroses, that prevent sufficient provisions for the presumptively universal needs from having their normal effect.

"Why just psychotherapy?" one might ask. Might not there be physical disabilities that implied special needs? Indeed there might be, but they are already accommodated by the allowance for variations in provisions under each head of need and the provision of medical care. Might not the obstacles be social ones? Indeed they might be—perhaps defective social arrangements that in family life or elsewhere placed some people under unbearable pressure. In the long run, social transformation might be a far better means of dealing with the derangement than psychotherapy, which is often ineffective anyway. However, the consequences of defective arrangements in the past and present would still have to be faced. Furthermore, possibly under any social arrangements whatever, people are going to have special psychic needs that fall outside the needs on the List or to be added to it; and psychotherapy will have some work to do for those people.

3.42* The Absence of Embarrassing Needs from the List

The second way in which the company of other needs matters normatively comes to light when it is noted that none of the needs on the List are undignified, embarrassing, or morally objectionable. They are all quite soberly respectable. What would people who invoke the concept of needs in its basic normative use make of such a suggestion as that human beings have a need to dominate others, which might carry so far as to imply preventing others from meeting their needs? Such a need is in itself morally objectionable, as none are in the List set forth, and (at least carried to the length indicated) it could not be admitted to the List without overturning the assumption of consistency. Yet philosophers and psychologists have made a case for there being such a need; some have held that it is universal. They may have been wrong. However, nothing can rule out a priori the possibility of finding, empirically, that unless this supposed need is met, people suffer from a derangement of function quite as visible as results from failing to meet any more respectable need. (A need to dominate may also play as big a part in explaining human actions, perhaps—just as Nietzsche and perhaps Hobbes would have been inclined to insist—a much bigger one than most other needs.)

I think that if people familiarly invoking the concept of needs in its basic normative application were confronted with evidence that established the existence of a need to dominate, they would be inclined to exclude it from the List as morally objectionable. If it were a need that arose from contingent social arrangements, including patterns of family life, which were subject to change, it could be excluded and yet temporized with, one of the ways, to be discussed later, of dealing with embarrassing needs and addictions. In time, given suitable social reforms, it would not have to be dealt with at all; the List would survive uncontaminated. Excluding it if, on the other hand, it could not be done away with would not be such a brilliant idea. Would it not have to be dealt with somehow? Would not excluding it just exhibit willful blindness toward reality? Yet even an attempt to exclude it would give the List of nonexcluded, approved needs a normative color that did not come from the Principle of Precedence. The effort would make it clear that only respectable needs belonged to the List, insofar as the List represents the ordinary conception of what is included under course-of-life needs.

As things stand, this color remains only potential; it is more hypothetical than real. How many people in any Self-govliset that we might have in view in the English-speaking world (or in other language communities) would have heard of Hobbes's or Nietzsche's or Adler's teachings I do not know. I should think, only a minority, few or none of whom have actually confronted anything like the issue whether a need to dominate should be on the List of Matters of Need invoked in the basic normative use of the concept of needs. Omitting to confront the issue does not imply neglectful or incoherent thinking. Very likely it can be explained by the absence (so far) of irresistible evidence that human beings do have a presumptively universal need to dominate. Such evidence may be absent for other needs that would be embarrassing if they were genuine.

The fact that the needs on the List are all respectable ones, then, though it is some evidence of the List's being surrounded by normative safeguards, does not therefore imply that the needs which do figure on it ever had to pass a normative test to gain or hold their places. Practice and the evidence known to date accord with a Criterion in which such a test is not implied. Without such an implication, my account of the concept of needs leaves it vulnerable to normative objections in cases of embarrassing needs. But this is a virtue of the account. The concept really is vulnerable to such objections, to the point of normative breakdown, as I shall fully acknowledge in my chapter on breakdowns, when I shall take up the subject of embarrassing needs again, together with addictions. I have confined myself here to maintaining that the List as it stands is wholly respectable and that one may doubt whether people relying on the concept have become generally convinced of the case for any embarrassing additions.

3.5 The Basic Account as a Schema for Expanded or Retracted Use

Derivation and conventionality and normativity, operating together, do not everywhere, or even in places where they most obviously affect assertions of need, make those assertions ill-founded, arbitrary, or inconsequential. The normative force of the assertions often persists notwithstanding, sustained in part by having attached to the assertions questions of fact that clearly demand observational evidence. Yet the complications that I have been discussing—in particular the closely associated complications of derivation and conventionality—do open up possibilities of fruitless disputation. People are bound to differ in the commitment that they feel to existing social arrangements, and in the energy that they will put into changing the arrangements. Some people, more than others, will view existing arrangements as susceptible to change regardless of their own efforts or wishes, because they differ in their estimates of the readiness of other people to make the change, and of the degree to which the arrangements are malleable in further respects. On all these different grounds, people are liable on occasion to fall into an interminable dispute about whether something that some of them recognize as a need should be so recognized.

The best way of dealing with this difficulty, without forfeiting the point that many needs will still, whether or not they have conventional features, stand on a firm nonconventional foundation, seems to be to treat the apparatus of my basic account—the List of Matters of Need, the Minimum Standards of Provision associated with these Matters, the Criterion, the Principle of Precedence—as a schema capable of more or less expansive use. Not only is it a schema reiterated as one moves from matters themselves on the List to derived needs, and there draws again—within a relatively retracted compass—a distinction between Matters of Need and Minimum Standards of Provision. It is also a schema subject to overall expansion and retraction. In a given discussion, in a given Selfgovliset, any substantial falling away from unanimous agreement on what are to be taken as needs requires retracting the discussion within a narrower use of the schema if it is to continue on the presupposition that it is needs that are being contemplated. The requirement operates more dramatically when the issue is accepting something as a basic Matter of Need. However, disagreement about what constitutes accepted Minimum Standards of Provision for a very specific derived Matter of Need, if the disagreement is blatant and persistent, will also drive the discussion back to a retracted schema, with minima lower than some people had been willing to advocate.

A modest use for a critique of needs lies simply in showing the way back to a retracted schema. For this purpose a critique might use the apparatus of the present account to identify the schema and follow up the implications of the present chapter in seeking to identify the grounds on which, in particular cases, purported needs are so widely rejected. Is it because the evidence tells against any connection with the Criterion? Then the assertions of need that are in question are discredited in the most trenchant way possible. There is no derangement of function to be feared. Is it because people are beginning to hesitate to keep up the conventions from which those purported needs are derived? Then just what conventions are to be set aside as no longer sufficiently compelling? Or is it because the derivation of one or another purported need was fallacious? What then are the needs that are validly derived from the same convention or conventions? Is the ground on which the purported need is rejected its failure to connect with anything beyond some person's idiosyncratic prejudice or fancy? Or with anything beyond the self-serving exhortations of advertisers? This, too, demands exposure by a critique. A critique, finally, should be able to give the disputants a reasonably adequate idea of what is left in the schema retracted from the purported needs examined— what Matters of Need, basic and derived, and what Minimum Standards of Provision.

Will the retracting ever go so far as to reduce the use of the schema to a short list of basic needs—to something like my two-part List, or even to something like the first part of it only, confined to needs physical or biological in cast?

Even if it did go so far, it would leave the concept of needs a substantial amount of work to do in guiding social policy. It would still cover matters that are expensive to provide for, and that in fact go unprovided for in all too many cases. Let us not forget those starving old ladies or those homeless people in New York and Chicago.

I see no reason to believe that in general retracting will go so far. Indeed, even in the Minimum Standards of Provision accepted for recipients of welfare in the United States and Canada, mean as those standards are compared with the standards of living for the middle class, and inefficient as social policy is in actually meeting them, a more expansive use of the schema is at work. It is accepted that people need indoor plumbing and central heating. Elsewhere, certainly in debates that do not involve the whole membership of a Selfgovliset, there must be innumerable instances in which by mutual consent the schema is used more expansively. Consider, for example, discussions of social policy at a conference of sociologists, or of professors of social work; or a meeting of parents in a prosperous town discussing the needs of their teen-age children.

Full commitment to the idea of an expansible and retractable schema discourages—properly discourages—attempts to answer at random questions about whether this or that is a need. Someone, knowing that I was writing about needs, turned to me in a discussion and asked, "Do people have a need for pornography?" Foolishly, I began to try to answer without any preliminaries regarding resort to the schema. But random questions turn out as often as not to be traps. They are the more insidious because sometimes, raising items that, like being safe from fire or fear, are strong candidates for inclusion on the basic List (perhaps assimiliated to other items already there) or among the associated Minimum Standards of Provision, they can be convincingly answered without mobilizing anything like my basic account and its complications. In general, however, before one proceeds with questions about individual items, one needs to ask where are we, questioner and respondent, with respect to the schema? And that question in turn requires us to ask, what are the issues of policy before us? Are they issues on which we are all, questioners and respondents, ready to use a relevantly expanded schema, or must we fall back on a retracted one? Then it may help to ask whether the issue is about a Matter of Need to be ascribed to the basic List or derived from it, or about the extent of the Minimum Standards to which we are to work in providing for a Matter of Need agreed-on. We must be prepared to find that on occasion we can determine what is to be counted as a need only in the context of a set of specific issues that are being dealt with inside a given Selfgovliset.

I do not think that this feature of the socially evaluative use of the concept of needs impairs the factuality of needs. On the contrary, once the schema has been fixed in respect to degree of expansion, all the needs that then come under it are provided for or not provided for as matters of observational evidence. The account I have given, treated as a schema expansible and retractable, may strike just the sort of balance that the conceptual situation requires. The practice of using the term "needs" has both firm foundations and fluid complications; and both these aspects must be attended to if the practice is to be accurately described over the whole range of its operation.

3.6 Abuses of the Concept of Needs

Arguing so pertinaciously on the side of vindicating the concept of needs all too easily begins to give the impression that I have lost sight of the abuses of the concept. That is far from my intention. I want to keep the abuses and possibilities of abuse firmly in mind. Derivation and conventionality and normativity, though not by any means inevitably abuses in themselves, do open opportunities for abuse that are commonly seized.

3.61 Reducing Abuses by Retracting Scope

The basic pattern of abuse is one in which the normativity of needs is invoked for needs that are at best derived needs, which depend by way of contingent social arrangements, or directly, upon questionable conventions. In the extreme, there may be no such conventions, just a personal inclination to believe that there is: I claim that I need a shirt with French cuffs and cuff links, too, to make a presentable appearance in public. Or, less flagrant, but still flagrant enough, the conventions may exist, and be untroubled by any widespread doubts that they should be persisted in, but not imply the purported need. (The conventions may, for example, allow for alternative forms of provision not of the description used to define the need.) Or, the conventions may have the implication, but the purported need may fail to connect also with the Criterion. Leaving it unmet may not cause derangement of function. Or, the conventions may have the implication, and the purported need the connection, but the conventions may have awakened widespread doubts, which are engendering or about to engender current debate on keeping the conventions up.

To a large extent, control of such abuses takes care of itself. The person or group that asserts the need will not gain the assent of the other members of the Selfgovliset. Without majority support, they will not have their way, unless they are disproportionately powerful or specially effective in manipulation. Even with majority support, they will not succeed in having the matter in question treated as a need so long as there is a substantial and articulate minority that rejects it as such. Just what makes taking the path of asserting needs politically attractive, namely, having what is accepted as needs treated as matters to be given such precedence that controversy is foregone and no vote is required to settle divisions upon them, proves unattainable in the given instance. If discussion is to continue under the same presuppositions regarding the concept of needs, all concerned, majority and minority, must retract the schema to a list of needs in which the controverted one does not appear (supposing that the controversy cannot be resolved in its favor).

Retracting the schema may eliminate abuses if it goes far enough, but will retraction always occur when it should? I have, up to this point, depended on outbreaks of disagreement to create a drive for retraction, which a critique of needs would assist. However, may not people be agreed as to certain things being needs that are not properly to be regarded as such? Everybody taking part in the discussion, even the whole membership of a Selfgovliset, may be trapped in a collective illusion. To be sure, it would be rare for a whole community to believe that it had a convention when no such convention existed. One may also doubt whether a whole community will often agree in a fallacious derivation from a convention; for some sorts of derivations, one might even doubt whether instances of fallacy were possible, since what the community agreed in deriving, in respect to minimum standards of housing, for example, would best be taken as further defining the convention or conventions from which the derivation proceeded.

However, it is relatively easy for a whole community to overlook some alternative forms of provision in any instance; to agree, fallaciously, for example, that people must have transportation to get to stores, when in fact it could be arranged to have mobile stores come to them. Frequent enough, one might suppose, would also be instances of collective illusion about purported needs that could go unmet without any substantial evidence of universal or near-universal derangement of function—without any physical weakness, without any loss in psychological powers. Advertising saturates us with tendencies to collective illusions of this kind as well as the other one just mentioned. Thus people could do without toothpaste, though I suppose this would commonly be agreed to be something needed; they could brush their teeth with baking soda, as consumers' magazines used to recommend with persistent austerity, or even forego brushing entirely in favor of flossing. They could do without citrus juice; though they need vitamin C, they could get if from rose-hip syrup, or from sauerkraut.

A whole community may concur in failing to perceive that there are more attractive alternatives to the convention or conventions from which certain needs derive—alternatives less rigid, less confining, less costly, less troubling, which assist in these and other ways the attainment of happier lives. A critique of needs capable of exposing the other sorts of error would have to be raised to a higher power to deal with this one. It would have to mobilize arguments from the comparative study of cultures, from social experiments with communes and other social forms, from empirical theories about constraints on social institutions, from utopian visions. It would also have to have comprehensive command of the principles of ethics, since, sometimes, purported needs are not only to be objected to as depending on conventions less effective than alternatives to the conventions. They are to be objected to on the grounds that meeting them is inevitably unjust or inhumane.

Given the web of conventions from which any convention would have to be extracted, a critique of needs could hardly hope for the luxury of dealing with conventions that it costs nothing to do away with. Yet it could hope to give on many occasions a comparative assessment of the costs of maintaining the conventions as against changing them. Moreover, while the critique would have much to learn from critiques with comparably comprehensive ambitions mounted in cases of social disagreement, cases of class conflict among them, it is capable of starting up whenever, in comparative studies or in theoretical speculation, a conjecture about the possibility of doing better achieves expression. Obviously, needs that survived such a critique would be more convincing than needs that, with their superordinate conventions, did not; and the needs on the basic List may well seem more likely to survive than any needs that depend on conventions for more than their conceptualization. On the other hand, the relatively greater possibility that it might fall before a critique does not by itself deprive a need derived from a convention of its factuality or its normative force.

3.62 Reducing Abuses by Relaxing Priority

Another way of reducing abuses of the concept of needs lies in shifting, under the Principle of Precedence, from strict final priority to something less exacting. I shall do this myself in the chapter to come on reconciling attention to needs with attention to preferences, where I shall concede that strict final priority is not the sort of priority that fits into a realistic picture of how the concept of needs is actually used in politics. Something less exacting that I call "role-relative precautionary priority" fits much better. It does so, however, at the cost of raising serious moral objections. A less exacting sort of priority cannot be so easily abused to give the full weight of needs to matters that should not be reckoned such. On the other hand, it has the drawback on occasion of not giving genuine needs their full weight. If such needs have essential parts to play in promoting justice and happiness, then not giving them full weight will be a moral dereliction in respect to these things. To see just what those essential parts may be, and hence just what the moral dereliction may amount to, I shall retain the assumption of strict final priority in the next two chapters, on justice and utilitarianism, respectively.

DIALOGUE

CRITICAL READER: *I'm dizzy with complications. Even the comfort of hearing that we'll persist with strict final priority for a time doesn't calm my fears. For sooner or later, strict final priority will come unstuck. I wonder, after that relaxation, will anything go? But maybe anything goes already—any consideration can be a need; and any amount of attention or neglect may be given it. How can one tell among the maze of considerations already produced?*

NOT-YET-REPENTANT AUTHOR: *Would you have been happier if I'd presented a necessary-and-sufficient-conditions definition of needs? I think I can make a further claim about the wisdom of evading the demand for a definition. The task is to describe a complex linguistic practice, and bundling the whole description into a definition would have been, to say the least, contrived, awkward, and indigestible.*

READER: *That's my trouble—there are enough complications anyway to give me mental indigestion.*

AUTHOR: *How could it be otherwise? We are trying to grasp a practice adapted to all the complications of social life. But, remember, in the face of the complications of the practice itself, an enormous number of considerations survive that do not figure on the List or among the Minimum Standards of Provision. They are not course-of-life needs, derived or underived. Some are special needs, marked off*

127

as not being presumptively universal from the needs that are embraced by my account. Some are adventitious needs, which command social attention, if they do, on a footing quite outside my account. If a man needs a spinnaker, that remains just an adventitious need.

READER: *But isn't every consideration a need of some sort or other?*

AUTHOR: *Even if every consideration were, that would not erase the boundaries of my account, or imply that relatively few considerations lay outside those boundaries. But you're forgetting, perhaps just because we've worked the term "needs" so hard, that all along innumerable considerations have been set aside as matters of preference only. Not a single good shown for sale in Frederic Wiseman's film about Neimann-Marcus (The Store) could plausibly be held to answer to a need, on my account of needs: not the sable jackets; not the dresses; not the perfumes; not the make-up; not the jewelry. I expect the same is true of goods advertised in any ordinary issue of* The New Yorker. *Who could possibly need a "$40,000 bracelet, set with over 1800 diamonds"?*

READER: *All the same, I'd think you'd be less ready to defend the concept after surveying the complications of the chapter we've just been through.*

AUTHOR: *My defense of the concept goes no further than to say that in spite of these complications it often works well. I'm not hiding the complications. So far, and for a number of chapters to follow, they won't be disastrous. I won't hide the disastrous complications, when their turn comes.*

READER: *Meanwhile, we're to pretend they don't exist?*

AUTHOR: *Meanwhile, we're to see enough of the range over which the concept works so that we won't take so much fright at the disasters when they come—the points of breakdown—as to think that they ruin the concept everywhere.*

F O U R

THE PLACE OF NEEDS IN
REASONING ABOUT JUSTICE

The concept of needs comes into reasoning about justice in two ways: contingently, in the train of rights; necessarily, in the train of a demand for equality. This position is weaker, in regard to rights, than many would expect. It is stronger in regard to equality. Indeed, put thus shortly, it is perhaps too strong. For some conceptions of justice, even some that by definition embrace a demand for equality (which not all conceptions of justice do), the necessity will turn out to be, not logical necessity, but practical. Nevertheless, it is even then a necessity that cannot be defied without jeopardizing the realization of the conceptions of justice in question. So it makes a strong connection between justice and the concept of needs. Whether it is practical only or logical as well, there is a strong connection of some sort over the whole range of plausible conceptions of justice. Properly nuanced, the position stated holds for all the families of conceptions falling within that range.

4.1 The Opportunity for Mutual Support

The Principle of Precedence for needs will contribute a good deal of force to any conception of justice that it is combined with. Does the force of the Principle itself require justification? I do not think justifying it would be easy. Here we seem to come to rock bottom in ethics just as with course-of-life needs we came to rock bottom in the application of the relational formula. It would be easy enough, to be sure, to supply a form of argument deducing the Principle from some principle more general, for example, Alan Donagan's principle, "It is impermissible not to promote the well-being of others by actions in themselves permissible, [insofar] as one can do so without proportionate inconvenience." But what strength would the Principle of Precedence gain from that? One might think that the support went the other way: Donagan's principle commands assent because more specific principles hover in the background, chief among them the Principle of Precedence.

Again, some think (I among them) that at the bottom of ethics there operates some principle or some relation between people in which they are found caring for one another, or at least ready to give mutual aid. The Principle of Precedence may serve to express this fundamental point. It may serve all the better because it does not require a generalized altruism that ignores the difference between other people's claims in respect to needs and their claims in respect to preferences.

Other principles, therefore, have a lot to lose from falling into conflict with the Principle of Precedence. In particular, will it not be a powerful argument against any conception of justice that it would tolerate some people's needs not being met, when there are the resources to meet them? (Suppose, if this is relevant, that the people in question have fulfilled all reasonable conditions about shouldering the burdens of production.)

Yet any contribution that the Principle of Precedence, and with it the concept of needs, makes to strengthening a conception of justice will be fully reciprocated. If anything did threaten acceptance of the Principle of Precedence from a moral point of view, would not the worst threat of all come from finding the Principle in conflict with justice? Showing that justice requires conformity to the Principle removes the threat and vindicates the Principle.

It is true, the force that justice has, when it has to do with needs, varies, like the force of the Principle of Precedence, with the footing of the needs in question. It will be greatest when that footing is firmest, which is the case when the schema has been retracted to embrace only the needs on the List, those conceptually entailed by them, and those derived from them when they are joined with scientific generalizations or other facts about natural circumstances. The following discussion will also apply to needs derived from social arrangements. However, for all the reasons that came to light in the previous chapter against giving uniform normative force to such needs, the demands of justice may not be so inexorable when those needs are in question. I shall draw the examples in this chapter chiefly from needs with the firmest possible footing, which most strongly invite being given strict final priority.

4.2 Needs Contingently Connected with Justice via Rights

What could have a stronger claim under justice than a need already firmly footed, which is also covered by a right, that is to say, a specific social device consisting in a standing combination of acknowledged social rules? (Some of these rules would have to do with the exercise of the right, some with acquiring or relinquishing the status of having the right to exercise; some rules would define the powers of the rightholders, some the obligations of other people.) Justice is commonly defined in terms of rights, as in the definition that Mill arrives at in Chapter 5 of *Utilitarianism*: "Justice consists in respecting, injustice in violating, a right held by an assignable person." Even people who might regard this definition as too narrow would be bound, if they recognized any rights at all, to look upon violating them as injustice; hence, if among the rights that they recognized, there were some that explicitly covered needs, they would be bound to consider failing to meet needs (some needs) as a species of injustice.

Let us waive for the moment the possibility that there

may be conceptions of justice that do not come hand in hand with the advocacy of any rights. The connection of needs with justice by way of rights is still only a contingent connection. For it is only contingently, when rights are recognized, that needs are covered by rights.

4.21* Analogies between Needs and Rights

This may well seem surprising, given the analogies between needs and rights that surface in my account of needs. On that account, the members of the Selfgovliset—people with the concept of needs—ascribe as matters of rebuttable presumption the needs on the basic List to all the members of a Reference Population—the people who have the needs. In doing so, the members of the Selfgovliset express their readiness to find, for every person in the Reference Population and every Matter of Need, some provisions required by that person as a Minimum Standard of Provision for that need.

However, it may turn out that, because they are physiologically or psychologically exceptional, some people in the Reference Population have no occasion to use any provisions for a given need; or, because they simply choose to use less, having adopted a deviant life-style, no occasion to use all the provisions that the members of the Selfgovliset are prepared to concede as needed under the Minimum Standards of Provision. Moreover, it will generally be left to the members of the Reference Population to take up, or not to take up, such provisions for their needs as are made available to them. It may even be left to them to decide whether such provisions shall be produced or assembled for their use.

As maximum allowable claims that can be pressed or waived by the people to whom they are conceded, the Minimum Standards of Provision look very much like provisions to which those people have rights. Certainly it is very easy to slide along the analogies from assertions about needs to assertions of rights. Nevertheless, though the possibility of waiving the provisions is genuine enough, the claims in question may not be claims of right but merely claims pressed in argument—and in argument not within the Reference Population but within the Selfgovliset.

4.22* Despite Analogies, Rights May Disregard Needs

Not all champions of rights—champions of justice, therefore, in regard to respecting rights—erect claims about needs into claims of rights. They may, like Nozick, at least Nozick abstracting from his Lockean Proviso against the total engrossment of the means of life, accept rights to acquiring, holding, and transferring private property, but not rights to having needs met. They may not even bother to defend the rights that they do recognize as having some merit as devices for enabling people to meet their own needs.

If the needs of the whole Reference Population demand any sort of explicit attention, these champions of rights may suggest that is something for private charity to take care of, not rights. Some members of the Selfgovliset may take this position, consistently with granting the existence of needs and Minimum Standards of Provision with all the analogies just mentioned. Others, perhaps more willing to acknowledge themselves to be bound by the Principle of Precedence, may argue that laissez faire or some other variety of self-help will work well enough in meeting needs to make any system of rights explicitly devoted to them superfluous.

4.23 Rights Themselves Dispensable

Even those members of the Selfgovliset who are champions of needs and in addition consider that justice requires meeting them may always contemplate using other devices besides rights. People need mates; people need food. However, could not a lottery or a system of computer

135

assignments share out the mates? Might not offering flour and eggs at multiple distribution points on a first-come, first-served basis serve to meet the need for food?

It is, to be sure, easier to see that such devices could take the place of rights, and the rights in question be entirely absent, when we take a culture-transcendent view. Let us consider a society not our own, though equally benevolent in its settled aims, if not more so, that might not use the device of rights at all. The authorities there could monitor the degree to which, in various regions, people's needs are being met at the Minimum Standards recognized. When the statistics for a given region looked bad, the authorities would pour resources into the region until the statistics began to look acceptable. More flour and eggs would be sent to the distribution points there; these points would be increased in number and scattered more widely.

In practice, it may be of the greatest importance to have needs covered by rights, because this may be the most efficacious way of making sure that the needs are met. The assumption that it is often seems to explain present policy. A part of the Reference Population, let us suppose, has provisions for food, clothing, and shelter inferior by far to those enjoyed by the rest. For those who regard this, under the Principle of Precedence, as an evil, one technique for remedying it would be to accord people in the impoverished part special rights, which they could enjoy so long as they had no alternative way of securing provisions. Another technique, which would come to much the same thing, would be to accord everybody rights to minimum provisions, and let them invoke the rights when they had occasion to. The U.S. federal food stamp program perhaps illustrates both techniques. All U.S. citizens have rights to minimum provisions; given these rights, they have under certain conditions rights to be issued food stamps.

Yet the assumption that rights are the most efficacious device is not to be taken for granted. The alternative procedures might in the end come as close to meeting the needs of everyone in the Reference Population as the device of rights. Suppose, however, that in the end there are some people to whom under the alternative procedures the provisions do not reach. They may be no more numerous— they might be less numerous—than the people who, given rights, would not have succeeded in exercising them. Certainly they have grounds for complaint. Would they not be asserting rights to the provisions if they made the complaints?

On a culture-immanent view, thinking as we think—say, in the English-speaking world at the present time—about needs and rights, we shall be powerfully inclined to say that at least the people who have not been reached should be able to invoke rights to the provisions; and inclined to move on from there to saying that they have the rights already, at least on a moral view. Our practices in other connections, especially where they have to do with emerging rights not yet fully formalized, make it difficult for us to take a moral stand against recognizing such rights here; and inevitably we shall have to take such a stand if we deny the rights.

On a culture-transcendent view, however, we can contemplate the possibility that another society, at least equally benevolent and equally concerned with people's needs, might refuse to grant such rights, mindful of the consequences in conflict, litigation, and administrative expenses. Those are real costs. How could a benevolent society be justified in ignoring them? But if after full deliberation that society does conclude that it would be best not to institute current social devices (paradigmatically, legal devices) answering to the case for recognizing such rights there, the case would have failed there. Moreover, unless one wished to hold that even full deliberation on these matters would necessarily be mistaken if it concluded against the rights, one must allow that there is possibly no longer a case to be made; in that society, there are no such rights, and there is no sense in asserting them, legally, morally, or in any other way.

4.24 Justice without Rights

Such a society, rejecting any use of the device of rights explicitly devoted to meeting needs, maybe rejecting any use of rights at all, might still consciously uphold a conception of justice; and thus realize the possibility, which earlier I set aside, of justice without rights. It might, for example, accept Rawls's Difference Principle as sufficing by itself to define a pattern of justice, namely, a distribution of income and power such that those in the worst-off stratum were on average as well off as those in the worst-off stratum under any feasible distribution. Clearly the policies pursued to establish that pattern might be policies subject only to a statistical test. The same thing holds for a conception of justice that insists more rigorously than the Difference Principle on equality of income and power, refusing to allow that equality may give way to inequality for the sake of having a more prosperous worst-off stratum.

So neither championing justice nor championing equality entails championing rights. Needs will therefore not come into justice either directly or indirectly by this route, except contingently. But may they not come in, with or without rights, in the train of equality, so far as equality counts as justice?

4.3 Equality Unattractive When It Leaves Needs Unmet

No logical inconsistency arises in championing equality— say, equality of income—regardless of whether needs are met or not. A pattern of equality can prevail in the respect advocated, and leave some needs of some persons unmet. In some circumstances, equality of income would no doubt give everyone the means of meeting needs; and give most people, or all, means to spare. Suppose, however, resources and circumstances are more straitened. Income has been distributed equally, without regard to needs, and some people end up with more than enough to meet their needs, while other people have too little. The Minimum Standards of Provision for them are higher; they are still hungry; or, to stop shivering and go to sleep, they need the extra blankets that are making other people hot.

One might well wonder whether in those circumstances equality of income retained any moral attractions. Can treating people equally, with no account taken of the differences between them in respect to needs, amount to treating them with equal respect? In the end, my argument that needs come in the train of equality will embrace even conceptions of justice that, however implausibly, favor equality in some sense while they disregard needs. For those conceptions can be captured by the same practical necessity that captures conceptions of justice which try to do without either equality or needs. Let us consider meanwhile, however, conceptions of justice in which equality figures in a more attractive guise.

The most attractive of these conceptions, I believe, are those that take a stand, not on equality of income or any other form of literal equality in goods to be distributed, but on meeting the needs of everyone in the Reference Population, with provisions for the needs varying from person to person as the Minimum Standards vary. Since everyone's needs, on this approach, are equally taken into account, what is aimed at may be called equality-in-meeting-needs.

Even literal equality becomes attractive to a degree, however, if it brings along with it a concern for meeting people's needs. Just this concern may furnish some people with their chief reason for seeking literal equality. Suppose a variety of benefits (and burdens) are to be officially distributed. Already, with the fact that some things are held to be benefits because they meet needs, and others burdens because they jeopardize meeting them, some chance appears (though it is far from a guarantee) that literal equality in the official distribution will result in meeting needs.

Moreover, by far the most important and most familiar application of literal equality lies in the equal division of money income (or of funds), leaving people to make their own decisions about spending. Given equal income and tolerably comfortable circumstances, it can easily be assumed that all the people sensible enough to want to will provide for meeting their needs, with due variation from person to person. The chance may now seem so good that the realization is taken for granted, and needs drop out as a reason for having equality, since the champion of equality will now see no occasion to express any concern about meeting needs. Such seems to be the case with one of the most notable current writers to make prominent use of the notion of literal equality, Ronald Dworkin. In a discussion of equality otherwise remarkably thorough, Dworkin sets up an ideal of an initial distribution, not quite of equal money income, but of equal money as spending power. People are to plan their whole lives with this as a start. Dworkin does not contemplate them as having to take any special precautions about meeting their needs.

4.4 Variable Favor for Needs under Literal-Equality-with-Exceptions

It is not, however, literal equality as such that one may expect champions of it to advocate. It is literal equality (in whatever is to be distributed) with exceptions. Besides having a strong claim to come in with literal equality if there are no exceptions, the concept of needs comes in with the exceptions, on any plausible account of the exceptions. Once the postulated initial distribution has occurred and people start producing for the market, Dworkin turns from literal equality to literal-equality-with-exceptions. But he omits several familiar heads of exception. The exceptions that he discusses, which license, indeed require departures from equality in the course of time to make the system of distribution "ambition-sensitive," fall under the heads of service and effort. People who prefer leisure to making further efforts to serve other people's wants through the market justly get less than people who are more active in production. One might comment that the argument for these exceptions becomes appreciably stronger if the efforts so rewarded are efforts to serve other people's needs. Needs come in more directly, however, under heads of exception that Dworkin does not treat separately, or treat at all.

4.41 A Logically Secure Place for Needs under Exceptions for Capacity

One of these heads is rights, considered as a separate head of exception, and not, like the right to property in distributive shares early or late, consolidated with Dworkin's prescriptions for initial equality and subsequent departures. Rights are sometimes set up as devices to make sure of people's being able to meet their needs, or at least to improve their chance of doing so. This makes, however, for reasons already considered, only a contingent connection between justice and needs.

For a truly necessary—conceptually necessary—connection, one must look to another familiar head of exceptions, namely, capacity to benefit, which Dworkin does not mention at all. Under this head, the only person around who can play a piano has a claim respected by justice to be given the only piano available, or at least some priority in using it while others learn to. Under this head, again, people with greater aptitude for legal studies justly gain admission to law school, while other people, however worthy in other respects, must accept rejection. It is under this head that needs come forward. If some people—children—need more protein, if some people—some single men or women—have more need of mates, if some people have more need of any provisions whatever, does not justice, at least justice other things being equal, sanction giving them more of the relevant goods in each case? There could hardly be a more compelling difference in capacity.

A conception of justice might make of capacity to benefit a head for exceptions either required or permitted. If it is made a head for required exceptions, it seems to me absurd to deny that in the ordinary view needs require to be considered as an instance of such capacity, falling under this head. What could possibly be more important to consider? It is true, one could perhaps have a conception of justice that fit the definition in embracing equality with exceptions but did not recognize capacity as a head for exceptions, or a conception that recognized capacity but did not consider needs an instance of capacity. Conceptions of these sorts, however, would be very far from making of the definition what current ordinary beliefs and practices make of exceptions to equality. Exceptions are commonly anticipated; and no head of exceptions is more familiar than capacity. Moreover, variable capacities of sorts other than needs, like the capacity to play a piano or to read a Bulgarian book, when both of these things have yet to be produced, would not have so familiar or so forceful a claim to be recognized as a required exception. If we think of capacity, more plausibly than the other heads, as a head for exceptions that are merely permitted, departures from equality to meet variations in needs have the strongest claim to being permitted. Here, too, the force of the Principle of Precedence comes to bear in a familiar way.

To sum up, if justice is conceived of as literal-equality-with-exceptions, capacity cannot reasonably be denied a place among the recognized heads of exception. But if capacity does have a place among the heads of exception, permitted or required, the concept of needs will have a secure place under capacity. So literal equality, made more reasonable by being recast as literal-equality-with-exceptions, leads, on any reasonable view of justice under this recasting, to a necessary connection with meeting needs.

4.42 But Will This Secure Place Give Needs Much Weight?

If meeting needs is only a permitted exception to literal equality, however, this connection may not in the end turn

out to make very much of meeting them. For other considerations, under capacity or under the other heads of exception, may be given so much weight as to leave little or no
resources to meet needs, even supposing (what might logically not be the case) that the Selfgovliset is ready to make
some use of the permission. If no other consideration by itself is given so much weight as needs, the other considerations together may still overwhelm the weight on needs.

Things will be different, and the attractions of justice as
literal-equality-with-exceptions will be at their brightest, if
meeting needs becomes a required exception and this exception at least is given strict final priority. Here, however,
we come to the verge of shifting from literal equality to
equality in the other sense that I distinguished—equality-
in-meeting-needs. For the effect in carrying out the Principle of Precedence is the same: Meet the needs of everyone
in the Reference Population first, then consider how,
whether equally or by exceptions from equality, to distribute the resources remaining to be distributed officially.

4.5 Needs Logically Front and Center
with Equality-in-Meeting-Needs

4.51* Familiarity of This Proposal

If familiarity implies being noticed and discussed by all, or
almost all notable recent writers on justice, some doubt may
arise as to whether equality-in-meeting-needs is a familiar
feature of any conception of justice.

Given its obvious attractions, especially when there is
any discrepancy between it and the position that people
find themselves in after a distribution literally equal or lit-
erally-equal-with-exceptions, one is tempted to construct
arguments for imputing it to writers who have not expressly mentioned it. Does not the cogency of the Difference Principle depend on assuming that it is to be applied
to current societies with large proportions of people living
in poverty and at risk in respect to meeting their needs? To

societies where literal equality would not do so well as literal inequality in enabling people in the worst-off stratum (hence everybody) to meet their needs? Why, besides being attracted to an ideal of equality in the first place, does Dworkin care so much that equality in initial spending power not work out to penalize people who because of various handicaps cannot hope to be specially successful, or even normally successful, in the market? May it not be because of some lurking notion that the handicapped may not be even successful enough to meet their needs?

Yet it would be more than a little incautious to infer equality-in-meeting-needs from the Difference Principle, which Rawls formulates as though it is to apply, strict lexicality and all, as much to societies wholly composed of millionaires as to societies where the poor are always with us. Dworkin is in formulations and preoccupations even further away, for, unlike Rawls, he follows the economists in their doubtful practice of defining "welfare" not by needs but by preferences or satisfactions. The explicit absence of any attention to equality-in-meeting-needs in Dworkin's writings is more striking than any surreptitious operation of the proposal. Perhaps one should say the same of Sidgwick. Sidgwick does explicitly endorse distributing the means of happiness in unequal quantities if this is the way to make them equally happy. But happiness belongs rather with the economists' sense of "welfare" than with the ordinary one. Moreover, Sidgwick—oddly, for so lucid and careful a writer—also, inconsistently, endorses literal equality in distributing the means of happiness.

Nevertheless, equality-in-meeting-needs is a familiar proposal. This I take to be established by the advocacy of it in the wittiest, most eloquent, and most convincing treatise produced by British socialism—perhaps produced by socialism anywhere—R. H. Tawney's evergreen book *Equality*. Tawney says,

Human beings have . . . different requirements and . . . these different requirements can be met satisfactorily only by varying forms of provision. But equality of provision is not identity of provision. It is to be achieved, not by treating different needs in the same way, but by devoting equal care to ensuring that they are met in the different ways most appropriate to them.

He has particularly in mind, in that passage, needs for medical care and education; and he does not there explicitly connect equality with justice. He is, in fact, very sparing throughout the book in his use of the term "justice." But I think it is clear that equality-in-meeting-needs does figure in his conception of justice. In another passage, Tawney maintains,

> The sentiment of justice is satisfied, not by offering to every man identical treatment, but by treating different individuals in the same way in so far as, being human, they have requirements which are the same, and in different ways in so far as . . . they have requirements which differ.

That statement comes from a passage conceding some inequality in rewards as incentives to production; and when the ellipsis is filled in with the phrase that I have left out, the last part of the statement will be seen to be qualified accordingly: "being concerned with different services." Even filled in, that part, however, is strikingly parallel to what one may presume Tawney would say to connect justice with meeting needs generally; and the preceding part of the statement is general already.

4.52 Carrying the Proposal Out

How the distribution of benefits is to be adjusted to variations in needs is easily understood, given my basic account of the concept of needs. People will be assured provisions for their needs that, in the case of each person, meet the Minimum Standards of Provision for that person. But how is the distribution of burdens to be adjusted? If we take work to be (insofar as it is onerous or disagreeable) at once the prototype of burdens and the most important category, we can found a rule for adjustment upon a rule for distributing work in conformity with the present standard of equality: Work and other burdens shall be so distributed, taking into account variations among persons in energy, strength, and psychological aptitude, as to constitute no more of a drawback or obstacle for one person to meeting needs than for another. (We may wish to add, No more of a drawback to heeding preferences, either.)

Now, the Minimum Standards of Provision, varying from person to person, have already been supposed to be adjusted to allow for variations in work, with ampler provisions of some sorts going to people doing more strenuous work. This adjustment, however, does not rule out the possibility of there being people, idlers, who more or less completely shirk the burdens of work. So the distribution of these burdens needs to be further refined if they are to be equalized as drawbacks to meeting needs. If this is not done, the degree to which the needs of the Reference Population are being met will be uncertain; and so will any claim based on the distribution of benefits alone that the needs are being met (in the present sense) equally. The demand that idleness be deterred or penalized can now be seen as a demand for the application of a basic standard of equality; and that standard has a foundation in the concept of justice.

As I showed in my basic account (Chapter 2), the extent to which needs are met can be measured in various ways, some of them quite straightforward. In many cases, it would be easy enough to measure the extent to which the need was met by the proportion of the required provision actually supplied: If miners are to get six liters of wine a day, and actually receive only five, they are getting five-sixths of what they need. However, to avoid a number of complications having to do, among other things, with judging the comparative significance of shortfalls of different proportions respecting different needs of different persons,

I shall suppose that what equality calls for, on this interpretation, is what the Principle of Precedence calls for under the only assumption for which I have fully defined it, namely, the assumption of sufficient resources. Every person's needs are to be met to the extent of actually reaching the Minimum Standard of Provision that is regarded as suitable for him or her in each Matter of Need. If anything is left over, after these Minimum Standards have been met, and we wish to persist in connecting justice with equality, we could revert to the literal interpretation of equality, dividing the surplus to be distributed into literally equal shares, or shares literally equal with certain exceptions. The possibility of thus using both interpretations, one at one stage and the other at another, helps explain why both interpretations survive.

4.53 Exceptions to Equality Displaced to Matters of Preference

One way or another, needs may have a certain priority with justice; but justice, when needs have been met, and there are still benefits and burdens to be distributed, must also deal with preferences. An important consequence of fixing firmly upon a definition of justice in which the standard of equality is invoked and interpreted in the first instance in terms of meeting needs is that the heads of exceptions, which offer such cogent arguments for departing from equality literally interpreted, are by and large displaced to second-instance issues of distribution. There matters of preference only will be in view, and no threat to meeting needs, which will have been provided for already, will attend departures from equality.

Were exceptions calling for increased benefits under any head to run counter to equality in meeting needs, they would look very questionable. What sort of capacity could be grounds for diverting resources required to meet people's needs? Other people might be willing to waive some part of the provisions for their needs to enable a person to have the instruments and training to develop a great musical talent. But the musician in question could hardly argue that the sacrifice was required by justice, or even permitted, if the others did not consent. What sort of competitive standing could be grounds for diverting resources? Questions would arise about whether social policy should make any room for competitions that would divert resources from meeting needs. Similar questions would arise about social policies that rewarded services at the expense of meeting needs—what sort of services would they be that did not do as much or more for meeting needs as the resources taken from needs to reward them? Returns to effort, where no service is performed for the community, are already circumscribed by the condition that the resources entering the returns be free for the taking, which implies, not preempted for more important uses. Rights call for the same treatment. For should not social policy be so managed as to avoid letting some people have rights that interfere with meeting other people's needs?

There may be some just departures under the head of rights even so, and under the head of service, whether doubling with rights or not. The displacement of the heads of exception to the sphere of matters of preference only is not perfect. The practice of recognizing a certain right may be generally useful as an instrument for meeting people's needs even if, in certain instances, respecting the exercise of the right may actually diminish provisions for needs. So may the practice of rewarding certain kinds of services, whether by right or not. Practices of these kinds may assist in protecting from theft or destruction the provisions assigned members of the Reference Population, or furnish indispensable incentives for producing the provisions in the first place, motivating some people to accept greater burdens in more strenuous work. At any rate, the possibility may be conceded that rights and rewards for services may in some instances conduce to meeting the needs of the Reference Population overall and yet demand departures from the fundamental standard of equality in meeting needs. Demonstrating empirically that such departures are actually necessary to obtaining the benefits in meeting needs gained generally by the practices is another matter. Better understood, or refined on various points, the practices might not license the departures.

Besides departures increasing benefits as a means of meeting needs more fully overall, justice with equality-in-meeting-needs accommodates departures reducing benefits, when these are necessary to deter outright interference (theft, for example) with arrangements providing for people's needs. Required exceptions to equality may occur in reductions to deter idleness, too. Making such exceptions, indeed, may be held to be indispensable to meeting the basic standard of equality in the distribution of benefits and burdens, adjusted to variations between people in needs. Making them also incidentally realizes the chief demand for justice on the side of production.

The exceptions may be called for, accordingly, even when they strike at meeting some people's needs. On the other hand, it would be more comfortable for everybody concerned, and in fact accord better with practices in affluent societies, to shift to the sphere of matters of preference only in introducing any inequalities in benefits and burdens that have to be introduced. Burdens, even if they were equalized, taking into account variations among persons, as drawbacks or obstacles to meeting needs, might still remain unequal as drawbacks or obstacles to heeding preferences, leaving some people, for example, less time for extra recreation than others. So justice on the production side may call for penalties or deterrents as means of equalizing burdens in the sphere of preferences. Moreover, industrious people, ready to resent the idleness of others, may be satisfied, if their own needs are securely met, with penalties and deterrents operating just in matters of preference only. They may not insist on penalties or deterrents in matters of need. In fact they do not insist on denying food and shelter (including heat) to criminals or to vagrants, though often, perhaps as a relic of more desperate times, when everyone was hard put to it to meet needs, the terms on which these things are made available seem deliberately humiliating.

4.6 Concern for Needs Imposed by Practical Necessity on Conceptions of Justice That Disregard Equality

The argument so far has captured, for the thesis that needs come into justice necessarily in the train of equality, all reasonable conceptions of justice that have a place for equality. Or so I would say. If the qualification "reasonable" seems uncertain in effect or question-begging, moreover, conceptions so far set aside as "unreasonable" will fall in with the argument in due course, when it winds up considering how practical necessity maintains a connection with needs in the case of all conceptions of justice whatever. Meanwhile, however, we may attend, not to conceptions that appear to rely on equality without regard to needs, but to conceptions of justice that disregard, or profess to disregard, equality entirely. I shall argue that such conceptions cannot in fact get away with disregarding equality; and, again, even in their case, needs come into the applications of the conceptions and come into the applications in the train of equality.

Current theorists of justice who set equality aside, among whom Nozick has received the most attention, typically advocate rights (though not rights to have needs met) and liberty instead. They seem ready to grant everybody the rights that they advocate—the rights to hold property, to make fair exchanges, to accumulate property. They seem ready, moreover, to profess a general concern for liberty, in which everybody is to share. Does it follow that they grant equality for everyone in respect to having rights or liberty? I think that something might be made of this point; but I shall not pursue it. The theorists that I have in mind clearly hold that having these rights is compatible with very great inequalities in the resources of those who exercise the rights. I wish to show that this position collapses into inconsistency; and that when it collapses, a place for considering needs is revealed. A conception of justice that relies on the rights mentioned cannot consistently ignore needs.

4.61 The Liberal Dialectic of Rights

As a preliminary observation, not part of the demonstration, I might point out that the position at issue ignores the dialectic of rights which helped transform classical liberalism into liberalism as it is now conceived, especially in North America. Beginning with the declarations of rights in the late eighteenth century and still working itself out in our own day (though in theory it was substantially complete with the work of T. H. Green in the mid-nineteenth century), this dialectic has continually insisted that if these rights are genuine and important then people must have the resources to exercise them. What was the right of property to people who would never escape from poverty by activity in the market, however strenuous?

For the majority of the population, who held only trifling amounts of property, the right of property remained formal and hypothetical rather than genuine and effective. Liberals who agreed that, dialectically, a serious advocacy of rights leads inevitably to advocacy that people have the resources to exercise the rights, found themselves compelled, dialectically, to reconsider the claims of economic liberalism. Was the market the most practical way of ensuring that everyone had the resources to exercise the rights? If it was not—and many liberals came to agree that by itself, with no more restraint and supplementation than classical liberalism had postulated, it was not—then to achieve those original aims of political liberalism that were expressed in the declarations of rights, various measures of intervention and redistribution were required, among them the establishment of additional rights, like rights to workers' compensation and unemployment insurance, and rights to fair employment opportunities.

4.62 Checking Inequality to Prevent Oppression

Like this dialectic of rights, my argument against a conception of justice that advocates certain rights regardless of equality in resources contrasts the position of people whose resources are scant with the position of people whose resources are ample. But I am not simply concerned with the possibility that people with scant resources are in no position to exercise the rights. I argue that, once the contrast becomes sufficiently stark, the people with ample resources are in a position to circumscribe the exercise of other people's rights, and even in a position to violate the rights. The people with scant resources become, not just worse off, but vulnerable; they face much more powerful people, who can exert power to make them worse off still.

Such vulnerability exists, it may be claimed, whenever there is a very unequal distribution of riches. It shows up, whenever a rich man has to deal with a poor one, in the greater chances of the rich man's getting favorable treatment from the courts or from officials, as well as in the rich man's greater capacity to wait out negotiations, and in other aspects of greater bargaining power (like having more information). I am willing to concede, however, that in modern democratic systems direct exertions of such powers by one person against another are uncommon, partly because it is uncommon for poor people to have to deal steadily, one on one, with any given rich people. Moreover, the laws of such systems are enforced against the rich effectively enough to discourage them from personally committing violence against the poor. A rich man in the United States and Canada could not retaliate against a fancied insult with the same impunity as the French "nobleman" who had Voltaire beaten up early in the eighteenth century.

Let us assume, then, a status quo in which inequality in

the distribution of resources, even a very great inequality, leads to relatively few instances in which the power conferred by ampler resources is exerted directly by one person against another, or, at any rate, to no more instances than are accepted as tolerable imperfections by almost everyone concerned. Such a status quo is liable to deteriorate. One might imagine circumstances—an ideal market, perhaps, with a random distribution of acumen over the whole population—in which everybody who, being rich, got richer, was offset by somebody who, being rich, lost riches, and in which everybody who rose to riches from poverty was offset by somebody who fell into poverty from riches. If, however, as in history has often enough happened, riches steadily accumulate in the hands of those already rich, the inequality of distribution and the discrepancy in power associated with it will grow. Is it tolerable for the discrepancy to grow indefinitely, until an enormously wealthy patriciate, with power that can easily be turned to oppressive uses, faces a poor rabble plebs, powerless to resist oppression, certainly powerless taken one by one?

I do not think that the advocates of justice founded on rights regardless of equality can get away without conceding some safeguard against this possibility; and the only adequate safeguard, given the power of wealth to corrupt governments and subvert laws, is at some point to check departures from equality.

The people who are most successful in exercising the rights to hold property, to make fair exchanges, and to accumulate property, may in time gain the power to circumscribe less successful people in further exercises by them of those same rights. Circumscribed, the less successful will have less bargaining power, less chance of favorable terms of exchange, less chance to accumulate. Had the advocates of these rights the least attachment to equality per se, they would have to agree that the unchecked exercise of the rights might in time wear away any feature of distribution that answered to the consideration of equality. Acting within the original defined scope of the rights would in time have consequences more and more objectionable to advocates of equality. It could have these consequences in time even if the actions were themselves perfectly honest and scrupulous in other ways. Thus, advocating these rights without the appropriate qualifications is inconsistent with continually giving even the least weight to equality.

That might be accepted, even defiantly asserted. What upsets unqualified advocacy is the fact that it is committed to viewing with equanimity the destruction for many people, maybe for most, of the rights at issue. For the power of unequal riches goes beyond circumscription. The patricians may act as a class to deprive the plebs of their rights; or, eventually, regardless of present practices, act individually, dealing with individual plebeians as they please, rights or no rights. How much liberty will the plebeians have then? They stand to lose everything in either case: wives, vineyards, liberty, too.

In the train of a concern to keep inequality from reaching that point must come a concern to meet people's needs. For it is people who are unable to meet their needs (unless they submit to the demands of other people who can block supplies of provisions, withhold employment, or frustrate efforts at self-help) that are most vulnerable to circumscription, violation, and oppression. A conception of justice that relies on the rights mentioned must, to have consistent comprehensive application, set some limit to inequality, and that limit must fall this side of an inequality so great that some people are able to reduce or extinguish the chances of others to meet their needs, including their chances of self-help. Any conception of justice that implies a persistent concern for personal liberty, whether or not it takes a stand on these rights, must set a limit there, too. But accepting such a limit implies a commitment to the Principle of Precedence. For justice will be insecure so long as even one member of the Reference Population is exposed to oppression by having her chances of meeting her needs in jeopardy.

4.7 Concern for Needs Imposed by Practical Necessity on All Conceptions of Justice

The argument from the possibility of oppression applies with special force and poignancy to conceptions of justice that, like Nozick's, waive equality to stress rights or liberty in the context of the market. The real-world market continually offers to some opportunities to gain resources so overweening that they endanger the very rights on which these conceptions set so much store, and the liberty. However, the practical necessity of assuring people of being able, free from oppressive conditions, to meet their needs, applies as a qualification also to conceptions of justice that aim at equality if they do so without regard for needs.

To be sure, achieving such equality may often provide incidentally for everyone's needs. When it does not, those people, if there are any, whose needs are met may have nothing to spare, so that they cannot drive any hard bargains with those whose needs are not met. Even so, they would be in a relatively favorable position, which they might abuse. They might, for example, use their greater health and strength to block the others from further supplies of the same insufficient provisions, thereby creating a surplus for themselves, and a basis for further oppression. If those whose needs are met do have something to spare, they may from the beginning compel the others to bargain away future provisions, future opportunities, even their future liberty. If they do not succeed in driving such hard bargains, they can bide their time, saving what they have to spare until they have enough to recruit as henchmen and "enforcers" some of those whose needs are not met.

Will it suffice simply to confiscate anything that the luckier people have to spare and anything that they save, or at least anything beyond a safe limit? But it could hardly be said that equality was then being maintained or approximated without any regard for meeting needs; it would have to be admitted that equality established without any regard for needs was continually, just for this reason, precarious. Precautions about meeting needs, indeed, precautions extending to meeting people's needs equally, have to be taken, if equality, taken to be the pattern of justice, is to be assured of persisting.

The practical necessity of taking such precautions holds, not only for the conceptions just discussed; it holds for any conception of justice whatever that requires some one person N to respect the position of another M. It holds for those conceptions that advocate literal equality only on condition that needs are met or accept meeting needs as a head or subhead of exceptions to literal equality. If needs come in in the former way, there is no issue. If they come in in the latter way, the weights given to other heads may permit the accumulation of very unequal amounts of wealth and power. So, again, some people will be in a position to oppress others. The argument for security in application comes in again with conceptions that already give a considerable place to needs. It insists that the place must be big enough to accommodate the Principle of Precedence.

Finally, moving entirely outside the range of conceptions of justice specifically considered so far, consider a conception according to which justice calls for a caste society, in which each caste has a different set of rights, and the lower castes have smaller, poorer sets, with rights less far-reaching. This conception, of which the limiting case is a society in which one person has all the rights, and the rest no rights at all, formally fits Mill's definition, though it is very far, of course, from anything that Mill's own beliefs about justice subordinated to the principle of utility would endorse. Let N be the one "assignable person" with "a sufficient claim to have something guaranteed" him by society, and let M be one of the other members of the society. Then any increase in resources on M's part begins to undermine N's right.

In this case, no doubt, most people would applaud the increase, since it would have the effect of enabling M to resist N's oppression. Nevertheless, the point holds that any increase in resources for one person relatively to another jeopardizes the pattern of justice established between them. The caste conception of justice is liable to jeopardy along with other conceptions.

I have relied on a less general point, suited to the more plausible conceptions of justice that I have discussed, that by increase in resources N may arrive at a position (if he is not already there) of being able to oppress M, who will be specially vulnerable to oppression if her needs have not been met. The more general point can be brought in to complete the argument, however. It is now complete: Every conception of justice is jeopardized in application by substantial shifts of resources that favor N vis-à-vis anyone M, whose position justice requires N to respect. Hence every conception of justice must, by practical necessity, ally itself in application with precautions against such shifts, qualifying in this connection any allowances that it makes for unequal shares.

Only a conception of justice that did not require any person N to respect some other person M's position would escape the argument. But that would be a conception that accepted any changes in relative positions, however brought about, as just; and that is no conception of justice at all. Among conceptions of justice, the more attractive the conception, the greater becomes the moral urgency of the precautions practically necessary. With the most plausible—the most defensible and morally attractive—conceptions of all, as many would hold them to be, the connection made by practical necessity runs alongside a connection of conceptual or definitional necessity that embraces meeting needs simultaneously with equality.

Those conceptions, which make of equality-in-meeting-needs enough directly to demand fulfillment of the Principle of Precedence, also make enough of needs to converge on many issues of practical politics with utilitarianism and its demands respecting the means of happiness. What would happen to utilitarianism if it were revised to incorporate the Principle of Precedence? We shall find that we would have a doctrine in the same neighborhood, a quasi-utilitarianism, which the argument of this chapter implies would be in a stronger position in the face of the claims of justice. I shall argue that it will be in a stronger position in other respects, too. Moreover, it will have a more direct title than utilitarianism itself to the historical achievements of utilitarianism in practical social policy.

DIALOGUE

CRITICAL READER: *Didn't I detect an inclination on your part to favor conceptions of justice that rely on equality-in-meeting-needs?*

NOT-YET-REPENTANT-AUTHOR: *Very likely. I'm not a model of perfect detachment. Nevertheless, the chief point of the chapter, that the concept of needs has a part to play over the whole range of conceptions of justice, is not affected by my favoring some conceptions over others. What's important is that the concept of needs is available to all these conceptions and, at points, indispensable.*

READER: *You're moving on to utilitarianism. What's your position there?*

AUTHOR: *Forget about my position. Think of my program. I want to show what the concept of needs does in the service of utilitarianism; or, at least, how it works as a surrogate. How I myself might defend utilitarianism can be guessed from what I'll say. I'd defend it only after revising it. But the defense of utilitarianism is not my immediate object.*

READER: *Which is?*

AUTHOR: *My immediate object continues to be, as in the last chapter, and now for two chapters further—to bring to light the place for needs in the neighborhood of the other chief ethical ideas used to assess social policies and social systems. The concept of needs ranks with them in importance, but philosophers don't usually give it credit for doing so. I aim to redress the balance.*

159

READER: *More specifically, in the chapter about to come, to explain how needs can serve in a surrogate for utilitarianism? But if utilitarianism requires a surrogate, can it actually be used to assess social policies?*

AUTHOR: *You put my point better—more boldly—than I did myself. Utilitarianism as such has never been more than a project for assessing policies. If it's had any credit for being effective, it's because the concept of needs has always been available, with procedures that actually work, to make up for the procedural deficiencies of utilitarianism. Perhaps surprisingly, it makes up at the same time for the chief moral deficiencies.*

FIVE

UTILITARIANISM WITHOUT
UTILITY

Meeting needs turned out to be an important, indeed essential consideration with all the conceptions of justice—families of conceptions—that I surveyed. Only with one family of conceptions, however, did it have by design a central place. Only here, where justice rested on equality-in-meeting-needs, did meeting needs stand equally supported by justice and the Principle of Precedence; and only here did these stand in a relation of full mutual support. With the conceptions of justice that professed no care for equality, meeting needs came in only as a means of maintaining the rights cherished as central, or the liberty. With conceptions relying on literal equality, meeting needs may have had a defined place among the recognized exceptions to literal equality; but so much weight might have been given to other matters among these exceptions as to leave needs neglected to some degree. There, too, meeting needs might have figured chiefly as a means of ensuring the security of a system of justice that aimed chiefly at achieving other things.

The conceptions of justice in which equality-in-meeting-needs centrally figures not only have more to do with needs; they run hand in hand with an approximation of utilitarianism—a quasi-utilitarianism, utilitarianism without utility—that calls for meeting needs in accordance with the Principle of Precedence and only then passes on to treat preferences, with no commitment to the notion of utility in that connection either. Other conceptions of justice must concede meeting needs enough importance to give pause to anyone who thinks there is an inevitable conflict between justice and utilitarianism. Are not needs likely to be the first consideration in pursuing happiness? With the conceptions resting on equality-in-meeting-needs, however, and with utilitarianism revised to rest on needs rather than on utility, justice and utilitarianism are so far from being opposed to one another as to become indistinguishable in operation, at any rate in operation over needs. Is utilitarianism so modified still utilitarianism? I have called it a "surrogate," "quasi-utilitarianism"; and if I refer to it as "utilitarianism without utility," I am conceding a paradox. Yet, as I shall show, utilitarianism without utility has a genuine claim to making the best of utilitarianism.

5.1 Censuses of Needs Replacing the Calculus of Utility

I shall be doing more than showing what needs can make of utilitarianism; or utilitarianism, of needs. I shall be at the same time filling out my account of the procedures for determining the bearing of needs upon social policies. So far, I have given an idea only of how it is established that everyone's needs—all the needs of everyone in the Reference Population—have been met. A census of the Reference Population would establish this. But censuses are also ultimately decisive for comparisons of policies imperfectly successful in providing for particular Matters of Need, and varying in degree of imperfection.

With the concept of needs and the Principle of Precedence, utilitarianism without utility incorporates the Census Notion rather than Bentham's felicific calculus as the basic device for bringing evidence about consequences to bear upon the choice of policies. With the Census Notion, it will be accepting certain rules for treating the evidence. These rules retain those features of Benthamite utilitarianism that forestalled certain objections: namely, that some people have been left out of account; or, worse, that some people have been eliminated in the course of calculating the evidence, just to make the evidence more favorable. The rules that come with the Census Notion do more. They secure the revised utilitarianism in which they figure against some powerful traditional objections that Benthamite utilitarianism is unprepared to meet. These have to do with the sacrifice of some people's happiness to promote other people's, sometimes people, maybe fewer in number, with greater capacity for happiness, sometimes just a greater number of people; or, even worse, with the sacrifice of some people's provisions for basic needs in favor of pleasures to be enjoyed by others. Utilitarianism without utility, in keeping with ordinary practices for evaluating policies, refuses to license the imposition of such sacrifices.

In general, the evidence collected under the Census Notion will consist, for every alternative action or policy considered, of a census of the Reference Population, showing its present condition or its prospects. If just one Matter of Need is in question, the census will show what proportion of the population can be classified under the given action or policy as having the Minimum Standards of Provision for that need (say, housing) and what proportion must be classified as not being provided for according to those standards.

	Policy A	Policy B
Need for housing met	95%	80%
Need for housing not met	5%	20%

In this illustration, the comparison of the two policies favors Policy A as coming closer to fulfilling the Principle of Precedence in respect to the need for housing. That is not because a majority—a larger majority—prefers A. One might expect a larger majority of those affected to prefer A; but they might not be called on to vote. The people affected belong to the Reference Population, and this may be wholly distinct from the Selfgovliset, where the policies are to be chosen and the vote taken. If the Reference Population and the Selfgovliset were identical, furthermore, the favor that the census gives to Policy A would stand regardless of whether 95% preferred A or voted for it. In fact, a majority might, against plausible expectations, vote against it, because they were confused, or because most people found the housing that they got under Policy B more comfortable, or because they preferred some other aspect of Policy B besides its consequences for housing.

So censuses and comparative censuses of needs are not equivalent to majority rule. Nor are they equivalent to the application of the Pareto welfare criterion. There the divergence may be even more dramatic: If Policy B is the present policy, and just one of the people among the 80% prefers having her need for housing met as it now is met to having it met as it would be met (supposing it would be) under Policy A, the move from B to A would contravene the Pareto welfare criterion.

If all Matters of Need are being considered at once, a census will divide the population between those provided for on all Matters of Need and those not provided for in respect to at least one. Strict final priority will have been realized when a policy is arrived at that leaves nobody in the latter classification. All along the way, the rules of evidence for the Census Notion will have sanctioned interpersonal comparisons, but they will have not have been comparisons of the sort that has been found so problematical for the concept of utility. They are straightforward comparisons, for example, of some people having heated rainproof shelters with flush toilets with other people not having shelters that meet the same standard. No introspection is called for; nor is any measurement of feeling, of strength of desire, or of satisfaction. This is so even in respect to the needs for companionship or for recreation. Being upset may be a sign that what the Criterion would endorse as the Minimum Standards of Provision for that person and those needs is not being met. The Criterion turns decisively, however, only on evidence of being able to perform the tasks in the four social roles, not evidence of upset as such; and the Standards call not for realizing some state of feelings but for supplying a quantity and variety of observable provisions that make it possible to perform the tasks without derangement of function.

If the censuses are to furnish the evidence required by the Principle of Precedence (and by ordinary notions of what is to be reckoned among the social consequences of policies), everyone in the Reference Population must be counted; and no one must be eliminated just to make the evidence bearing upon a given action or policy look better. To violate either of these conditions amounts to tampering with the evidence. But if these two conditions, which the Census Notion shares with Bentham's felicific calculus, are fulfilled, then two prime candidates for being peremptory considerations—as it happens, two important points of justice—are automatically taken care of in applications of the Principle of Precedence. One might well want more than these conditions in the way of respect for life and respect for persons, but the conditions do assure a minimum of respect for both.

Furthermore, utilitarianism without utility, incorporating the Principle of Precedence and with it the Census Notion, fulfills more than a minimum condition of respect for persons. The felicific calculus begs the fatal ambiguity of the slogan, "The greatest happiness of the greatest number," in favor of maximizing utility regardless of its distribution whether to the greatest number or not. The Census Notion waives the calculations that lead to such results. By contrast with the calculus, it puts distributional considerations first, both when it points to unambiguous improvements and when it stops short of doing this. And since, as we are about to see, it comes with safeguards against changing

165

people's positions for the worse, it does so without prescribing, in the place of sacrificing the happiness of some people to the greatest happiness, that similar sacrifices shall be made to the happiness of the greatest number.

The Census Notion may give ambiguous—intractable—results when on a comparison of policies it appears that one benefits a few people a great deal and the other a great number of people moderately. This intractability is easier to see when happiness is in question than when the issue is meeting needs, and in any case occurs only when we turn from a two-place census to one with three or more categories.

	Policy C	Policy D
Supremely Happy	15%	0%
Happy	60%	80%
So-so	25%	20%

Does the advantage with Policy C of having 150 people out of a thousand supremely happy more than outweigh the disadvantage of leaving 50 more people, if not miserable, still in a condition that observers would not be prepared to call clearly happy? The rules of evidence for Census Notion do not tell us one way or the other, which may be taken as a caution forestalling any gratuitous sacrifices of some people's prospects to improve others, and, as well, a further ground for distinguishing between the Census Notion and majority rule.

5.2 The Census Notion at Work with the Principle of Precedence in the Revisionary Process

If we shift back to the perspective of needs, the comparison of proportions like those just inspected become more tractable, but this is because in the perspective of needs the Census Notion gets some extra help from the Principle of Precedence.

	Policy E	Policy F
Need for housing amply met	15%	0%
Need for housing barely met	60%	80%
Need for housing unmet	25%	20%

Here the Principle of Precedence, insisting on meeting the Minimum Standards of Provision for as many members of the Reference Population as possible, calls for Policy F. Ampler housing for anybody must wait until everyone has housing that will at least serve.

Even in the perspective of needs, however, such clear advice will fail if the difference between the policies entails a change of persons. Suppose the 200 people whose need for housing will go unmet under Policy F are all people whose need for it is now met or met amply under Policy E. Neither the Census Notion by itself nor the Census Notion helped out by the Principle of Precedence unambiguously recommends Policy F now. It would be different if the point of departure was one in which nobody's need for housing was met even barely; different again, if Policy E had to be given up in any case, and Policy F was the best, in respect to housing, of the remaining options. Suppose, however, that as things stand Policy E is the present policy and Policy F is just the first alternative that has come to light. Then the Census Notion cautions against accepting it as an improvement.

What is the best way of approaching the fulfillment of the Principle of Precedence, given this caution? The best standard way seems to be, during operations short of fulfillment, to keep on providing for people whose needs are now provided for and add to their number, rather than simply to change to any policy that promises to meet the needs of a greater number of people, whoever those people may be. Occasionally, opportunities may come up to move more quickly to fulfillment on a route of mixed changes; and in emergencies, when the restoration of status quo fulfillment

167

is at issue, these opportunities may be especially compelling. Distributing full rations to people in regions stricken by drought may justify reducing, temporarily, the provisions going to people elsewhere. Over relatively long periods of time, however, the risks may increase of not being able to restore the positions of the people whose provisions have been sacrificed. Retaining the present measure of success and building upon it will present itself as the less risky strategy, as well as the surest means of respecting the intractability of each mixed change in itself.

Moreover, following such a strategy is a means of forestalling gratuitous sacrifices, and avoiding deprivations that, if they are unnecessary, would be regarded by many as tyrannical impositions. In practice, proceeding this way not only avoids the moral objections that such things provoke; it also minimizes social conflict, which might otherwise rise so high as to jeopardize any advance in meeting the needs of those with needs unmet.

Proceeding this way, partly for the same reasons, is also the most propitious strategy for dealing with intractability of another sort: Census comparisons taking into account several needs at once may find policies that do best on one need do less than best on others. Different people may be favored in each case; and people may differ about which needs to deal with first. Are not these intractabilities, too, best treated with respectful caution, with movement ahead sought not by taking sides but by meeting the demands of both sides? Driving under the Principle of Precedence for strict final priority for all needs together, the strategy of steady cumulative change will call for a succession of policies that go on providing for all people and all needs currently met and in addition cover people and needs not met hitherto.

Will a policy of this sort be available, however? None with such consequences may have been proposed. What the Principle of Precedence calls for then is that such a policy be formulated. Some people have thought the fact that the Census Notion may give—indeed, may often give—intractable results shows that it is not very useful in arriving at policies. That impression betrays a misunderstanding of how policy-making is normally carried on. Contrary to the standard assumptions of formal theories of decision, both personal and social, the choice of policies is not normally limited to any given set of proposals. The set is always finite (indeed, normally quite small) and open to revision by amalgamating features (say, the best features) of different proposals already in the set, or by adding some proposal that may take a completely new approach. The Principle of Precedence, with strict final priority for needs, is to be looked upon as something that guides this Revisionary Process and insists upon its continuing until all the needs of everybody in the Reference Population have been met. Given the resources normally available to the Selfgovliset for delivery to the Reference Population and given normal adjustment of the recognized needs (in respect, among other things, to Minimum Standards in such potentially elastic connections as safety) to the resources normally available, the insistence is practical enough.

When the Census Notion gives intractable results respecting needs, then, these results are not to be looked upon as breakdowns in evaluating policies, but as intermediate stages in which revision and invention are incited, with every chance in normal circumstances of advancing under the Principle of Precedence to improved policies. Will there not be abnormal times when there is no choice but to meet some people's needs at the cost of not meeting others? Or times when the revisions called for, taking into account a number of different needs, met with various success by different policies, are more complicated than any that I have illustrated? Those times may require meeting some needs of some people at the cost of not meeting other needs of theirs, to say nothing of meeting the needs of other people. Such times may come about in either of two ways. A disaster may descend upon the Selfgovliset or the Reference Population, or both—maybe the climate changes in a drastic way, so that resources previously adequate to house the Reference Population, or to raise food for it, are outstripped; maybe the resources shrink or vanish though the demands on them remain constant. Resources may get out of match with needs in another way, however. The concept may be extended so far as to make demands that the resources are first just on the margin of being able to meet and then fall marginally short of meeting, or further.

In the second sort of case, though normal operation of the Principle of Precedence cannot continue, normal operation can be restored by revising the set of needs on a plan that I have already discussed. That is to retire within the scheme for expanded or contracted discussion offered by the concept toward the firm ground of the basic List and more stringent Minimum Standards of Provision. Restoring normal operation in the first sort of case, where, let us suppose, the concept has been used conservatively, so that some firm ground would have to be given up if it were revised, will not be so easy. In such a case, the concept of needs, as an instrument for evaluating policies, will have broken down at once in two different ways: It will have been brought into conflict with itself, with no good means to be drawn from any critique of needs for resolving the conflict, since on both sides of the conflict there will be a firmly founded need. Moreover, the methods of arriving at social policies normally used with the concept—the Principle of Precedence, driving with the Census Notion for strict final priority, and the Revisionary Process, responding to the Principle, offer no way out of the conflict either.

The Principle of Precedence offers no help toward resolving conflicts of needs. When some needs must go unmet if other needs are to be provided for, the Principle does not imply anything about priorities among people or among needs. Principles can be found that do, but the ones that I am aware of are principles for use in short-run emergencies (when it will be more urgent, say, to see to shelter, and only

170

then to the food supply, because the danger to life from exposure to the cold is more imminent) rather than in continuous monitoring and evaluation of social policies. These principles do not, moreover, derogate very much from the possibility that personal orderings of priority for different needs may vary so much that the several policies meeting each of three needs might be ordered every whichway by the various people concerned. Then, even in short-run emergencies, conflict of needs would lead to confrontation with Arrow's theorem and related difficulties in social choice theory as much as conflict of preferences would.

Does an occasional breakdown, in times of disaster, imply that the concept of needs is an inconvenient or ineligible instrument for evaluating policies and choosing between them? Or discredit utilitarianism without utility as a normative doctrine? I do not think so. Other things being equal, a principle that gave determinate results in every possible—in every imaginable—case would be preferable to one that did not. Philosophers may be expected to persist in being dissatisfied with any principle that does not. It does not follow that a principle that works in most cases is not to be valued; in frequency of determinate and satisfactory results, it may excel any alternative principle. Compared with principles that in practice do not work at all, even a principle for which no more could be claimed than that it works sometimes would deserve a good deal of respect.

5.3 Defects of the Concept of Utility as Compared with the Concept of Needs

Utilitarianism without utility, relying on the concept of needs, the Principle of Precedence, and the Revisionary Process, thus shines by comparison with any form of utilitarianism that relies on the concept of utility. Outside the theoretical discussions of economists and philosophers, the concept of utility is not in current use. It creates problems about measurement that the Census Notion, in continual practical operation, does not have to face, and systematically by-passes. If one grants (in spite of various difficulties) that the von Neumann-Morgenstern technique can in principle give measures of utility valid for persons taken one by one, the fact remains that no one has drawn up anything like a full schedule of even a single person's utilities, and there is no prospect of anyone's ever doing so. Moreover, the problem of translating these measurements into interpersonal comparisons remains. The current suggestion that the problem of interpersonal comparisons be resolved by simply assuming that human beings are sufficiently alike for us to use any one person's scale as a basis for comparing all the rest, whatever its other merits or demerits, hardly gets to the starting gate in practical affairs. We do not and will not have the measurements for any one person, to say nothing of all the rest: 24 million in Canada; 240 million in the United States. Meanwhile the Census Notion is away and running.

Utilitarianism with utility might escape the difficulties of social choice theory if it incorporated a revisionary process. Arrow's theorem, for example, applies only to sets of alternative policies once the membership of these sets has been established, and thus does not stand in the way of constructing new policies deliberately designed to escape any deadlock or paradox created by the set first proposed. Relying on utility, such a utilitarianism would still, by comparison with a utilitarianism without utility relying on the Principle of Precedence for needs, be up in the air, in Cloud Cuckooland.

What does the concept of utility accomplish in real disputes about policy? Nothing, I would say, unless it is taken as a device for talking about other matters better talked about in a straightforward way. For example, the traditional effort to justify progressive taxation by the hypothesis of diminishing marginal utility for income has the disadvantage that no conclusive evidence can be produced for the hypothesis. It can be claimed that rich women with sensitive tastes becoming continually more sensitive, are getting as much utility out of marginal dollars that they spend on fashion as poor women of uncultivated tastes and phlegmatic disposition out of marginal dollars spent on baking soda; and would lose more utility if proportionately more dollars were taken from them. Far better to say, in defense of progressive taxation, that the poor find it difficult to cover their basic needs, while the rich can indulge in the most frivolous preferences. This is something that can readily be established by a census. If it is agreed that the issue is whether larger incomes leave a larger surplus (supposing any incomes did) over meeting basic needs with standard forms of provision, the census results will be a foregone conclusion.

How did utilitarianism accomplish anything in real disputes while it relied on the concept of utility? The most expeditious means of throwing light on this question, it seems to me, is to consider the history of the concept. I shall offer only a rudimentary sketch, but that will suffice for the purpose. The distance of the concept from practice was present in the theory of Benthamite utilitarianism from the beginning. What saved the doctrine from conflict with ordinary practice in policy-making, and indeed enabled it to have some practical efficacy, was just the assumption that matters subject to census comparisons, checking crime, building sewers, regulating factory hours, etc., would have results in gains for happiness that would be corroborated by the felicific calculus were the calculus ever to be made usable and put to use. In principle, however, the calculus not only ignored the divergent prescriptions signified by the phrases "the greatest happiness" and "the greatest number"; it overrode any distinction between matters of need and matters of preference only, in favor of treating pleasure or satisfaction, wherever it was gathered, as the same in kind and in moral value. (Simultaneously, utility ceased to be just the general property of suitable means for obtaining pleasure or satisfaction, and became in conception their equivalent.) John Stuart Mill offered strongly felt though somewhat ambiguous advocacy for taking another path. However, the discrepancy from ordinary practice on the distinction between needs and mere preferences has been continually disregarded throughout the history of utility in economics and in the branches of the Liberal tradition with which economics has been most closely allied. So has any other standard for discriminating between preferences or the objects of preferences.

For economics, the history of this disregard begins at once in an alliance with Benthamism on the side of moral advice and on the side of descriptive theory with the decision (itself sensible enough) to treat demand as being equally effective in the market no matter what the character of the wants giving rise to it. So the classical economists, even when they are not talking about utility, use the term "wants" and the term "needs," too, indifferently to refer both to matters of need proper and to matters of preference only. Marx is notably emphatic on this point (in one of his two views of "needs"). When economists began to rely on utility, they were already prepared to treat it as having the same character wherever it was found insofar as they had been allied with Benthamism. Insofar as they had not been allied, the use of "needs" over the whole range of human wants would have prepared them; and the same aim of having a unified theory of demand, of course, carried them forward.

Not much difficulty about the discrepancy between promoting the greatest happiness and promoting the happiness of the greatest number could be expected while the assumption that marginal utility declined with income was in force; nor would much difficulty arise about giving people's needs some sort of priority over attending to anyone's preferences. The biggest returns in utility would be found in bettering the condition of the many poor, not in bettering the condition of the few rich; and, at least if the poor had the dispositions most essential to their own survival, they could be expected to find big gains in utility in further provisions for what Marx called their "primary needs" or "necessary needs"—the Matters of Need on my basic List. If they were not assumed to have such dispositions, the argument for the progressive income tax lost a good deal of its force—what would have been the point of letting the poor keep proportionately more money if they were all going to use it to kill themselves with drink?

5.4* *Liberalism Led Astray from Needs by the Pareto Welfare Criterion*

When confidence in the interpersonal measurability of utility finally collapsed, economists might, in normative connections, have fallen back on needs; and would have done better had they done so. Instead, they fell back on preferences. Perhaps in charity it might be allowed that implicitly they were setting aside certain preferences as morally unacceptable, like a preference for roasted human flesh over strawberry jam, or even for more strawberry jam instead of more justice. Officially and explicitly, however, they have continued to this day to treat preferences on the same plan as they had treated wants, that is to say, on an equal footing whatever their character and whosesoever they might be. The Pareto welfare criterion, understood literally, sanctions a change of policy only if the change thwarts nobody's preferences. The preferences of the rich for gold-plated doorknobs and peacock fans call for as much respect on this approach as the preferences of the poor for enough food, for a minimum of clothing, for a sound roof over their heads.

The Pareto welfare criterion may nevertheless be regarded as an extreme of Liberalism as well as the extreme point reached by economists in their attempt to abdicate from moral judgments. For Liberalism has always (to its credit) had a special care for people's preferences; and what could be more scrupulous than the Pareto welfare criterion in this respect? There certainly is no danger of its singling out any objects of preference as less meritorious than any others. A preference for roasted human flesh will get just as much respect as a preference for works of charity, but no more. So will the preference for the status quo of someone with a vested interest in maintaining it, as compared with the preference of someone whose future depends on changing it. The Pareto welfare criterion does not fall into the ambiguity that sets "the greatest happiness" at times against "the happiness of the greatest number"; it is not committed to pursuing either.

The Liberalism of the Pareto welfare criterion, however, is a caricature of historical Liberalism. When the maharajah's preferences conflict with those of his ten million subjects, it allows the maharajah to block reform, even though what is at stake for the subjects is elementary survival. Historically, whatever its bad faith in office from time to time, Liberalism in practice has been more sensitive to matters of need. In theory, moreover, it has favored people's being free to exercise significant choices over wider ranges of goods rather than smaller ones. What reality would there be in the political rights so cherished by Liberals if people did not have enough relief from the pressures of struggling for bare subsistence to inform themselves and take time to act on the information? Once Liberalism had raised the banner of rights, it was launched upon a dialectic about fulfilling the conditions of giving the rights reality.

Even if its distaste for political oppression did not bring it down on the side of the maharajah's subjects rather than on the side of the maharajah and the Pareto welfare criterion, it could hardly have granted him or anyone else privileged by the status quo power to veto changes in it. Historical Liberalism could not have accepted the Pareto welfare criterion and carry out its program of promoting competition and discouraging reliance by businesses on government favor, much less the macro-economic policies that some Liberals found themselves advocating in the Keynesian era. In all of these connections, the Pareto welfare criterion would have found insuperable obstacles in some people's preferences for their economic positions in the status quo.

5.5* *Utilitarianism, without Utility, Reunited with Liberalism*

In the practice of Liberalism and in the theoretical development to which it is susceptible, then, there have always been present some grounds for reservation about treating all preferences equally. Needs figure among these grounds. What could be more compelling grounds for discriminating between preferences of different character? It cannot be just the preferences of a greater or smaller number of people that are to have their way; they might all be frivolous, and the one person's preferences that stood against them might be about vital matters. If one is justified in overriding the Pareto welfare criterion in either direction—in favor of a minority, or in favor of a majority—it must be because morally more important matters have to be attended to on the other side.

These will chiefly be needs, which come forward here as the most convincing justification for overriding the Pareto criterion and the best ultimate explanation of why people think that it is justifiable to override it. In corroboration of this explanation, needs also come forward as the matters that the economists who are boldest in abandoning the self-stultifying restrictions of the Pareto criterion turn to. Quite in accordance with the historic concerns of Liberalism, these matters are needs in the dress of social indicators. But the concerns of Liberalism with these matters are just the concerns that utilitarianism has had in its practical applications. Thus, in utilitarianism without utility, incorporating the Principle of Precedence, Liberalism, the most relevant advice of economists, and ordinary practices of evaluating policies are substantially united again. I say "substantially," because there are currents in Liberalism that, with Pareto, would make more of heeding preferences than utilitarianism without utility can, though it can make quite a lot, as we shall see in a moment. Moreover, the currents that join in the union become, on one side, downstream, hard to distinguish from socialism. That did not prevent Liberals in those currents from formerly advocating laissez faire as what looked like the most promising means of meeting people's needs. There are, no doubt, some Liberals—on the other side of downstream—who still believe this; and it is a logically possible position in the union that I am referring to.

The utilitarianism in this union is, just because of the priority that it gives to needs, ready to face one of the most telling lines of objection that, implicitly or explicitly, exploits the arbitrariness of sacrificing some people's mere pleasures in favor of mere pleasures for other people. At its most poignant, this objection plays upon the gratuitousness of sacrificing some people's provisions for needs—relegating those people to hardship and suffering—in favor of other people's provisions for matters of preference only. Shall even one innocent child be tortured as a means of making all mankind happy forever? The felicific calculus might sanction such an action; or sanction a demand for self-sacrifice running far beyond any reasonable demand for altruism in ethics. The Principle of Precedence, with strict final priority, never will. Utilitarianism without utility is going to have to do something about preferences, but the Principle of Precedence prevents it from sacrificing anyone's needs to heed them.

What the Principle of Precedence, with strict final priority, will sometimes sanction is sacrificing some people's pleasures—overriding their preferences in matters of preference only—in order to meet other people's needs. Even here, the Revisionary Process will in practice avoid calling for the sacrifice if the sacrifice can be avoided. If it cannot be avoided, however, is not the demand morally compelling? At the very least, it cannot be dismissed as a gratuitous prescription favoring some people's pleasures, and made into an objection of that sort to utilitarianism. In some cases, it may run against the prescriptions of justice on the production side, so as to raise an issue about reducing the pleasures of those who have contributed their share of production in order to meet the needs of those who have not. Utilitarianism itself, with the Principle of Precedence, might argue, from considerations about meeting needs in the long run, against the demand here. However, if the incentives for production can be taken care of entirely by awardings and withholdings within the sphere of matters of preference only, such considerations would not apply, and the demand would stand. We do not, in fact, in the reasonably civilized societies on hand in the world, deliberately penalize even criminal behavior, much less mere idleness, by withholding provisions for needs.

5.6* Provision for Preferences under Strict Final Priority for Needs

What, however, is utilitarianism without utility to do about matters of preference only? It would be a very incomplete utilitarianism, or analogue of utilitarianism, and a very illiberal one, if it did not undertake to say how to make the best of matters there, too. In the end, what it is to say, if this is to be reconciled with certain demands for liberty, personal and political, and adapted to the weight given to needs by real political processes, will require shifting from strict final priority for the Principle of Precedence to a looser condition—role-relative precautionary priority, which I shall introduce in the next chapter. Even given strict final priority, however, utilitarianism without utility can make substantial provision for matters of preference only, compatibly with the Principle of Precedence.

The provision can be ampler the more surplus productive capacity the Selfgovliset has available apart from the capacity committed to meeting needs. In any case, however, observing strict final priority for needs will in a sense make it easier to provide for preferences. With strict final priority the tendency is as fully realized as it ever will be to use the concept of needs to collect a number of matters of action and set them apart as decided, with no further collective decision to be made about this status by aggregating personal preferences. Conflicts about the policies to be adopted as means to meeting the needs thus agreed upon may remain, as well as conflicts about matters of preference only. It is settled, however, that as matters of prior importance the agreed-on needs (along with any peremptory considerations regarded as having yet higher priority) will be met without prejudice by any measures taken respecting matters of preference only. Not so much hangs upon attention to these matters, therefore, and imperfect measures respecting them will be more tolerable. Will it not be foolish, then, in the absence of any effective rival concept, to belittle needs because they solve only part of our difficulties? They will have solved the most important part.

5.61* Packets of Discretionary Income: Private Goods

Indeed, if we could suppose that matters of preference only concerned nothing but private goods, consumed by individual persons (or households) to the exclusion of other persons, like the apples that they eat or the shoes that they wear, strict final priority for needs might make utilitarians content to waive any refined problems about aggregating preferences there. Quite straightforward measures might serve well enough. One such measure would be to distribute in equal packets money income for expenditure on matters of preference only. Then individual citizens could decide for themselves how much they wanted to spend on more elaborate provisions for meeting their needs than those guaranteed by the Minimum Standards of Provision. Some would pass up the hamburger that they could have anyway in favor of calves' liver or Wienerschnitzel. Individual citizens would simultaneously decide for themselves how much they would spend on goods that did not enter into the Minimum Standard of Provisions for needs: a bottle of fine port; a sports car; a trip to the Caribbean.

Everyone might become better off if, as an alternative measure, Rawls's Difference Principle were adopted, to apply to the sphere of matters of preference only by applying to the packets of discretionary income made available for expenditure there. Larger packets would be given to some to just the extent that they furnished incentives for greater production and that those worse off in the Reference Population enjoyed, through sharing in the output, a higher standard of living than they would under a regime of equal packets. Thus those who, being worst off, would be the most urgent cases to check for possible victimization, could in fact freely and rationally consent to an unequal distribution. Strictly speaking, some could perhaps argue that they themselves would not be among the worst off under other arrangements, but this argument would lose some foundation if under the present ones they had had a fair opportunity to try out for better paid work. Even if the argument survived, facts about the course of past history and about institutional inertia might persuade the people for whom it survived that it was unrealistic to demand any of the other arrangements. They might also be persuaded that other arrangements would have equally arbitrary results for other people; and that to make anything of the issue would start up an interminably distracting hunt among speculatively possible arrangements.

Strict literal egalitarians, even if they saw some sense in these points and in consent by the worst off to the described application of the Difference Principle, might resist the application notwithstanding. So might Marxists, holding that the Difference Principle would have attractions only for people whose motivations lay still within "the narrow horizon of bourgeois right," not yet generous enough to adhere to the ultimate principle of "From each according to his ability, to each according to his needs!" Utilitarians would no doubt think that some concession from strict equality was justified, provided that the inequalities were not carried so far as to engender apprehensions about concentrations of power or to begin losing—for this or other reasons—more in unhappiness about the inequalities than it gained for happiness by increased production.

5.62* Incentives for Full Efforts in Production

Neither equal packets of discretionary income nor packets distributed on the Difference Principle ensure by themselves that the people receiving the packets will be putting forth full efforts in production, by some standard, high or low, of what efforts are expected. Perhaps, when everybody can meet needs and can make, under a regime of equal packets or under the Difference Principle, what he regards as a just amount of provision for matters of preference only, no problem about motivation to work will remain. Everybody will be happy to put forth a full effort. Or if some do not—if some are bone idle—those that do will not worry about it; they will wonder that others do not enjoy work as much as they do, and maybe pity the others a little for not being able to. "We work," says Delacroix, "not just to produce, but to give value to time."

5.63* Preferences for Public Goods

The measures that I have discussed for dealing with private goods in matters of preference only have the advantage of being able to devolve the decisions about which goods are to be bought by any individual person, and hence which of his preferences in these matters are to be heeded, upon that person with the packet of discretionary income that is his to spend. This advantage disappears when we consider that public goods, too—art galleries, parks, concert halls—will figure among matters of preference only. Public goods, like air freed from pollution, also figure among Matters of Need; when they do, we are assuming that social policy makes sure that they are provided in quantities sufficient to meet the relevant Minimum Standards of Provision. However, choices among public goods, even choices within the sphere of matters of preference only, cannot easily be devolved upon individual persons; nor can choices about how the output available in the sphere of matters of preference only is to be divided between private goods and public goods.

Treated as a question of defining and achieving an economic optimum, having to take public goods into account makes achievement distinctly more remote. Private firms have incentives to produce private goods; they have no incentive to produce fully public goods, from the consumption of which no one can be excluded, whether she pays a price or not. Governments can arrange to produce them and collect taxes to pay for them; but governments are not in a position to ascertain just how the benefits that individual consumers get from the goods vary (in accordance with the consumers' preferences) from consumer to consumer. An optimum can be defined over public goods in which every consumer pays for a public good a fraction of its marginal cost proportionate to the consumer's marginal benefit. However, governments are not in a position to charge in taxes amounts proportionate to different consumers' benefits; and not in a position, either, to determine how much of any public good should be produced. They cannot determine the benefits; and consumers have an incentive to conceal what the benefits really are. Hence a government may be taxing many people who never visit national parks unjustifiably large amounts, while it taxes a relative few who use the parks continually unjustifiably small ones. Yet taxation is the only way of making sure that no one entirely escapes as a free rider from paying for the public goods that he enjoys. Leaving the goods to be provided by private charities raising funds from voluntary contributions simply gives carte blanche to free riders.

5.64* The Difficulties Raised by Social Choice Theory

A satisfactory theoretical solution—not to speak of a satisfactory practical one—of the economic question about public goods is yet to be reached. Nor is a satisfactory theoretical solution available on a political approach to public goods. Agreeing to meet needs (as well as to take care of even more fundamental peremptory questions) before attending to matters of preference only may have extricated the most important questions from the difficulties of social choice theory. Some writers would object even so that the operation of social choice had been unduly restricted in the course of doing this. They would have some backing in those versions of Liberalism that call for maximum consultation of personal preferences. Some writers—some of the same writers—would object to any attempt to reduce the difficulties of social choice theory in the sphere of matters of preference only by devolving as many choices among private goods as possible upon individual persons. Could this really be regarded as putting those choices outside the field of social choice? Social choice, it might be claimed, would still be operating to endorse them and back them, and in doing so, it will be beset by paradoxes like Sen's Paradox of Liberalism, which makes it appear that giving individual persons even the most limited discretion endorsed by social choice runs counter to letting unanimous preferences govern in all cases.

Even someone ready to shake off these objections would have to face the difficulties of social choice theory when public goods are brought into matters of preference only; would lack a refined solution to those difficulties; and would have to concede that though various ways can be found of living with the difficulties, no ideal theoretical solution has been found. With needs taken care of, we have the best reasons possible for holding that personal preference orderings ought to be free to vary every whichway;

but if they do, Arrow's conditions for an intelligible reflection of such orderings in social choice cannot be met; and we have not settled upon what conditions to adopt instead. So we do not know how best to proceed from personal orderings to a social ordering of any set of given alternatives more than three in number.

In practice, of course, as I have noted in my discussions of the Revisionary Process, we always face sets of alternatives that are incomplete. If the sets are unsatisfactory in any way—falling short of levels of aspiration; generating paradoxes in social choice—we can search for further alternatives that rise above them, being designed specifically to meet the points of dissatisfaction. Often we can find such alternatives, though we cannot generally expect that doing so will have resolved the issues in question permanently. We may be content to deal with our present difficulties about public goods by postulating the same practical process. To fit meeting needs to the attention given preferences in real political processes is going to require further adjustments anyway, among them abandoning strict final priority for needs in favor of a much looser sort of priority (an adjustment that I shall consider in the next chapter).

At a given time, we suppose that the Selfgovliset arrives at a social choice that specifies how much of the output available for matters of preference only is to be set aside for public goods to be bought from public revenue, and how much is to be devoted to private goods bought from the packets of discretionary income distributed to the members of the Reference Population. Those members of the Selfgovliset who want a larger amount of public revenue spent on public goods than is decided upon may if they wish arrange to have more public goods produced with funds assembled from private charitable contributions, some or all of which might be volunteered as outlays by members of the Reference Population from their packets of discretionary income.

There will be no telling whether the total output of public

goods will fall short of the theoretical optimum, or over-shoot it; but a substantial amount of them may be produced nevertheless. Private charitable contributions alone might pay for a substantial amount. In Great Britain in the latter part of the nineteenth century, private charitable contributions to all causes ran at annual rates equal to the annual outlays from public funds on the Royal Navy. Moreover, the decision, arrived at itself perhaps by revising the first proposals, will be subject to reconsideration and supersession, if in time the mix of private and public goods in matters of preference only ceases to correspond in an acceptable way to the preferences in those matters of a decisive number of members of the Selfgovliset.

The upshot of these reflections is that utilitarianism without utility can go, in favorable circumstances, a good deal of the distance toward heeding preferences that would be expected from following the precepts of any form of utilitarianism. It is, moreover, always poised and ready to make a further advance when a widely persuasive case for one surfaces. All the while, the strict final priority given to meeting needs ensures that no sacrifices in unmet needs will be imposed in favor of heeding someone's—someone other's—preferences. The scope allowed for heeding preferences, therefore, is both extensive and defensible. At least one current conception of justice converges in its precepts with utilitarianism without utility; and one of the most serious moral objections to standard forms of utilitarianism is forestalled entirely, at its most poignant.

Even so, some will reasonably think, moving with certain currents of Liberalism, that preferences have not yet been assured of full attention.

DIALOGUE

CRITICAL READER: *You seem surprisingly ready to make use of the market. How is this consistent with holding that needs override preferences? Isn't the market just the place where preferences override needs?*

NOT-YET-REPENTANT AUTHOR: *Indeed it is, so far as it operates without constraints. At least, apart from constraints, everyone has the option of preferring other things to meeting her needs. Furthermore, I'm going to make even greater allowances for the operation of the market. I'm far from done with conceding all that in practice may have to be conceded to preferences.*

READER: *But then what's going to happen to priority for needs?*

AUTHOR: *It's going, as foretold, to weaken, though not simply because other considerations are brought in. I've been bringing in other considerations while strict final priority was still assumed. There has been lots of room for heeding preferences even so; and I'll say more about this. Put another way, there's lots of room for the market to operate, but under strict final priority the room is constrained by the concept of needs. We check to see from time to time whether the market is, however incidentally, meeting needs; and we take measures to offset and correct the market if it is not.*

READER: *Aren't we now on the point of abandoning these constraints?*

AUTHOR: *We're on the point of loosening them to accord with the fate of the concept of needs in real political processes. We're loosening them to accord at the same time with arguments coming forward under liberty and demanding more scope for preferences than strict final priority licenses. I loosen the constraints without myself endorsing the loosening; or, if you like, I am not ready to say how far any endorsement that I might give would carry. Until the extreme limit of loosening is reached, the concept of needs will still count for something.*

READER: *But something maybe a far cry from strict final priority?*

AUTHOR: *Maybe. But over most of the range of the loosening, strict final priority will still operate as a moral ideal, something that we would not qualify except under the pressure of other considerations, including political tactics. It defines the standard for measuring the shortcomings of loosened policy choices.*

S I X

ATTENTION TO NEEDS WITH
FURTHER ATTENTION TO
PREFERENCES

The extent to which preferences can be allowed for, compatibly with strict final priority for meeting needs under the Principle of Precedence, does not stop with packets of discretionary income. Nevertheless, the allowances compatible with strict final priority do not go far enough to reconcile attention to needs with all the principles that I and others would like to see reflected in social policies. In particular, liberty, understood as ruling out paternalism among other things, stands as yet unreconciled. Nor do the allowances go far enough to show how my account of the concept of needs must be adjusted if it is to present accurately even in broad outline how the concept is actually used in the Self-govlisets of the world today most sensitive to issues about needs.

The obstacles to maintaining strict final priority cast their shadow even upon the introduction of that notion in my basic account. Their weight became more perceptible immediately afterward, with the complications about derivation, conventionality, and normativity that I discussed in Chapter Three. These complications—especially the first two—inevitably detract from strict final priority, by opening up grounds or pretexts for ignoring the needs invested with the complications. For if a need derives from an existing social arrangement and thus depends on conventions, it loses some of its ineluctability. One has the option of repudiating the arrangement and the conventions. The option is, I argued, often more fanciful than practical. Yet the normative force of a need is always weakened to some degree by the presence of such an option; and, often enough to cause misgivings about strict final priority, the option is real and the weakening is substantial. How can we be justified in insisting that the Minimum Standard of Provision for a certain need be met for everybody in the Reference Population before anybody's preferences are considered, if there is a genuine possibility of doing away with the arrangement and conventions on which the need depends, and thus with the need?

We might have taken our leave of strict final priority as soon as the unsettling effects of those complications had made themselves felt. However, it would have been premature to have done so. The place of needs in justice and utilitarianism is not only more easily made out when the Principle of Precedence is assumed to carry with it strict final priority; the conception of justice in which needs figure most prominently really does call for such priority, and so does the form of utilitarianism that converges with that conception.

That is awkward. Heavy-handed anyway, the concept of needs bears down heaviest with strict final priority. But if we give strict final priority up, justice falls into jeopardy, and with it, the convergent realization of justice and (quasi-) utilitarianism. Full allowance for attention to preferences, if it requires giving up strict final priority for needs, cannot therefore be had without incurring significant moral costs.

6.1 The Demands of Liberty

Liberty in particular instances, the liberties to perform particular actions, may run athwart priority for needs. Suspicions about paternalism start up a whole family of instances. Perhaps not everything called paternalism will prove morally troubling, but enough things will, supported by strict final priority for needs. Enough particular liberties will be threatened or sacrificed in other connections to imply that strict final priority for needs imposes significant moral costs of its own.

6.11* Interlocking Arguments for Preferences and Needs

Yet, as the discussion in the last chapter of the room for heeding preferences under utilitarianism without utility implied, conflict between liberty and needs does not occur everywhere in the range of those concepts; nor does conflict between liberty and justice. Heeding preferences can go hand in hand with meeting needs. Indeed, the arguments for heeding preferences are themselves, in part at least, arguments for meeting needs. If it is granted that people have a need—a candidate for being one of the needs on the basic List—to have some at least of their preferences heeded, then to ignore preferences entirely would be inconsistent with giving precedence to meeting needs. Here the argument for meeting needs implies an argument for heeding preferences.

Preferences beyond the minimum to be heeded as a need demand attention morally—partly because gratuitously unpleasant consequences in frustration and resentment are likely to follow from ignoring them; partly because trying them out and finally settling upon suitable ones, which then require continued attention, are crucial to self-development. Still assuming a List and Minimum Standards of Provision governed by the Criterion of performance in the four basic social roles, I am not here postulating a need for self-development. Self-development can be understood to be an important moral consideration without being taken to be a need. It can be so understood, furthermore, without choosing—and I do not mean to be choosing—between various theories and doctrines of self-development.

Consider, for instance, any version of utilitarianism foresighted enough to recognize that preferences can develop

191

for better or worse. Such a utilitarianism would call for development for the better, and would find in such development a reason, in addition to the concern that it would have with pleasures and preferences anyway, for insisting on preferences being given wide effect. In this insistence it would be joined by other ethical doctrines that supported free self-development. Suppose there is such a variety of temperaments that people may be expected to fulfill themselves and enjoy their lives on many different plans. Then such ethical doctrines must prescribe that people have as much scope for preferences as they require to identify achievements and enjoyments that suit them, to arrive at life-plans in which such achievements and enjoyments predominate, and to carry out such life-plans.

Here, too, however, heeding preferences does not go against meeting needs, at least when resources are available for doing both. Meeting needs may be looked upon as meeting the conditions for having any preferred life-plans succeed. For the plans cannot succeed unless people live while they are carrying them out; and it is at least implausible to suppose that unless the plans in question essentially involve debilitating experiences (like taking certain drugs) they can succeed if people cannot function smoothly in the way required by the Criterion of performing basic social tasks. Here the argument for heeding preferences implies an argument for meeting needs.

Ethical doctrines concerned with free self-development must further require, however, that needs be met without reducing the scope for preferences in avoidable ways. That requirement amounts to requiring both that preferences be heeded in the forms of provision supplied to meet needs and that (compatibly with so heeding them) preferences be heeded in the goods supplied in surplus to meeting needs. From these requirements it follows once more that some sort of reasonable balance must be struck between heeding preferences in forms of provision for needs and heeding preferences in surplus goods.

I have assumed all along that a need was provided for if the persons concerned had provisions in hand or assigned to them, regardless of whether they actually used the provisions. So in the sense, appropriate to social policy, in which I have been using "meeting a need," people whose needs are met still have the choice, according to their preferences, of bringing the provisions to consummation. Moreover, if we exploit an equivocation in the claim that provisions have been made available, we can slightly extend the discretion for preferences by treating needs as met when provision had been made available, whether or not the persons concerned have taken up the provisions. Then, as they prefer and choose, they can both leave the provisions in the warehouse or not, and, if not, use the provisions or refrain from using them.

On this point, however, some possibility of a conflict between liberty and justice appears. People fail to take up provisions for their needs because of ignorance—sometimes cultivated by bureaucrats trying to cut the costs of programs; or because they cannot cope with the bureaucrats and the regulations, as the bureaucrats interpret them, for releasing provisions; or because they cannot make their way to the places where the provisions can be had. There have been cases in New York City of people who have not taken up welfare provisions because they feared their furniture would be stolen were they to leave their apartments. To rely on having provisions available, leaving it to people to take them up or not, may amount in practice to tolerating quite a considerable amount of injustice.

The conflict here is not—unlike others that we shall soon come upon—insoluble in principle. In principle we could stipulate that only when we were sure that the people concerned were in a position to take up the provisions, or not, as they preferred, and knew themselves to be in such a position, should failure to take up the provisions be disregarded in judging whether the needs had been met. Only then, we might say further, would the people concerned be entirely free to follow their preferences about taking up the provisions. Then not only is the in-principle solution for justice compatible with the in-principle solution for liberty; the two solutions coincide. The provisions are available; and the people concerned are free, and know that they are free, to take them up. That is as much liberty as is at stake in the issue.

Liberty and justice may coincide elsewhere, too. Liberty can be treated as a good that like other goods is to be distributed with literal equality unless recognized exceptions prevail. Something like the same coincidence could be brought about under equality-in-meeting-needs by treating liberty as something needed; the need to have some at least of one's preferences heeded would cover part of the ground. Under either interpretation, the goods that join to liberty the resources which make having it worthwhile are already a central concern of justice. But, of course, some at least of those goods are a central concern in meeting needs. Meeting needs may both by itself go some distance toward satisfying the demands raised by the subject of liberty (both as to discretion and as to power) and satisfy those demands coincidentally with satisfying the demands of justice.

6.12* Remaining Openings for Paternalism or Tyranny

Some possibilities of conflict between meeting needs and respecting liberty are left. They obtrude most acutely in the possibilities of carrying projects of meeting needs so far as to fall into paternalism. Here the possibilities may threaten a sort of tyranny. James Fishkin would have us consider as instances of tyranny the imposition of social policies that prevent some people from satisfying wants for themselves that they regard as important, when there is a feasible alternative policy that will not have this effect on them (or anyone else) now or in the future. The wants may involve needs; in that case the Principle of Precedence and Fishkin's principle of opposing such instances of tyranny coincide in

194

what they prescribe. However, the wants may express preferences that do not correspond to needs. Suppose the preferences at issue on either hand do not conflict with needs, whether by rejecting provisions for needs or by diverting resources indispensable for such provisions. Fishkin's principle then goes beyond the Principle of Precedence (which has nothing to say about heeding preferences, when preferences only are in question). The two principles are still compatible, however, and Fishkin's principle is to be welcomed.

The fact that here preferences only are at stake, which are by the Principle of Precedence less important than needs, may create some transient confusion. A moment's reflection will show, however, that not only may people feel intensely about "mere" preferences, as directed upon things important to them and their life-plans. People will justifiably resent gratuitous obstruction of such preferences. Some important features of a good life may be at issue with them. So the word "tyranny" is applied with perfect propriety to such obstruction, so resented.

What is to be said of the case remaining, in which the wants express preferences that do conflict with needs? Even here Fishkin's principle is not always opposed to the Principle of Precedence; for when meeting needs requires overriding intense preferences, yet not meeting them has the same drawback, Fishkin does not charge tyranny.

Suppose, however, one policy would meet needs that are not regarded as important by the people who have them. Simultaneously the policy would deprive them or others of things not meeting needs, things that they wanted for themselves and did regard as important. The alternative is open meanwhile to produce those things, accommodating all the intense preferences in the group, while the needs are disregarded. The Principle of Precedence calls for the first policy; and thus it fails to accord with Fishkin's principle, which requires the second one.

Moreover, whether it is the preferences of the people

with the needs or other people's preferences that are to be overridden, the Principle of Precedence leads here to paternalism. Having the good intention of meeting people's needs may somewhat mitigate the charge of tyranny; it does nothing to dispel the impression of paternalism. How could it? It is paternalism to meet people's needs when they prefer not to have them met (or met in that way); and paternalism, too, though a less direct variety, to disregard some people's intense wants, even if these wants express preferences only, to meet needs of other people who do not care whether the needs are met. In both cases, the policy-makers following the Principle of Precedence would be supplanting the judgment of the people affected with their own. Except in special cases themselves to be treated with sensitive caution (dealing with children or the mentally infirm) to do so is to presume too much, even if the policy-makers have correctly discerned the needs in question (which they may not have done).

Indeed, it must be added that paternalism may arise in cases that slip through Fishkin's escape clause about overriding preferences either way. Suppose one policy would meet some people's needs, and the only alternative is one that does not, though it has effects that those people intensely prefer. Suppose further that other people intensely prefer the first policy, though neither has any effect on their needs. It is paternalism, if it is not tyranny, to push the first policy through, unless there are grounds, quite separate from any issue about needs, for deciding between the policies according to the preferences of the second set of people (who may, for example, be more numerous). Yet this paternalism, again, is something that the Principle of Precedence, with strict final priority, will lead to in the circumstances assumed.

That is not to say that the Principle of Precedence and strict final priority are inherently paternalistic. Notoriously, some people (people in both Liberal and socialist systems) have been willing to set themselves up as experts on other people's interests, including needs. They have considered that their expertness entitled them to force provisions of their choice upon those people, or at least to prevent those people from providing for themselves in other ways. Yet I do not think that the Principle of Precedence, taken as reflecting one important aspect of the observed use of the concept of needs, is to be read as entailing paternalism. Understood as conferring strict final priority on needs, it is compatible with laissez faire or other arrangements for self-help. For though this requires evidence, and periodic checking, they may be the most effective means for realizing strict final priority. Social output, under any other system, might fall short.

6.13 Safeguards for Preferences

The most that can be said against the Principle of Precedence is that it does not exclude paternalism. When meeting the needs of the Reference Population conflicts to any extent with heeding the preferences, the Principle may be invoked by people who are prepared, paternalistically, to override the preferences. This is bad enough; and it is something that can be avoided only by giving up strict final priority and making fuller allowances for preferences.

The members of the Reference Population have so far been given no say about whether provisions for their needs should be made available in the first place. They might prefer to have other things produced. In allowing for their preferences here, the Selfgovliset, which in some cases may be wholly different from the Reference Population, must not be assumed to be obliged to supply goods and services that answer to those preferences. When it is not, avoidance of paternalism reduces to refraining from thwarting the preferences. The Selfgovliset refrains from removing opportunities that do not require its active assistance. Even when the Reference Population and the Selfgovliset at least roughly coincide, it will be paternalism (or, worse than paternalism, tyranny) to override people's preferences should these preferences run counter to giving strict final priority to needs. The preferences will require safeguards, including safeguards against majority rule.

6.2 A Dead-End Path: The Misguided Attempt to Have "Preferences" Entirely Supplant "Needs"

If these fuller allowances and safeguards are to be instituted, on top of considerable allowances compatible with strict final priority, it might be asked in some quarters, why bother with priority for needs at all? Why take up the problem of balancing the allowances for preferences against the priority for needs when preferences might serve as the sole basis for assessing social policy? Economists have on this point—ironically, in view of the host of difficulties about giving effect to preferences in social choice that economists themselves have turned up—persuaded many that it is a convenient simplification to ignore needs except as these find expression in preferences. This approach is nevertheless a dead-end path. Needs resist reduction. They retain a sort of priority, even when strict final priority gives way to fuller allowances for preferences.

To be sure, one reason why it is incongruous to insist upon strict final priority for needs in social policy is that individual persons, whether members of the Selfgovliset or the Reference Population, rarely, if ever, insist upon it in the private budgets that are generated by their preferences. Economists will be quick to point out that some people do not in fact give needs any special precedence; some people deliberately flout such precedence by indulging in dangerous drugs or by going in for dangerous adventures. One might expect basic needs to be represented in most people's cases by preferences more adamant than others. However, whether people do have preferences for meeting their needs, and how strong those preferences are, should be treated as empirical matters. Needs becomes a superfluous

198

concept, both for individual persons and for societies. At most, it may be conceded, Matters of Need can be treated as conditions of having further preferences heeded. However, it will again be an empirical matter, which will show up in a comprehensive treatment of preferences, how many people give special weight to meeting those conditions, and how much weight they give to them. Whatever difficulties there may be about aggregating preferences, separate attention to needs seems from this point of view just a gratuitous complication, which should not be temporized with in the name of liberty or accurate description, but jettisoned in the name of both.

I certainly do not deny that people's preferences may, and frequently do, run counter to the conditions for having further preferences heeded. I take it that for their part the economists would not deny that failing to meet those conditions might be very damaging to the persons involved. This point of resemblance to needs is what makes the suggestion that "needs" give way to "conditions for having further preferences heeded" plausible.

6.21* Nothing Accomplished by Defining Needs as Preferences

It is not so easy to replace the concept of needs. One might ask whether the concepts really have been changed. Is "the conditions of having further preferences heeded" at best anything more than a way of defining needs? If the Matters of Need that satisfy the Criterion in my basic account are not provided for, the people concerned will suffer impaired functioning in four basic social roles; hence the range of preferences that they have the capacity to heed acting in those roles will shrink. If we shift to another criterion, in the family of recognizably appropriate criteria, the approach to equivalence is even closer. People will not have any opportunity to have further preferences heeded if the needs that their biological functioning and survival imply go unmet.

However, is the definition in question much help? Once we have a List of basic needs in hand, supplied according to the Criterion of functioning in the basic social roles, they certainly appear to be very probable conditions for having any preferences about further matters heeded. But could we use being a condition for having further preferences heeded as a criterion itself for generating a List of basic needs, or of anything likely to command the same attention? I think not. What are the bounds of "the conditions of having further preferences heeded"? The project of definition founders, I think, on the impossibility of drawing any bounds; so we shall not have to consider whether once drawn they encompass all those needs, and only those needs, that are course-of-life needs on the basic List, or firmly derived therefrom, satisfying the Criterion in either case (or at least some criterion from the family of criteria).

To give the project of definition a fair chance, however, let us suppose that the conditions in question at least resemble those course-of-life needs in being conditions for everybody in the Reference Population. We shall take the further preferences, accordingly, to include whatever further preferences anybody might have. Thus we shall not have the conditions varying with the further preferences, as would follow from adopting David Miller's view of needs as relativized to people's varying life-plans. That view mixes up adventitious needs with course-of-life needs, and exposes the concept to criticism that challenges it and the life-plans on the basis of an indiscriminate use of the relational formula. Miller's view does not, therefore, give so steady a foundation for the concept in evaluating social policy as the presumptively universal course-of-life needs established by the Criterion.

Let us confine ourselves to necessary conditions and to conditions that can be identified with observable features of persons and their physical circumstances. Consider an activity that falls outside the four social roles embraced by the Criterion—for example, body-building. Some people certainly have preferences for body-building; some, for winning prizes in body-building competitions. A condition for having these preferences heeded is having a set of weights to lift or other means for specially strenuous exercises. Is this condition within the bounds of the basic conditions of having further preferences heeded? If it is, they evidently include conditions that cannot be identified with course-of-life needs; the possession of a set of weights to lift is at most an adventitious need for people who indulge in body-building as a matter of preference. If conditions like this one, that are conditions for heeding not any further preferences whatever but subsets of possible further preferences, are allowed in, the set of basic conditions will at once become too populous.

But suppose that possessing a set of weights is ruled out of bounds. In the subset of further preferences to which possessing a set of weights relates, however, there may be some preferences for meeting basic needs, like the need for exercise, which is in part at least a need for coordinated exercise. The basic conditions now seem, under the stipulation that they must each serve all further preferences, to have shrunk within such narrow bounds that they not only do not coincide with basic needs, but do not even guarantee that when they are met all basic needs are, too. Nor can this conclusion be escaped by holding that any basic need will come within the bounds in its own right, as identical with one of the basic conditions. For such a need may itself serve the fulfillment of only a subset of further preferences. To be able to choose between sleeping late and getting up early, one does not have to have companions.

A way out of these difficulties would be to stipulate that the bounds of the conditions are to be taken just to be the bounds of basic needs; and that the criteria for basic needs are to be used as criteria for establishing the conditions. This would, of course, give the game away. Moreover, a difficulty would remain. Suppose that at the beginning of a period of consumption some person prefers to forfeit any opportunities to have other preferences heeded. The concept of needs handles such a case quite easily: There is no contradiction between a person having a set of needs and her preferring not to have any of them met; people can and do prefer on occasion not to go on living, and they act on that preference precisely by disregarding their needs, even when they are fully informed about their needs and the consequences, near and remote, of not meeting them. But what condition for having further preferences, that is to say, preferences other than preferences for having such a condition met, does such a person's preference require meeting? It is logically impossible to define a set of conditions all of which have to be met if further preferences of every kind are to be heeded.

6.22 Preferences Incapable of Supplanting Needs in the Definition of Interests.

The possibility of expressing conflicts between needs and preferences is also at stake in moves that would eliminate needs in favor of preferences when defining people's interests. Political scientists are especially prone to adopt such definitions—for example, a definition that identifies people's interests with their fully informed preferences, or with the objects of these preferences. People's interests will then depend on the alternatives that they actually have in view. Change the set of alternatives by subtracting or adding some other alternative, and what is in their interest may change, too. Sometimes this does happen; the alternative subtracted or added may, for example, be more lucrative than any other in the set. In other cases the result of applying the definition is at odds with the ordinary conception of interest; and the definition prevents us from making an important distinction. The alternative subtracted or added is a very risky gamble; a fascinating but predatory lover; a gastronomic tour of Germany, with heavy meals at every stop. Even a fully informed person might prefer any of these things, and choose them, prepared to suffer the probable consequences. Yet if, among the remaining alternatives, there is one that enables him to meet his needs and assures him of keeping his money, even of getting more, the preference in each case runs counter to the person's interest.

Shall we say that though fully informed, a person with such a preference must be irrational, and only rational preferences define what is in one's interest? But this suggestion brings back the concept of needs as part of a criterion for being rational; people are rational only if they prefer to meet their needs, so far as they can. Moreover, the suggestion confuses being rational with being prudent. In favor of short, adventurous, and dissolute lives, people do defiantly repudiate bourgeois prescriptions for living, and with them any assurance of meeting their needs and increasing their riches. Whole social classes, whole societies, agreeing in their preferences, may repudiate any assurance. They are certainly imprudent; but how is it irrational for them, weighing the advantages and disadvantages, to prefer such lives? We have said the most that is to be said in objection to their preferences, supposing that no obligations to other people are at issue, when we have pointed out that the preferences conflict with their interests.

The attempt to define interests in terms of fully informed preferences creates trouble also with the notion of common interests. Suppose people agree in preferring one social policy to another; then, according to the definition, they have a common interest in having that policy adopted. Now add to the set of alternatives a policy that some prefer even more, while others do not. It follows from the definition that they no longer have a common interest. That is not a happy entailment. For the policy on which they were first agreed may continue to answer to their interest by meeting their needs and assuring their enrichment. A notion of honor or national pride, more or less far-fetched, perhaps not far-fetched at all, leads some people to hold nevertheless that the whole group should seize a new opportunity to break with present economic arrangements and declare its independence.

Those people will, of course, be loath to admit that seizing the opportunity conflicts with the group's interest. Even if seizing it portends a drop in their standard of living, it will be said that there is more to the group's interest than keeping up their standard of living, more even than meeting their material needs. They have higher needs, among them (as would be said in Quebec, for example) the need to preserve their own culture. The connection between interests and needs may thus be maintained by expanding the concept of needs to suit. If this way of talking is adopted, people in the group can be described as having several common interests, some of which call for incompatible policies. Dividing on those policies, some people prefer one; some prefer another. On both sides there are interests that preferences do not match.

Finally, preferences, fully informed preferences, may conflict with interests in cases of self-sacrifice that it is of some importance to have the means of noticing. Before they themselves choose what to do, people frequently want to know what other people prefer. Their preferences could hardly be fully informed if they were denied this knowledge. Nor in many cases is any harm done by their adapting their preferences and their choices to their discoveries in this connection. Yet in some cases, when a person defers to another's preferences, she is sacrificing provisions for her own needs. Out of fear perhaps, perhaps out of love, she is acting against her own interests. If she does so repeatedly— in some cases, if she does so just once—there are grounds for thinking that she is being exploited. Her interests are being disregarded, though she prefers them to be.

6.3 Another Path: From Strict Final Priority for Needs to Precautionary Priority

Would identifying needs with the conditions of having further preferences heeded, even if it were not a dead-end path, solve the problem of what sort of priority those needs or conditions are to have—and solve it in a way that substantially reduces paternalism? If it is not strict final priority, could it be just the priority that can be shown with indifference curves on economists' maps of people's preferences? Taking preferences to be revealed or implied in the actual choices that people make in various circumstances, economists would claim that a consistent picture of preferences for any agent can be built up in which references to needs are replaced simply by indications that for the agent the initial increments of provision of certain goods have an extremely high value. The agent will steadily prefer those increments to the most alluring combinations of other goods. He will not give up his minimal ration of water for a dozen, even a hundred camels, if he has his wits about him and is convinced that there is no chance of getting more water before the month is out.

6.31 Too Little Priority with Indifference Curves, Too Much with Lexicographical Ordering

This is hardly priority enough, either for needs or for conditions of having further preferences heeded. In maps with indifference curves of the usual shape, asymptotic to the axes and rounded throughout their course so that they do not turn straight up and down anywhere short of infinity, the possibility lingers of trading away even the initial increments of water, if the offer of camels gets large enough—rises, let us say, to a thousand camels. No prudent consumer would countenance such a possibility.

A trenchant remedy for this inadequacy, which certainly makes sure that a prudent person's preference for his minimal ration of water holds up against whatever number of camels come forward to tempt him, is to abandon indifference curves and utility functions of the usual sort in favor of a lexicographical ordering, at least a lexicographical ordering with satiation limits. This move, it may be claimed, stays within the field of preferences—it just leads to acknowledging that some preferences are such that the agent insists on heeding them before he is willing to consider using his resources for any other purpose.

This is too much priority for reasons touched on earlier. Even prudent people do not rank their needs so firmly that they will insist on meeting the Minimum Standard of Provision for one if it means foregoing any provision at all for needs ranked lower. Moreover, in circumstances in which they could not meet all their needs, they would be hard-pressed to carry on their lives; but they might be able to do something to minimize the disaster if they balanced scant resources among different needs.

If we say, the lexicographical ordering that we seek is an ordering with a satiation limit for all matters of need taken together—so that the Minimum Standards of Provision are satisfied for them all—we come back to strict final priority. That, too, is too strict to ascribe to individual persons or to Selfgovlisets. It is too strict in two ways. It implies that, before the Minimum Standards of Provision have been met, even the tiniest increment of provisions for needs will offset any amount of provision for other things. The upper bounds of the Minimum Standards of Provision are not sharp enough or firm enough to sustain such an implication. It cannot hold in the face of the conventionality of those upper bounds as they are currently understood in English-speaking societies and indeed (I expect) in every other. Nowhere are those Standards cut to the bone, where physical survival itself is indisputably jeopardized. Would the upper bounds be sharp even then?

The second way in which lexicographical priority for all Matters of Need taken together is too strict lies in its failing to allow for temporary marginal adjustments. It is possible, even probable, as a consequence in part of the looseness of the upper bounds, that at least in short-run emergencies, when resources shrink to just barely covering needs at the Minimum Standards of Provision, the precedence asserted by the Principle will give way a little. Some expenditures—

some uses of resources—not strictly required to meet needs will continue, while some needs are deliberately neglected, to a degree. A man might let the rain wet him in order to keep his stamp collection dry.

What sort of priority, however, can then be left for the Principle of Precedence to assert? If we can define this priority for persons dealing individually with their own needs, we may be able to transpose it for use in social decisions. But how is it to be defined for persons?

The best way to approach defining the priority in question starts, it seems to me, with considering whether lexicographical priority, at least, lexicographical priority with satiation limits, for the needs ranked one by one of any individual person or for all her needs together, can be saved as something not applying strictly and always, but as something normally manifested in her personal preference schedule. It cannot be; it is never a plausible current representation of the choices that an individual person is prepared to make. Yet, amid the wreckage of the project of making it one, we shall arrive at a notion of priority for needs that may be reasonably imputed to individual persons and by analogy to societies—Selfgovlisets—too.

Assume that income and consumption occur together in sequences of distinguishable cycles, C_j, C_k, etc.

Then suppose, first, that for a given need there is just one form of provision (the need for salt, derived from the need for food and water, might serve as an example; or the need for water). In the last cycle C_n of some sequence, e.g., in an emergency, with a shortage of resources, the agent accepts less than the Minimum Standard of Provision for this need in exchange for retaining something desired as a matter of preference—a more attractive rather than a less attractive form of provision for some other need; or some good that does not answer to a need at all. Nevertheless, we might try to say, in every cycle preceding, $C_1 \ldots C_{(n-1)}$, a minimum provision of salt or water was obtained and insisted upon as something accorded lexicographical priority. However, what would it mean to assert lexicographical priority for a preceding cycle? If we imagine that the agent's preference schedule during a preceding cycle showed such priority, we must concede that at best the basis for drawing up the schedule that way would have been our conjecture or the agent's testimony about what would be done in a less favorable situation. As soon as the conjecture or the testimony was put to a real test, in cycle C_n, it was discredited.

Suppose, second, that we have in view some need for which there are a number of forms of provision, varying in attractiveness. Can we find any better purchase for the notion of lexicographical priority? It might seem that we could; for the sequence $C_1 \ldots C_{(n-1)}$ might exhibit a history of the agent's substituting forms of provision less and less attractive to him as the more attractive ones, turn by turn, grew too expensive or perhaps disappeared from the market altogether. We could cite this history as evidence of the need's having lexicographical priority all along, until the onset of a final emergency in cycle C_n. But the priority would not show up on a preference map holding for any cycle in the sequence. Even if the map changed from cycle to cycle, showing successively higher values for different forms of provision for the need as these forms came in turn to be relied on to meet the need, it would not show lexicographical priority for any of the forms, since further substitutes would be available until the end, and then, in C_n, a compromise would be struck between meeting the need at the minimum standard regularly attained theretofore and using resources for other things.

6.32 Precautionary Priority in Parts of Behavior Usually Unmapped

What I am seeking to define as priority for needs slips through preference maps for forms of provision and cannot be represented as lexicographical priority for any such forms, even tentative or temporary priority. Yet it is now clear where the priority given needs is to be found. It is to be found in the parts of behavior that economists, by habit and convention, generally omit to map—the parts to which one must turn for ultimate explanations of why higher values are placed upon certain goods than others, indeed very high values on the initial provisions of them. In that unmapped behavior, preferences have histories. Agents plan, take precautions, and draw up budgets. In the course of doing so, they may give precautionary priority to a given need n_i by first setting aside—mentally or physically—all combinations of goods offered that include less than the Minimum Standards of Provision for n_i. Only after they have done this for each need to which they give priority would they survey the remaining combinations, seeking among these the combination with the most attractions in other respects. To speak more realistically, the agents may satisfice in the choice of other attractions. Yet the other attractions would not thereby receive treatment symmetrical with n_i, since the agents' level of aspiration for them will rise or fall while the Minimum Standard of Provision for n_i remains relatively fixed. The attractions in other respects may include, of course, having more attractive rather than less attractive forms of provision for n_i.

Thus in the plans that agents lay, they may take precautions, mental or physical, that answer to strict final priority for their needs. Hence this notion continues to figure as a feature of a more relaxed priority. However, the precautions must be supposed to be only tentative, however normal it may be for them to have effect. Face-to-face with the circumstances in which the plans in the end have to operate, the agents may deviate from them, though large deviations would be very improbable. Normally, the agents may be taking precautions in the ways described, and normally those precautions may bear fruit.

The precautions consist in setting aside provisions for needs. The condition of precautionary priority will be equally well satisfied if the combinations set aside are goods already in being, perhaps capable of being physically sorted on the spot, or simply projected outputs, which resources applied one way or another might give rise to. The agents must always assume that resources suffice to cover provisions of the kind that they have in mind for the need to which they give precautionary priority. Especially when they are choosing among projected outputs, the assumption may be incorrect; yet their behavior may still exhibit the priority in the plans that they choose. Moreover, their giving precautionary priority to needs can show itself in the previous history of their choices and attempted choices, even in those cases where the priority breaks down, because of emergencies and shrunken resources, or, sometimes, possibly, in the fact of unexpected opportunities for sensational gains answering to preferences. If the people concerned know that there is no chance of replacing their minimal rations of water, they will not, I suppose, consider giving them up; but they might try, for example, to get along without entirely adequate winter clothing, if that would make it possible to take up a bargain in video-cassette tape recorders.

6.4 From Precautionary Priority to Role-Relative Precautionary Priority

Precautionary priority, in attribution to individual persons, as I have just described it, will normally lead to their meeting their needs. It is a priority that lapses only in exceptional circumstances—short-run emergencies; rare and dazzling offers. It lapses only temporarily, probably only slightly, with the lapse followed by a resumed pattern of comprehensive provision for needs. Precautionary priority in the same sense carries over from persons dealing individually with their own needs to societies dealing with their needs in social policy. On the social plane, however, realism and accurate description require taking on a further complication—the differences in roles that people play when they are taking part in social decisions. Hence, on the social plane, simple precautionary priority gives way to precautionary priority that is role-relative—upheld by some people, in some roles, generally with some effect favorable to needs in final outcomes of social policy; but subject, in the actions of some people playing other roles, to deviations from priority.

Role-relative precautionary priority may in upshot deviate dramatically from strict final priority. Even in the roles in which people give needs precautionary priority in social policy they may give them less than strict final priority; and deviations from precautionary priority in other roles may leave little net priority in the end. Role-relative precautionary priority is not something to be attributed to societies idly; it must make a difference to social policy, increasing the chances that the needs of any Reference Population at issue will be met. However, it may not have the successful effects that one can expect, steadily and normally, from precautionary priority practiced by individual persons. It may not have such effects even when the Selfgovliset has, as much as the individual persons, the wherewithal most of the time to meet the needs at issue—for the Selfgovliset, the needs of the Reference Population. It is perhaps only partial compensation that the discrepancies between roles which may undermine expectations of success in matching outcomes to precautions can be justified in the name of liberty.

6.41 Priority for Needs Varying with Roles: Planners, Citizens, Consumers

In particular, discrepancies may arise between the roles of planners, citizens, and consumers. These may be different people. Citizens will be members for sure of the Selfgovliset. Consumers—the people who will consume the provisions for needs implied by the social policies at issue for the Selfgovliset—will be members for sure of the Reference Population. But in the issues about these policies the Selfgovliset may be contemplating an external Reference Population, the consumers in which do not intersect at all with the citizens in the Selfgovliset contemplating them. If the sets differ in this way, planners could be members of either, or even, possibly, consultants external to both.

On the other hand, the membership of all three sets may coincide, without eliminating the discrepancies between the three roles or the complications arising from those discrepancies. There are grounds for thinking that the discrepancies and complications will be greater the more disparate are the groups playing the three roles cited. For then fewer people will have to consider whether their actions are consistent over all three roles; so any weight and advantage that this consideration might have will be lost. However, important discrepancies may come up even when the sets of people who are planners, citizens, and consumers are substantially, or even perfectly, identical. What people do in their capacities as citizens may frustrate the precautions that they called for in their capacities as planners; what they do in their capacities as consumers may frustrate the precautions that they endorsed in their capacities as citizens.

One can easily imagine arrangements that would minimize the discrepancies between planners and citizens: Let all the planning be done in plenary sessions that end with the adoption as policies of the Selfgovliset of the plans that have been arrived at. Then the citizens would have to face the demand that they be consistent in their votes for policies with the positions that they took as planners; indeed, the positions that they finally took as planners might, under given arrangements, be expressed in their votes for policies.

6.42 Role-Relative Precautionary Priority

Suppose that, officially, at a plenary session of citizens, a majority is found for prohibiting the consumption of alcoholic beverages; but in practice, consumption goes on, even increases. Or, officially, a policy is adopted for meeting a certain need, say, a diet that provides for all the essential components of nutrition. The provisions are actually made available to everyone in the Reference Population—to all the consumers in the Selfgovliset; but many of the people who can make their own provisions do not and many of the people who cannot do not take up the public provisions. Most people, with their children, continue to subsist on junk food; or to substitute booze for part of the food that they should be eating.

Can we conclude in such cases that in the end the society in question does not give any priority to meeting needs? I think that would be unwarranted. It may not be in every respect consistent for people in one role to call for what they fail to do in another; but it is intelligible that they do, since they play the roles in different contexts. Thus, acting as a citizen contemplating an action concerted with other people, to be adopted on public-spirited grounds, a person may support every effort short of gross interferences with personal liberty to stop people from drinking or smoking. As a consumer, however, in the absence of fully effective legislation, with no means of coordination available, the same person may reason that to go on smoking and drinking himself will make only a negligible difference to the overall results.

Given the sort of shortcoming that I have just mentioned, the most that we should expect to find in the way of priority actually given needs is role-relative priority. This will take the form, in the first instance, of precautions, which may themselves answer to strict final priority, but which may be undone during the succession of roles played by various sets of people in the working-out of social policies. Different societies, on different issues, will come closer than others to minimizing the discrepancy between the priorities given in one role and the priorities given in others. So long, however, as we can find one important role—the planners' role in policy-making, for example, extending to recommending precautions that make sufficient provisions available—in which priorities are given to needs, and find that these priorities raise the chances of needs being met by the actions taken in other roles, we should be ready to acknowledge that they count for something in the workings of the society. Of course, they will count for more the more the choices made in the end accord with them. So long as deviations in the other roles are forestalled to some degree by adherence in the role or roles played earlier, however, precautionary priority for needs may be ascribed to the society in question. The qualification, "role-relative," points to the multiplicity of roles that must be taken into account as opening up room for deviations to occur and to persist.

The deviations have to be allowed for to get accurate and realistic descriptions of the use of the concept of needs in real political processes. Some of them—I am not trying to decide just which—have to be allowed for to meet the demands of liberty. Hence the notion of role-relative precautionary priority opens up room, with the deviations that it allows for, for both descriptive and normative concessions that strict final priority for needs rules out. I do not say that the deviations which actually occur will always have the same claim to fit within the normative concessions as they will to fit within the descriptive ones. A sense of justice and attachment to the Principle of Precedence will limit the normative concessions—at different points for different people.

In spite of the deviations, if role-relative precautionary priority can be ascribed to the Selfgovliset, then the concept of needs escapes being reserved for an idle and pointless use, for example, in *ex post* evaluations that have no followup. It has some cutting power in social choice. It may not be given all the use that the Principle of Precedence, or justice, may demand. It is given an opportunity that can lead to outcomes fully consistent with the Principle of Precedence and strict final priority. How much comes of the opportunity depends on the authority which the planners have to

214

follow the Principle and on the resolution with which the consumers play their parts after the planners and citizens have played theirs. Moreover, *ex post* evaluations will (though, again, not inevitably) affect planning in the next stage, encouraging renewed, more vigorous efforts to make sure of meeting needs, if priority for needs has strong enough backing.

Role-relative precautionary priority is imperfect in another way. It is normal priority. Short-run emergencies and dazzling opportunities may lead planners, citizens, and consumers to abandon temporarily, together, or somewhere in the succession of roles, precautions that most of the time the Selfgovliset does take. Resources or provisions normally allocated to meeting needs are diverted to other uses, and some people in whose cases the Minimum Standards of Provision for certain needs would normally be met, go without some part of the provisions that in most periods they obtain. A sharp rise in the price of home heating oil, at a time when a small country has embarked on ambitious preparations for the Winter Olympics, may lead to consumers' putting up with colder houses so that money can be raised to build facilities for figure-skating.

6.43 Removing Discrepancies in Priority across the Three Roles

A Selfgovliset that is sufficiently affluent and sufficiently efficient will no doubt take precautions against having to abandon any normal precautions. It will have reserves of various kinds, including reserves of money, so that even unexpected emergencies and opportunities do not jeopardize meeting needs in the regular degree.

A well-governed Selfgovliset may also be expected to try to make priority more effective by removing the discrepancies between what its members do in one role and what they do in others. Suppose that, however taken aback the citizens are by the total amount of resources that the planners call for to meet needs, the citizens do not quarrel with the facts on which any recommendation respecting a particular need are founded. Would the typical problem about discrepancies then be a problem about reducing the discrepancies between citizens' decisions and consumers' actions?

The prospect of these discrepancies, however, will create discrepancies also between citizens' decisions and planners' recommendations. Acting privately, consumers will not heed the views about needs that they adopt as citizens, deciding upon concerted action in a context that encourages public-spiritedness. Moreover, in the views that give final shape to their public decisions, citizens cannot help but be influenced by what they expect—by what each expects of herself; by what each expects of others—they will do as consumers. They may be willing, as citizens, to push ahead of what they would do as consumers, without the role of citizens to play, in circumstances unmodified by decisions taken in that role. They will not be willing to impose an intolerable burden on themselves; they ought not be willing to impose an intolerable burden, acting in a majority, on a minority within them. So, without disputing any particular recommendation, they refuse to go along with the combined demand for resources; and they set aside, or honor only in part, some of the particular recommendations put forward by the planners.

How are these discrepancies to be reduced? They will persist so long as people have divided minds; or do not agree on Matters of Need and Minimum Standards of Provision; or do not (in some cases) wish to meet their needs, however fully acknowledged as such. The techniques for reducing the discrepancies, to mention some of the chief ones that come to mind, include circulating information about needs, Minimum Standards of Provision (like the minimum daily requirements of vitamins published by the United States government), and the effects on health and performance of meeting needs; mounting campaigns, like safety campaigns, that awaken or revive attention to Matters of Need among members of the Reference Population and enlist joint commitments to providing for them; encouraging the formation of mutual support groups of people undertaking to abide by a needs-meeting regimen (Alcoholics Anonymous and Weightwatchers supply precedents). The techniques include, besides, finding incidental, inconspicuous, and inevitable ways of furnishing provisions, illustrated by iodized salt, pasteurized milk, and (sadly vexed though this example has been by misinformed criticism) fluoridated water. Citizens, approving such techniques, approve of making it not worth the effort for themselves as consumers to evade the effects. The minority of citizens who do not approve lose something in liberty, but they can, in favorable cases with relatively little trouble, find means of evading if they wish. Finally, I might mention, equally broadly described and thus equally standing for a diversity of particularized techniques, making the forms of provision for needs more attractive, given comparable prices; or making forms already attractive cheaper. In pursuit of these objectives, the planners might recommend and the citizens authorize supplying small amounts of seed money from public funds as capital for entrepreneurs proposing innovations; or public funds might be used to set up competitions in design, with prizes for the most promising. This technique, too, would, like the others, divert to meet needs some resources that minorities among the citizens and consumers would wish to put to other uses. Yet there would, in many societies, be plenty of room to use all the techniques simultaneously without coming anywhere near diverting so much in resources that the minorities would begin thinking it not worthwhile to continue belonging to the system.

To some extent—perhaps, in favorable circumstances, to a very great extent—the technique of making forms of provision for needs more attractive given the prices or cheaper given the attractions is something that can be entrusted to the spontaneous operations of the market. Indeed, it might be asked again, might not the market take care of meeting needs entirely? I think that in principle it might; one possible answer to the question, "What policy shall be adopted to meet the needs of the Reference Population?" is "Laissez faire." If this question were raised and so answered by a Selfgovliset informed that laissez faire was not only an adequate policy but the most effective one, role-relative precautionary policy would stop there, provided that there was some sort of institutional provision for monitoring the policy, to corroborate the hypothesis that the case for it was well-founded and continued to be. Even without raising and settling the question, a society that fell into the practice of laissez faire might coincidentally meet all the needs of the Reference Population. However, it would not then have deliberately given any sort of priority to needs, any more than an individual person would have, who met his needs by happy accident—liking his whisky with soda, and so getting enough water. I would not ascribe precautionary priority to either.

6.5 Planners Differing from Consumers Both in Roles and in Persons: The Erosion of Priority

Planners will seldom in reality be all the same people as citizens. Even a Selfgovliset small enough to meet in plenary session and vote on policies might be too large to do the committee work required to arrive at definite plans. Probably all of the Selfgovlisets that are in the world are too large to find a place for every citizen on some committee of planners or other. Planners will be at best a small subset of citizens. Nor are citizens likely to be just the same set of people as consumers. At the extreme, the Reference Population—and thus the set of consumers that is currently at issue in making policies about needs—may entirely differ in membership from the Selfgovliset. Will these disparities make any difference to the findings about reconciling attention to needs with attention to preferences just reached in the discussion of a simpler situation in which planners, citizens, and consumers could be assumed to be all the same people? I do not think they make much difference to the general lines of the preceding argument, though they may make important—frightful—differences to what is actually done to meet needs or heed preferences. The previous issues, however, with the adjustments to be made, and the basic techniques for making them, persist. Even if, as before, the discrepancies between roles in decisions about needs are reduced by bringing the consumers and the citizens to match the planners in supporting precautions that the planners prescribe, removing the discrepancies will remove some possibilities of paternalism. Moreover, the techniques for removing them, when they were not educative and facilitative rather than insistently paternalistic, were imposed only after democratic discussion and democratic decision. This at least reduced the scope for paternalism on the part of the planners; and the same sort of reduction might be effected with an external Reference Population by waiting for their democratic consent.

When people as well as roles differ, new possibilities of the planners being at odds with the citizens open up. For good or ill the institutions entrusted with planning are likely to be more complex. The institutions embodying and expressing the citizens' will are likely to be more complex still.

The citizens—the great majority of citizens—will not be under the same internalized pressure to decide consistently with the planners' recommendations if they are not the same people as the planners. Moreover, the institutional means of expressing the will of the citizens may be so complex and uncertain in operation that decisive expressions are hard to come by. All the difficulties that political science finds in controlling elites may beset the citizens. If the planners escape control, they will sometimes be able to impose provisions for needs, paternalistically, upon a body of citizens with different views. The imposition of metricization in Canada has been a classic example of such paternalism, a measure much more useful in respect to needs in the planners' eyes than in the citizens' (or the consumers'), who, by and large, have seen nothing necessary in it at all.

6.51 Imposed Priority: Majority Paternalism

A majority of citizens in the Selfgovliset might accept for themselves as consumers in the Reference Population the prescriptions of an elite company of planners. So might a majority of an external Reference Population accept the policies respecting their needs agreed to between the planners and citizens in the Selfgovliset. In both cases, however, a minority of the people whose needs are at issue might dissent.

Is it paternalism to the minority for the majority to adopt the combined policy of meeting needs? Not so far. Everything depends on how the minority fellow-citizens are treated in their capacity as consumers (members of the Reference Population). Suppose they are restricted, in the goods and services that they get, to provisions for needs, with perhaps in addition a share of any surplus output devoted to matters of preference only, but no opportunity to increase that share. Then the members of the minority are being dealt with paternalistically; they are being compelled to deal with their needs as the majority sees fit for everybody to deal with them. This is so, even if they retain the liberty not to bring the provisions for needs to consummation; or even if they retain the liberty not to take the provisions up. At the other end of the range of possibilities, paternalism vanishes if the members of the minority are left free to provide for their needs or not, as they themselves individually see fit, and have available to them comparable amounts of resources per capita to apply to uses that they choose themselves. One might imagine, after the vote, dividing up the resources available to the Reference Population proportionately, and letting majority and minority go their separate ways. Even then the minority's capacity to depart from meeting needs might be restricted by not being in the same position as the majority to realize economies of scale in production. This would be a painful restriction if the minority was a very small one. It is not paternalism, however, for the majority to refuse to give active assistance to the minority's purposes.

In a complex industrial society it will not be feasible to divide up resources neatly. For this reason alone the solution to the problem of paternalism is going to be untidy and imperfect. The minority, if it is to have a proportionate benefit of them, will have to stay on hand and make use of common facilities—power plants, steel mills, railroads, networks for distributing vegetables in and out of season. One possibility, which may be sufficient to avoid paternalism if the minority is not too large and the output surplus to meeting needs is substantial, is to have everybody supplied with provisions for meeting needs (not just resources that could be converted into such provisions), but to leave everybody at liberty to trade these provisions away for other goods and services. Of course, the members of the majority must be willing to accept more goods and services of the kinds that provide for needs in exchange for goods and services answering to matters of preference only.

The members of the majority may themselves, acting individually in their capacities as consumers, deviate from meeting their needs in accordance with the combined measures that they legislated in their capacities as citizens of the Selfgovliset or at least of the Reference Population. Would it be paternalism to prevent the members of the majority from deviating? I think it would be. They might, as citizens, require of those who favored the legislation pledges to abide by it as consumers, and set up some agency to make sure that the pledges were kept. So they consent to being prevented; but consent does not do away with the paternalism. Nor, I think, does the fact that they are consenting to have an agency prevent them that is of their own devising. Are they not to have the same liberty as the members of the minority, including the liberty to change their minds at one stage or another? The pledges, a partisan of continuing liberty might say, should not be taken in the first place. We are not talking about commitments to uphold social institutions; or to pay taxes to pay for public goods, including those involved in meeting needs. We are talking about pledges, when all taxes have been paid, to take up and consume provisions for needs, or, at least, failing consummation, not to trade them away. And to insist upon these, with the weight of majority legislation coming to bear on individual members of the majority, is a serious invasion of personal liberty.

6.52* Defection and Sabotage Confronted Internally

The planners will not be able to get away with anything that they please to do, even if it is something that would be done in high-minded attention to needs. Resistance by the consumers within the Selfgovliset raises for planners' policies dangers of defection or sabotage. The likelihood of defection varies with the opportunity to form coalitions for production or trading that, operating contrary to the policies, improve the position of the members in respect to preferred forms of provision for needs or in respect to satisfactions, whether connected with needs or not. Those who form such a coalition would presumably withdraw all—or at least a substantial part—of the resources that would have been available for use under the policies; and the policies themselves may be ruined as a consequence. However, to safeguard the policies by preventing people from entering into coalitions implies the use of measures of repression, inevitably objectionable and ugly, so far as they go; and resentment against such measures may show up in sabotage and other forms of resistance, which may themselves frustrate the plan.

The best course for the planners—their only practical course if they are democrats themselves, unwilling to go in for repression—may be to strive, in planning or by letting the market actually operate, to have the allocation of resources and distribution of output represent a coalition-proof solution of the equilibrium problem for the economy, that is to say, a solution in the core for the economy regarded as an *n*-person game. Depending on the degree to which the potential members of coalitions insist upon preferences at odds with their needs, this solution may still conform to constraints that exclude production of such things as tobacco and other debilitating substances.

In general, however, one cannot count on people's preferences being so well behaved. Moreover, even if the constraints on producing certain categories of good are respected, a core solution, if one were available, might be a considerable departure from the needs standard. The departure might be of the same sort as could be expected to result from retrading after rationing (which indeed might be one route to a core solution). Yet the discrepancy might be something that one should cheerfully accept for the sake of liberty. No doubt one might hope that it could be worn away by various processes of education; but people fond of liberty and wary of paternalism might accept the discrepancy regardless.

It may seem far-fetched to assert now that even role-relative precautionary priority is being given needs. Should we wonder at this, however? If so much care has to be taken to guard against coalitions that would undermine any policies which ignored them, we are very far away from having any sort of consensus on meeting needs or the Principle of Precedence. Yet what the planners in fact do may be the best that can be done to meet needs, and may be endorsed by the citizens on just that ground, far though it may be from any ideal solution endorsed by the Principle of Precedence.

Supported to a greater or lesser degree and more or less

effectively by citizens, planners may strive without substantial paternalism to reduce the final shortcomings in
meeting needs by any of the techniques and means mentioned earlier: education in various forms; inconspicuous
and incidental provisions; more attractive forms of provision. A more complex and more populous society would offer in addition opportunities to set up a greater variety of institutional arrangements. For example, planning and
policy-making could devolve upon a number of jurisdictions, divided not necessarily geographically, perhaps in
different ways for different purposes. The jurisdictions
could nevertheless participate, according to their several
policies, in a general market for public goods and other provisions for needs. Minorities could then move from one ju-
risdiction to another, seeking one in which the balance
struck between needs and preferences was most to their liking. Such arrangements have been advocated both by economists of the Chicago school and (in *The Civil War in France*)
by Marx; this is another point upon which Liberalism and
Marxism converge.

6.53 Dealing with the Preferences of External Reference Populations: Paternalism Again

Consumers in an external Reference Population can be offered education; inconspicuous provisions; more attractive
forms of provision. They can be encouraged to sort themselves out into different jurisdictions, too. There are the
same possibilities of infringing upon personal liberty; and
hence the same opportunities for respecting liberty and
avoiding paternalism. The Selfgovliset makes resources
available, but does not impose its views about how the resources are to be used.

Some Reference Populations, wholly external to the Selfgovliset, may have a right to active assistance and to such
treatment along with it. Gurkhas retired from service with
the British Army have a right to their pensions and a right

to spend them as they please. Other external Reference Populations may be given such treatment. The Selfgovliset may be generously accommodating in these respects; or persuaded that its efforts to meet the needs of the Reference Population will fail if they do not take due account of contrary preferences. However, do all external Reference Populations have a right to such treatment? And is it paternalism to refuse to give such treatment when there is no right?

I do not think so. It is true—even when the ground on which the Selfgovliset has accepted responsibility for meeting (or helping to meet) the needs of the Reference Population is that otherwise the needs will go unmet—that the Selfgovliset will be limiting the liberty of the members of that population insofar as it does not adapt its aid to their preferences. If it confines itself to providing just the means of meeting needs, it will be denying those people the liberty to choose to be provided with means answering to matters of preference instead. Furthermore, the Selfgovliset will in this connection be overriding, in favor of its own view of the importance of meeting needs, the view taken by members of the Reference Population.

On the other hand, in its offer of aid, the Selfgovliset is not thwarting their preferences by removing opportunities that they would have without its active assistance. On the contrary, it has increased the liberty of members of the Reference Population by making available to them an alternative that presumably they could not obtain by themselves. Furthermore, that the Selfgovliset should on demand furnish aid of another sort is not merely something not entailed by accepting a responsibility to meet needs; it is inconsistent with a claim for aid founded on needs to demand, instead of provisions that will meet the needs, provisions that will not. By hypothesis, the members of the Reference Population are here relying on a claim founded on needs. They are not fellow citizens, whose preferences must be given the same weight as those of any other citizens, and who stand in a complex relation of reciprocal obligation transcending any immediate issues about needs. Nor, like retired Gurkhas or Indians in Canada and the United States, are they owed compensation for service to the Crown or by right of treaty obligations. Their liberty is sufficiently respected, in the absence of such obligations, by leaving them the option, which is not in question, of refusing to take up the provisions for needs that are offered them.

One could leave the matter there, were it not for the danger that the argument may furnish a pretext for smugly belittling people who are not right-thinking about needs; or, worse, a pretext for not making reasonable adaptations to deep-seated preferences—offering pork to devout Muslims—or, even worse, a pretext for not making any serious effort to meet the needs of the Reference Population at all. Pork will be offered, knowing that it will be refused; or, by way of an excuse for not offering anything, it will be said that the people concerned would just waste anything offered them. They will make whisky, given corn; use bathtubs to store their winter coal. In fact there may be techniques—including techniques already mentioned—for inducing them, step by step, to give more weight to meeting their needs, until finally they are ready to meet them entirely.

6.6 Attention to Preferences at Odds with Justice

Given the considerations that I have discussed, the reconciliation of attention to needs with attention to preferences may be expected to be untidy. Some minorities may have to go along with prevailing views, which they do not themselves share, about meeting needs, and in consequence accept reduced opportunities to give effect to their preferences about the use of various resources. But the sacrifice may run the other way, too, and maybe run the other way simultaneously. Some minorities may have to accept inadequate provisions for their needs if they go along in policies with prevailing views about the relative weights to be given matters of need (for everybody) and matters of preference only (perhaps only for the privileged).

The possibility thus arises that allowances for preferences and liberty, even when they are imperfect, will create injustices by the disregard of the needs of some members of the Reference Population. This possibility can be realized without the crassest sort of disregard of those needs and those members. The people who put policies through may not insist on first making sure of meeting their own needs, and then, in favor of luxuries for themselves, sacrifice meeting the needs of others. The majority—or the decisive set, the people in power whether a majority or not—may be ready to undercut Minimum Standards of Provision for their own needs to keep television going, to carry on harness racing, to build an absinthe distillery. In these cases, too, other people, who would prefer to have their needs met, yet are denied resources to do so, will suffer an injustice.

Even if the members of the Reference Population all concur in the policy of diverting resources from needs to the absinthe distillery, so that the sacrifice is voluntary for everybody, justice will fall into some jeopardy. For such a decision is bound to detract from the importance of meeting needs; and a succession of such decisions will tend to inure members of the Selfgovliset to the spectacle of needs not being met. Then, if circumstances turn desperate for some members of the Reference Population, involuntary and unjust sacrifices are likely to be imposed on them. The members of the majority—of the decisive set—still amply provided for with shelter, will go on indulging themselves in absinthe and other goods, matters of preference only though not necessarily so destructive, while perhaps tens of thousand of people find themselves homeless.

Allowances for preferences and liberty as full as I have contemplated have another serious drawback. Besides creating problems about justice, they stand in the way of making use of an expanded concept of needs. But it may be in people's interest to adopt an expanded concept of needs and use it, in the schema for using the concept of needs, with high priority—with in the end relatively high role-relative precautionary priority—throughout the succession of roles. For otherwise, it may be argued, they will not discover and develop life-plans as rich and as ambitious and as coherent as they might; they will be settling for narrower and less satisfying lives than they might enjoy. All the arguments against imposing policies under the concept of needs come up again, of course, against imposing policies under an expanded concept, and hold with at least as much force. Nevertheless, one might reasonably wish to persuade people that they should not use the allowances for preferences and liberty in such a way as to block themselves from exploring the orientation on life that an expanded concept of needs might give. They should not think that, once needs narrowly conceived have been taken care of, everything is best settled as a matter of preference—even of correct preference, based on informed taste.

DIALOGUE

CRITICAL READER: *You said that you weren't going to endorse all the loosening that you were going to describe as possible in practice. Does that mean that you don't endorse confining the concept of needs to role-relative precautionary priority?*

NOT-YET-REPENTANT AUTHOR: *It certainly does, since that priority is variable just in respect to how much loosening away from strict final priority occurs.*

READER: *But—come clean—how far are you willing to go along with role-relative precautionary priority?*

AUTHOR: *Just far enough to concede that some further allowance for liberty may be demanded as a moral claim, beyond the allowance compatible with strict final priority. I'm not prepared here to refute any particular claim even though I may not wish to make the larger claims myself.*

READER: *Wasn't the chapter just past inevitably more normative—less detached—than that?*

AUTHOR: *I suppose so. I think it was normative of me to show, so far as I did, how the concept of needs can be reconciled with the concept of liberty given larger and larger claims for liberty. Don't forget, though, that equally important was my descriptive aim of showing in outline how the concept is used if we concede that it's not used with strict final priority.*

READER: *But isn't the form of reconciliation with liberty normatively controversial, even putting aside the possibility of extreme departures from strict final priority?*

AUTHOR: *It is. Begin conceding more to liberty than strict final priority allows and you begin jeopardizing justice. But vice versa: make too much of strict final priority and you jeopardize liberty. I don't think there is any neat solution. I don't think I can say, more liberty than I would insist on is too much liberty to demand, reasonably and morally.*

READER: *But haven't you argued that failing to meet needs undermines liberty and thus makes people vulnerable to injustice? Maybe the concessions to liberty are self-limiting; if you go too far, you begin jeopardizing liberty itself with the concessions.*

AUTHOR: *Sometimes one will be able to make a stand against the concessions for just that reason. I doubt whether it's a general solution.*

READER: *Won't the expansion of needs, which you're now about to take up, aggravate the problem? Won't it demand a good deal more under needs, which will be strenuously resisted on the part of liberty?*

AUTHOR: *That's a real danger. On the other hand, if the expansion comes about with mutual consent, it will so far accord with liberty rather than thwart it. Moreover, within the new categories of need reached by expansion one may expect there to be room—required room—for increases in liberty.*

SEVEN

THE EXPANSION OF NEEDS

My treatment of the concept of needs so far will have struck some readers, I expect, as not conservative enough. Not only is the allowance for derived needs too broad for them; they incline to reject the less physically oriented needs on the second part of the basic List. Their dissatisfaction will have offered some resistance to my discussions of justice and utilitarianism, even though derived needs were there informally set aside. It will have persisted through my discussion of reconciling needs with preferences, though little was made of derived needs there, and the priority for basic needs was relaxed. The dissatisfaction will not have been laid to rest by my readiness to restore unanimous consent on the list of needs by moving back toward the basic List (or another list equally basic). Readiness is not performance, though that strategy is, notwithstanding, the one that I would follow, all the way to emending the basic List if necessary, were I to find myself in actual politics dealing with people so restrictive in their use of the concept.

Other readers will have found my treatment much too conservative. They will point out that if the Criterion of functioning adequately in the four social roles is used rigorously, the Minimum Standards of Provision for the Matters of Need on the basic List may call for very low levels of provision—a monotonous diet; one companion; one brief period of recreation per week. Do not people need more than that for full lives, or for happy and fulfilled ones? If the Criterion does not support their having more, is it the right Criterion for the concept of needs? The same readers will

231

remind us, moreover, that even so the Criterion would endorse many needs that do not figure in the List as it stands—the need for establishing a sense of identity, for social orientation, for some stress (the agonistic aspect of life), for some liberty, at least as much as would embrace having some of one's preferences heeded. Other matters would seem to these readers to press for attention just about as urgently, whether or not the Criterion endorsed them—besides ampler provisions on the points mentioned a moment ago, being able to travel just a little, out of their houses, off the block, around their home towns, none of which is covered for sure by anything in the List; or having satisfying work, which is not covered either. Even adding all of these things would not assure feminists of attention under the concept of needs to the matters that have most concerned them: equality; participation. They certainly would not accept having these things treated casually as matters of preference only and might not wish to treat them solely as abstract points of justice either. Everything covered by the List, even by a List expanded to take into account the previous suggestions, might be furnished a woman, and leave her a victimized wife, suffering visibly from her deprivations.

I think the position of the second set of readers is stronger, though it has the disadvantage of opening up opportunities for abuse of the concept and, with or without abuse, of multiplying the occasions for disagreement about its application.

7.1 Is the Two-Part List Unduly Narrow?

Those readers for whom my treatment so far has not been conservative enough would argue that once the physically oriented needs of the first part of the List have been left behind the subject becomes too controversial for any cogent assertions. I do not agree. The two parts of the List (as I noted when the List was introduced) do not neatly separate. Failure to meet needs in the second part can have physical consequences, for example, in psychosomatic diseases. Social conventions play an important part in determining what are acceptable—even, in dietary cases, physically acceptable—forms of provision for the needs in the first part. Can a devout Muslim eat pork sausage without gagging? The two parts of the List do not neatly separate in cogency either. Allowing for the variation between persons, and for rebuttable presumptions sometimes fulfilled short of true universality, few things attach to human beings more firmly than their needs for companionship, social recognition, and recreation. It is also surely rather backward to suggest, a century after Freud began his work, that they do not have a need for sexual activity, which, unmet or denied, has disruptive repercussions in many, even most aspects of their lives.

If we reserved the first and second parts of the List for needs like these, which firm evidence brings under the Criterion of functioning without derangement, we might open up a third part for matters that we might want to consider needs whether or not they satisfied the Criterion. Having some opportunity to travel and a variety of friends might figure here. Without conceding out-of-hand that the Criterion must be abandoned or at least amended, the third part of the List might ascend from the conditions for a minimally full human life toward the conditions for achieving a happy and completely fulfilled one. If having someone—indeed, a family circle—to cherish that deserves being cherished is finally indispensable to a human being's happiness, does not that being need to have such a condition realized, along perhaps with accomplishments to be proud of? We might add chances to accomplish noble ambitions, or at least chances to fail nobly in striving for such accomplishments. At this point, we may have flown too high for the concept of needs. Nevertheless, during the ascent, there will be a place for the need stoutly asserted recently in Canada by the National Council of Welfare: the need in a person's work for "the challenge of growth-potential experience"; and a place for the need—one supposes, closely related—for satisfying, absorbing, engrossing work, a need which has been continually, surprisingly neglected in the thinking about needs characteristic of liberal democracies.

Were it not for that neglect, both the needs just mentioned might have come up earlier. The List was drawn up with a certain strategy in mind—the strategy of trying for something approaching unanimous agreement from people in English-speaking Selfgovlisets, or communities like them, to something like the most far-reaching list (taking into account derived needs) on which unanimity could be expected. Neither the List nor the Criterion inducible from it contemplates people's having any needs that are centrally and indispensably fulfilled at work, though, of course, people may while at work incidentally meet their needs for exercise, companionship, social status and recognition, even recreation. The point of view taken in the first two parts of the List, as the Criterion makes unmistakably plain, is that these needs have to be met for people just to keep going; and the Criterion proposes to test, among other things, whether they are kept going at work. Marx and his followers have had reason to suspect that this test was in fact central in bourgeois eyes; and its being so central may do something to discredit the concept of needs. Certainly there is no suggestion in the List that people need to have satisfying work, or that to be satisfying, it must offer something like "the challenge of growth-potential experience." Marxists, by contrast, have given needs for such things due emphasis. (Marx himself does not, however, explain how meeting the need is going to be reconciled with what he foresees in some passages as the virtual elimination of work by advances in automation.)

Moreover, the Criterion, and with it the concept of needs, even given reasonably high Minimum Standards of Provision, lends support to a narrow and ungenerous view of what social policy requires. It is not so narrow as to ig-

234

nore entirely the needs of those whose provisions are in jeopardy. One may strive, with the Criterion and the concept of needs, even strive officiously, to keep people alive; but, if social conscience goes no further, one may leave people, most people, leading very circumscribed lives. If some people are content nevertheless, does that excuse arrangements and policies that go no further? A friend of mine came across a woman who spent all her working hours—the best part of her waking hours—as a cleaner in a public latrine, yet said, when asked, that she was happy. She should not have been.

Either the concept of needs must expand into a robust third part of the List, or it must be firmly recognized as covering no more than the preliminaries to adequate social policies and a good society. So Marxists would say, along with other critics more concerned with the abuses of narrowness than with the abuses of expansion. They would say it, moreover, with some scepticism about whether either alternative will be realized under present arrangements. The concept of needs, in their eyes, may be a trap for social conscience that current social conscience cannot extricate itself from.

7.2 The Advantages of Expansion

The preceding chapter, on reconciling attention to needs with attention to preferences, may be taken to have explored the alternative of recognizing needs as no more than preliminaries to other matters important to social policy. Those matters could all be brought up under the head of preferences. Are there any advantages to the other approach—to expanding the concept of needs? I think there are a number worth considering.

One advantage is contingent and precautionary: If the concept of needs is going to be used to select social policies, and it looks as though social policies will not go much further than to meet needs, the partisans of generous policies will want to make sure that the concept is not too restrictive. So they may openly argue for a number of additions to the List.

Four other advantages, not contingent on circumstances, may be expected from judicious expansion, that is to say, expansion grounded either on the Criterion or on a carefully amended one.

The first of these is that such expansion encourages people ready to act on the Principle of Precedence to be more sensitive to other people's fates. To transfer something from the sphere of matters of preference only to the sphere of needs invests it with a more urgent claim to attention. If being able to travel about town is just a matter of preference, understandably it might be an agreeable thing to have the opportunity to do so, and it might be highly valued by all sorts of people, but as a matter of preference it ranks among optional pleasures. As a Matter of Need, it cannot on the face of it be denied without causing some significant damage, physical or psychological, which can be ascribed to all members of the Reference Population, or to all human beings, with presumptive universality. I am supposing that either the unamended Criterion can be invoked in support of it, or an amended Criterion that has the effect of enlarging the range of relevant damage to include, for example, further substantial impairments to life-plans. Treated as a Matter of Need increases the chances that the item brought in by expansion will be taken seriously; attended to under justice; given the specific protection of the social device of rights.

The increased sensitivity accompanying an expanded use of the concept of needs is not, however, just an effect of having something covered under needs that was formerly covered under preferences. As the List expands, one may expect that to whatever degree the relation with the Criterion is kept up, the disturbances in functioning that are recognized as signs of deprivation in respect to needs will embrace continually subtler phenomena. What would have

236

been ignored as bad temper or mere eccentricity in one age becomes in a more affluent, more expansive age a neurosis calling for remedy.

The second of the four noncontingent advantages is that the increase in sensitivity which may be expected to accompany the expansion of needs is sensitivity to matters in which human beings have parallel concerns. It is too simple to say that needs unite humankind while preferences divide. If the means of meeting everybody's needs are absent, needs may engender desperate, bitter struggles among human beings. Hume thought that in such circumstances, where justice was unattainable, justice was an idle notion. However, while it must be acknowledged that in preferences other people may be so different as to be hardly understood, much less sympathized with, needs unite human beings in their conception of themselves.

In favorable circumstances—when, among other things, it can be assumed that the means of meeting the needs are available—they supply a reliable basis for fellow-feeling. They also furnish nonmonetary incentives consonant with true, fraternal cooperation. An important part of the satisfactions of work lie in meeting other people's needs. How useful can a person feel producing things that he deems to be trivial or even harmful, like a jingle designed to increase the sales of soda pop? Preferences may be shared, too; but this is more a matter of accident, and less reliable. The basic List concerns needs ascribed to not just one Reference Population or another, but to all such populations, including any Selfgovliset in question, with presumptive universality. Thus, simultaneously with accepting into the List an added Matter of Need as something to be ascribed other people, people accept it as something to be ascribed themselves, and recognize that in this respect their fates and the others' turn on having parallel provisions.

The third noncontingent advantage of expanding the basic List lies in the consensus on policy that it implies. This amounts, of course, simply to carrying forward with the expansion the consensus, extending at least to role-relative precautionary priority, that I have repeatedly noted as a feature of the concept of needs when that concept is given distinctive use. With this consensus, and so long as the priority is kept in mind, the matter at issue is removed from politics in the sense that whether it should be provided for is no longer debated. Debate shifts to the cost of alternative methods of supplying forms of provision; the cost of the forms of provision themselves, where there are alternative forms; the degree to which attention to everybody's preferences can be reconciled with the provision.

Consensus may not be achieved. If there is widespread opposition to counting something as a Matter of Need, then the concept is not being given its distinctive use. However, the fourth noncontingent advantage of expanding the List is that by associating the added matters with the Criterion or something like the Criterion people can be helped toward consensus by founding the added matters, like the matters already there, on objective, observational knowledge. The Criterion, calling for such knowledge, opens up further work for that part of the critique of preferences which points out the disadvantages of having preferences at odds with needs. Started up perhaps just given consensus that some matters are Matters of Need, the critique can carry on, after further matters have been assimilated to the needs originally agreed upon, to argue for adapting preferences to these matters, too. The Criterion gives the critique an explicit basis for bringing about the assimilation.

How far will expansion on such an objective basis extend? To answer this question we must consider more closely the various forms that expansion might take.

7.3 The Courses Expansion May Take

Needs are capable of expanding dramatically in the sense that derived needs may multiply under new social arrangements as technology, growing more complex, becomes capable of producing new sorts of goods, and, growing more efficient, becomes capable of supplying goods both old and new in greater abundance. This may have been something that Marx had in mind when, like Fourastié, he asserted that needs are infinitely expansible. However, there is good reason to believe that both of them were thinking of the expansion of wants, whether or not the wants answered to needs, rather than of the expansion of needs strictly speaking, derived or otherwise. They are writing in languages (German and French) that do not, like English, compel them to choose, in choosing or not choosing to use the word for "need," one side or the other of the distinction: "Bedürfnisse" and "besoin" are perhaps better translated by "need" than by "want" in most cases, but here "want" would give more plausible results. It would also give results more suited to Marx's generalized use of the German and French words as technical terms to keep company with "use value": An object has a use value (which is a necessary condition of its having an exchange value) if and only if it answers to a want.

7.31* Derived Needs Brought in with Changes in Technology

Nevertheless, the growth of technology may well lead to additional derived needs as well as to additional wants not answering to needs. Social arrangements, springing up to take advantage of technological developments, in time become so far consolidated that use of the new product becomes unavoidable. People can hardly get along without a telephone, or without a radio, though their needs for communication are still partly served by pen and paper and by the press. Growing affluence may have similar effects, either indirectly by fostering new social arrangements (dishes with knives, forks, and spoons where once people used their hands and knives to feed from common trenchers) or directly by inducing rises in the Minimum Standards of Provisions. These rises, as I pointed out in Chapter Three, can often be regarded equally well as bringing in new derived needs. Having a telephone, for example, is equally a need derived under certain social arrangements from the need for companionship (though not necessarily from this need alone) and an ingredient in raised Minimum Standards of Provision for that need.

Can derived needs multiply without limit or Minimum Standards of Provision rise without resistance? The resistance may be formidable. As resources increase, a greater proportion of the population may become more affluent. Yet, forgetting the poverty of the past, working harder under the incitement of expanded wants, and unable to obtain "positional" values (like uncrowded beach space) available to the rich in the past, these people may feel harassed, dissatisfied, far from comfortably rich themselves, and ungenerous—unwilling therefore to recognize higher Minimum Standards of Provision. Moreover, Marx for one has to have some ground (though he would not wish to rely on ungenerous feelings as such a ground) for holding that needs will not expand so fast as to outrun resources. If they did they would forestall the coming of abundance, with all the beneficial effects that Marx expected of abundance, including an end to conflict of interests and to the state as an indispensable means of repressing the disorder to which such conflict gives rise.

Marx would not endorse every derived need that might be added with the growth of technology and consequent changes in social arrangements. Technology may work—it has worked in the past—toward the privatization of households and against joint activities on behalf of communal purposes. The sense of community may diminish under new social arrangements brought in with increasing resources. This helps no doubt to explain why the Principle of Precedence continues to go unfulfilled and why the affluent so complacently enjoy their privileges while large parts of the population, jobless, even homeless, suffer all sorts of indignities. Derived needs that block dealing with these matters may well represent, with the social arrangements on which they depend, questionable adaptations to technology. Marx, in the occasional passages where he opposes "truly human needs" to "animal needs," and, much more explicitly, some of Marx's followers, have contended that the needs accepted as such in the transformed society to come will be needs that satisfy a thoroughgoing critique of needs. They hold, moreover, that such a critique will give due place to unifying, communal purposes.

7.32* Marxist Expectations Regarding Humanly Enlarged Needs

The needs recognized in the new society will escape the distortions that afflict needs accepted as such hitherto. They will not be distorted to serve class privileges, or to serve a structure of domination that rests on libidinal sacrifices which are now excessive if they were not always so. They will be authentic needs, because they will be needs freely arrived at: People will not be coerced or deceived into postulating them as needs and conducting their lives accordingly.

Even if (revised, perhaps drastically) some needs now recognized survive in the transformed society, the needs there will be viewed differently. Different forms of provision from those now demanded will seem suitable. The relations of the needs and the forms of provision for them will differ, too. Where now, for example, it is common for people to find recreation and companionship for the most part off the job, there everybody, or nearly everybody, will have such work, and such a variety of work, that little of these needs will remain to be met outside of it. The new pattern will be better, too, because it will be pervaded with communal purposes tending to bring people together in their activities, rather than setting them apart. Instead of competing to assemble private collections of valuable objects to own and display—a characteristic higher cultural activity of bourgeois society—people will devote themselves exclusively to building up public collections and to assist in the active public use of them.

It would be an extravagance, and a mystification, to claim that the novelties on these points would transform currently accepted needs entirely, so that, for example, none of the needs now in the basic List would survive. Here, as in other cross-cultural comparisons, we can perfectly well identify some needs—the need for exercise, the need for companionship; indeed, all the needs in the basic List—in terms so general as to transcend existing social arrangements or personality structures. Exercise may take different forms after social transformation; but the need for exercise will still be there. Moreover, Marx and Marxism have a use for those needs in criticizing capitalism as well as in explaining the benefits to be expected in the new society. Capitalism would stand condemned in Marx's eyes even if it did meet present needs; but it is in his eyes a significant additional failure of the system, and further reason to condemn it, that it fails to meet the needs—even the "animal needs"—of everybody. The new, transformed society, for its part, must do more than meet basic needs if not meeting them, or the fear of not meeting them, is to be removed as a prime source of conflict. It must meet them at as high Minimum Standards of Provision as capitalism has ever achieved; indeed, do persistently better with respect to at least some matters of need and some Standards. Some followers of Marx have looked forward to a society more austere than capitalism with its diffuse comforts during prosperous periods. Marx himself, however, was no champion of austerity, any more than a typical worker is. Failure to match, even surpass capitalism in respect to Minimum Standards of Provision would remove one of the direct attractions of the transformed society.

Marx would eliminate present social arrangements and the needs distinctively derived from them. But doing this would surely tend to reduce the number of needs rather than multiply them. So would the recovery from the sphere of needs and its constraints of ground lost through the extension of convention to matters best treated as matters of preference only. Such recovery would occur as an incident of repudiating social arrangements, unless new arrangements came in with as extensive and as inexorable a set of derived needs as before. It might also occur to some extent independently of repudiating social arrangements wholesale, as something brought about by a critique of needs aiming to show there is more room for preference even in living with present arrangements than people, hard-pressed by their own misconceptions, commonly realize.

The net results of accepting new derived needs with new social arrangements thus seem indeterminate, since simultaneously a greater or lesser number of other derived needs will be discarded. The results seem indeterminate for another reason as well: We do not have any very certain principles for individuating needs, so that neither the new needs nor the old ones could be counted. We could get determinate answers, in the absence of complete counts, only if all the old needs survived and others—not reducible to any of the old ones—were added; but that is ruled out by the assumption that there will be change at once in both directions.

7.33* Additions to Basic Needs Following Advances in Science and Technological Capacity

Might we, on a Marxist approach or otherwise, look for benefits from more fundamental changes in the set of needs than any confined to derived needs alone? Will there be any expansion in the basic List of Matters of Need? Here, at least at first sight, the assertions about expansion seem very implausible. There is, admittedly, as remarked earlier, some reason to believe that neither the first nor the second part of the List given is complete or could be completed. We may always make further discoveries about people's basic needs, sometimes with the help of new concepts. The need that human beings have to be under some stress, rising to having to have a course of life with agonistic features, may be cited again as an example of such a discovery. However, needs added to the basic List this way, like the needs that already figure there, can evidently be ascribed with presumptive universality to human beings regardless of differences in culture or circumstances. They are founded on persistent features of human biology and psychology. Differences between cultures enjoying material abundance and cultures not so well off have already been taken into account, as well as differences of wealth among the members of any given culture.

Natural science, and technology advancing with natural science, might add to the number of needs in the course of finding means of doing things that people were not able to have done before. It is a notable fact about the current List of basic needs that there are known sorts of provisions, normally, or at least frequently, available for meeting them. Our knowledge of provisions may change, however. A vaccine against dental decay, if it did not have the drawback of changing the microflora and microfauna of the mouth for the worse, would render obsolete any need for the present procedures and materials of reparative dentistry. But would it not do more than that? Would not its becoming available lead to its being needed? And if the corresponding need did not count as a new Matter of Need on its own bottom, but rather as (again) a revised feature of the Minimum Standards of Provision for keeping the body intact, it could still serve as a model of what it would be like to have an advance in technology establish something as a new need, basic or derived.

Transformed social arrangements may enable science and technology to do even more than they have been doing to expand needs in the senses just mentioned. So such needs fit in with Marxist expectations about the benefits of transformed arrangements. They do not, however, squarely answer to the expansion of needs as envisaged by Marx, or, for that matter, by Fourastié. They are not needs that imply any sort of development or transformation in the people to whom they are ascribed. They are, in particular, not, as Marx evidently would have it, needs that are generated in the people to whom they are ascribed at least in part by the fact that needs recognized earlier have been met.

7.34 An Amended Criterion Aiming at Full Personal Development

To identify additional needs of this sort, which is at the same time to focus on the most problematic aspect of expansion, it is convenient to consider opening up a third part of the basic List on the basis of an amended Criterion. The amended Criterion would bring to bear on this part the notion of the full development of human personality. I invoke this notion without settling upon anything rich or exact enough to define it. Indeed, I want, characteristically, to allow for radically different variants of the notion, some, for instance, assuming greater quantities and varieties of goods as a foundation for self-development, others implying new needs independent of further increases in consumption. I do so, furthermore, without precluding the possibility, which I shall discuss in due course, that some of the needs introduced under these variants will be found to satisfy after all the unamended Criterion of underanged functioning.

It is reasonable to suppose, with Marx and others, that the level which personal development can reach is subject to change with fundamental transformations of society; and will rise if the transformations are favorable. Some persons in the past may have developed to a level not easily surpassed—Plato, perhaps, or Socrates, Leonardo, Goethe. The thesis of higher development is still plausible, taken in a statistical sense, as applying to the opportunities for development available to the average man and woman—or to the worst-off ones; and perhaps the greatest excellencies of the future will surpass the exceptional excellencies of the past after all.

"Expansion of needs" suggests expansion of consumption. Operating on a larger, more affluent plan, people may require more in goods and services as provisions for new, more complex and sophisticated needs: more musical instruments, more sports equipment, more motorcycles, more camping gear, more scientific apparatus—a telescope in every backyard, more public works to maintain the environment, more concerts, more art exhibitions, more sustained and thorough guidance in exploring the psyche, or at least special facilities for this pursuit and active cooperation from others.

Operating on a larger plan, people may require more just to keep going, since perhaps the commitment to the larger plan prevents them from making sure of capacity and smooth functioning with just the needs met in the first two parts of the List as received, and met according to the received Minimum Standards of Provision. The provisions for recreation, for example, will have to be more extensive, more elaborate, subtler; and new needs may emerge for high cultural stimulation, perhaps, and for self-expression.

The implied rise in the Minimum Standards of Provision for recreation may, however, be typical. Even though the expansion makes a genuine and important difference, the expansion of needs, in the ways just illustrated, may be accommodated entirely by rises in those Standards for matters already in the basic List. This is so, moreover, even if we associate with the vague notion of living on a larger plan a notion, more susceptible perhaps of exact description, of a change in personality structure. Used to living at a higher level of civilization, people become more sensitive, hence more easily deranged in functioning. They therefore require ampler and subtler provisions. People from comfortable middle-class circles proved more vulnerable to the indignities practiced upon them in Nazi concentration camps, and broke down much more fully than other prisoners. This phenomenon seems to imply a difference in personality structure of the sort at issue here. (The increased vulnerability is not a flaw in the personality structure; it is a further indictment of the distance to which the concentration camps departed from the standards and expectations of civilized life.)

Marx seems to have thought of self-development in the transformed society as founded on greater affluence; and Simmel, teaching that self-development proceeds by incorporating experiences of various objects into the developing self, offers a view that is so far consistent with Marx's. In an early text, Marx declaims, "To take the place of wealth and poverty as political economy knows it, there comes forward the rich man, fitted out with rich human exigencies. The rich man is at the same time the man who, to live, has need of a totality of human manifestations, the man for whom his own realization is an interior necessity, a need." The richness of human exigencies here is readily associated with a demand for a rich variety of goods.

Yet the "interior necessity" of self-realization may not depend on having such a variety, or on greater affluence. The suggestion running from the expansion of needs to an expansion of consumption stumbles at this point, and awakens arguments showing that in certain instances at least the two phenomena are independent. From Simmel one can even draw an argument to the effect that the expansion of output—the production of a greater quantity and a greater variety of goods—obstructs self-development, by presenting too many possibilities of experience. Instead of making music part of her life and self by devoting herself to playing the recorder, a person flits from one instrument and from one sort of ensemble to another and yet another, or allows easily available recordings of virtuoso performances to daunt her so much that she ceases trying to become as proficient as she could be on any instrument.

Expansion, it seems clear, may take a course toward new needs that do not require the person with the needs to consume more goods and services. Fourastié suggests that technological developments have created a new need for tranquility. Another example might be found in a need for the opposite—a need for adventure, going far beyond a need for stress and some agonistic features of life. Surfing and whitewater canoeing are adventurous, and make small demands in material goods. The need for adventure may break entirely out of a prudent, bourgeois attachment to meeting the needs on the List. James Graham, Marquis of Montrose, was thinking of chances in love when he wrote,

> He either fears his fate too much,
> Or his deserts are small,
> That dares not put it to the touch,
> To gain or lose it all.

However, the sentiment typifies an aristocratic outlook on life generally, and self-development may take an aristocratic course rather than a bourgeois one. The consequence of meeting needs in the first two parts of the List and of securely providing besides for compatibly moderate, comfortable pleasures may be, for many people, not satisfaction but boredom. A tidy life on that pattern may seem to them tame, circumscribed, petty-minded. In my mind I can hear Nietzsche, dressed up in his absurd uniform, tripping over his sword as he rushes on stage to agree. He might think that the possibility discredits the concept of needs; but to be fit for adventures people must first meet their needs.

More congenial to bourgeois sentiment, but equally capable of moving in a direction other than that of expanded consumption is the need for a person or persons, for example, a family circle, cherished and cherishing, which might be supposed to carry beyond the need for companionship to depths of intimacy and mutual identification not easily accommodated under that need even with heightened Minimum Standards of Provision. More elusive in definition, yet equally clearly a candidate for addition to the basic List, is the need commonly expressed in the resort to psychoanalysis, to come to terms with oneself; to discover one's identity; to have full self-knowledge and full command of oneself. Some of the techniques for meeting this need, which may be regarded as central to self-development, are, like psychoanalysis, expensive. Even they, though along with the need they may figure in more affluent plans of life, will not always require a net increase in the consumption of goods and services by the person meeting the need; he may give up holidays in Martinique and more luxurious automobiles to pay his psychoanalyst. Other techniques, like meditation in the Zen tradition, are inherently inexpensive and indeed aim at less concern with material goods and less time spent with them.

7.35* The Need for Satisfying Work

The need for satisfying work is a candidate for addition to the basic List that can be backed by notions of self-development throughout the range considered, from those assuming increased consumption to those assuming nothing of the kind. People can function without derangement even at work that is far from satisfying. All along, however, it is indispensable to their full development that they have opportunities at work to enlarge their views, test their talents, and attain a sense of significant accomplishment. Here the need for satisfying work, as a condition of full personal development, intersects with another candidate—the need for multiple accomplishments, answering at least to a variety of the talents that a given person may have, some of them distinctive to a degree.

Among other reasons because it fits with many different notions of self-development, the need for satisfying work may be the clearest and most convincing case of a new need to be assigned to the third part of the List. When the pressures of other needs have been dealt with, and the opportunity arises to provide for the full development of the human personality, will not satisfying work become a leading consideration? I suppose that people who are hard-pressed just to keep their heads above water will not worry much about satisfying work or become upset about not having it. Will not their outlook and condition, and their needs, change, however, once the grip of necessity relaxes? So at least many social critics and prophets have thought, prominent among them, Marx, who looked forward to the time when "labour has become not only a means of life but life's prime want."

There are no grounds for denying that activities apart from work—play—will be a source, too, indeed an increasing source of satisfaction; or that the satisfactions found there will in large part be the same as those of work—challenges to strength, ingenuity, and responsibility surmounted by elegant demonstrations of masterly skill. Yet many people—most people, as they are now constituted in our society and may be expected to be constituted for some generations to come—would find the fullest measure of these satisfactions in work, if the work were commensurately challenging.

Ironically, the satisfactions of even the most challenging work will lose their distinctive foundation if the work is not needed; and the surest way of establishing that it is needed is to show that it serves, directly or indirectly, but in any case indispensably, one or another of the needs in the basic List. If the needs currently in the basic List are going to be met easily, with advances in technology and affluence, it would be reassuring to find that those needs will increase, giving more scope for work. It would be somewhat paradoxical, however, giving an appearance of circular futility, if the increase was confined to the need for satisfying work itself. However, if we recall the needs of people outside the affluent societies, and the possibility that conservation may compel us to do more work to meet needs generally, we shall have less to fear in that paradox; there may be needs enough just in that connection for work to meet, besides the need for work itself.

The need for satisfying work turns out to fit the unamended Criterion. The Canadian National Council of Welfare cites evidence from an American study that people who are not offered at work "the challenge of growth-potential experience" manifest boredom, discontent, absenteeism, alcoholism. These effects fall readily among the effects looked for by the unamended Criterion invoked in the first two parts of the basic List—incapacity and derangement of functioning in the tasks assigned by the basic combination of social roles.

With less concrete evidence to invoke, one may argue that some of the other needs that an amended Criterion contemplating the full development of human personality would bring into a third part of the List fit the unamended Criterion, too. With the change in personality structure adapted to living on a larger plan, people become more sensitive, and liable to be deranged in functioning, not only by not having ampler and subtler provisions answering to higher Minimum Standards but also by having unmet needs for significant accomplishments, or for having not just companions but a life partner or a family circle, cherished and worth cherishing.

If the unamended Criterion will serve after all, is there any point left in recognizing a third part of the basic List? We came by a roundabout route, using the notion of full development of personality. In the end, however, we see how the needs in the first and second parts might expand, perhaps indefinitely, not just through rises in the Minimum Standards of Provision for needs already there, and not just through revisions and additions consequent upon scientific discoveries of needs or provisions, but through changes in personality structure following changes in circumstances and culture. Some differences in culture connect causally, by way of changes in personality structure, with capacity and smooth functioning in ways that give grounds for adding Matters of Need.

7.36* Persistent Advantages of a Third Part of the List and an Amended Criterion

Advantages nevertheless can be found in maintaining a third part of the List to which these needs might be assigned. They come later to recognition than the needs originally accepted as such in the first and second parts. The fact that they fit the unamended Criterion might be taken as a bonus. One might well be inclined to make a case for them anyway, invoking the full development of human personality. If that inclination were given full weight by assigning the needs to a third part, which in principle could be added to the List by the consideration of full development, the third part would be open for additions which could rely on that consideration alone.

Inevitably, discussing the third part of the List as an option, I have made it seem, contrary to what I held in Chapter 3, that whether or not something is a Matter of Need is a question for debate and decision in a way that establishing a matter of fact is not. Yet what I have been saying in this chapter can be reconciled with the position that I took earlier. I said there that it would be an anomalous departure from our use of the concept of needs to say that something could now, with the coming of affluence, be thought of as a need, though it was not a need earlier. The option that I have been concerned with here is in part an option for philosophers in the analysis of the concept of needs. Can that analysis be comprehensive if it is not prepared to see the Criterion amended? For the rest, the option may be reckoned as one that is taken, if it is taken, by people generally, in the process of development and reorientation described earlier, in which people with power, becoming more secure with affluence, gradually become more generous. I am, in my discussion, making some things explicit that go on without explicit discussion and decision in the course of this development. I can admit that, however, without having to concede that my discussion has somehow supplanted the development as a primary phenomenon. For people engaged in the development in the ordinary way, it will seem in retrospect that added needs, to whatever part of the List they may be assigned, were needs all along. Neglect of them earlier was due either to lack of enlightenment or to lack of means.

Having a third part of the List would be the most dramatic way of vindicating Fourastié's contention that new needs will spring up after the earlier ones have been met; and Marx's assertion, which is perhaps only at first sight stronger, that meeting the earlier ones causes the new ones to appear. At the same time, so far as the unamended Criterion serves for the third part, too, the opportunity of invoking a change in personality structure in the causal explanation here and elsewhere remains.

On one view of this change, its character would be foreordained with great specificity. People may be endowed by nature with a hierarchy of needs, some of which press for attention only after the others have been met. The needs themselves, however, even the latest-comers, would invariably appear, in very different cultures, once suitably abundant provisions became available. The conception of such a hierarchy was a familiar theme of economics in the mid-nineteenth century, and Marx may have had something like it in mind. Yet it accords better with the strain in Marxist theory that emphasizes the cultural plasticity of human nature to interpret his thesis about the expansion of needs as referring to phenomena of another sort, in which once rudimentary needs are met, and the way is clear for other needs to develop, these develop in culturally specific ways. On this view, the changed personality structures would take different forms in different cultures.

7.4 The Risks of Expansion

Some expansion of the concept of needs, in all the ways that I have surveyed, many people will perhaps find congenial straightaway. Others, apprized of the possibilities and the advantages that I have described, may be persuaded to accept the expansion. Yet it will not occur without risks. In the eyes of many thinkers it will inflate the concept well beyond the point, if there is a point, to which they are ready to go in joining a consensus on the Principle of Precedence.

For some of these skeptics expansion of the concept may serve as an occasion for renewing their insistence on the relational formula. "N needs x in order to y." In every case, they will say again, whether there is a need for x depends on whether N wants y, or whether people concerned with N want it for her, which is just a contingent fact about N or them. Expansion, taking the concept into regions formerly left to human variations in matters of preference only, reveals this contingency more starkly; but it can and should be carried back, these skeptics would argue, to the use of the concept in its narrowest beginnings.

Whatever the risks that the concept of needs runs with expansion, I do not think that succumbing to this adverse use of the relational formula is one of them. People may be found who do not want full personal development; but that end comes almost as much, noncontingently, at the end of justifications, with no call for its being justified itself, as does the Criterion of capacity and smooth functioning, or any of the alternative criteria that might be used for the first two parts of the List. Furthermore, as I have shown, the unamended Criterion of functioning without derangement applies to the most plausible current candidates for entry in a third part of the List, as it does to matters of need added to the first and second parts following scientific discovery of needs and provisions.

Even so there is a sense, fully admitted throughout my

discussion, in which the use of the concept of needs depends on preferences that may be less readily forthcoming for expanded use. Going along with the way of thinking that the concept entails, that is to say, joining in the consensus that puts needs out of politics insofar at least as giving them role-relative precautionary priority for an entire Reference Population goes, is something that one may prefer not to do. The presence of this option does not, in the face of a robust Criterion, make any needs matters of preference only in the sense of detaching them from support by the Criterion. Yet considering the commitments that going along may bring in its train, more and more members of the Selfgovliset may withdraw from the consensus as the concept is expanded. If the consensus is seriously undermined, however, the concept will no longer operate to discriminate among policies solely on the basis of factual considerations acknowledged as relevant in the consensus. It will at best single out a set of considerations championed by a partisan majority. The majority will have arguments to show that all these supposed needs, even needs brought in by expansion, have an objective foundation corresponding to the Criterion, amended or unamended; but for the moment at least those arguments will not have succeeded everywhere, and they may be inherently less compelling applied to the expanded set than to an unexpanded one.

Covering more as Matters of Need, the expanded use may lend itself more easily to corrupt uses. It will be easier to smuggle in considerations that are not entitled to the status of needs at all. There is also a danger that some people—a fraction both of the Selfgovliset and of the Reference Population—may attain a standard of living that comports with an expanded use before the rest of the Reference Population has met needs on a narrower list; and may defend that standard as leaving them no room beyond their needs to aid the rest. In other words, the expanded use may soften or blur the discrepancy between their standard and the standard of the rest. On this account, one might hesitate to

welcome any expansion until all the matters on an unexpanded list had been provided for throughout the Reference Population.

To make sure of these basic provisions, one might wish
to have them accorded strict final priority, reserving for
needs that came in only with more expansive use of the
concept any relaxation that role-relative precautionary
priority would introduce. But this position is already allowed for, in the sense that role-relative precautionary
priority might work out to such a result, if members of the
Selfgovliset so insist. On the other hand, for all the reasons
brought up in the preceding chapter to explain the shift to
role-relative precautionary priority, such insistence cannot
be continually expected, even when the members' own
basic needs are at stake.

Another risk and drawback of expansion lies in its restrictive impact on people's conduct of their own lives. Needs
demand priority. As they multiply, people may find them
absorbing so many resources that fewer and fewer are left
over to be treated frankly and freely as means of pursuing
preferences. No doubt there will be less to this objection the
more authentic the connection between the needs added
during expansion, on the one hand, and, on the other, the
full development of human personality in happy and completely fulfilled lives. Moreover, needs added in this connection will, one might expect, generate preferences for
free exploration as much as displace them. Nevertheless,
some confusion about these matters is to be expected, given
the degree of exploration that they have had hitherto; and
amid the confusion people may persist under the grip of
conceptions of need that they would do better to free themselves of.

All these drawbacks are real. The most substantial of
them, however, remains the risk of demanding so much
under the Principle of Precedence that members of the Selfgovliset will rather repudiate the concept than pay the
costs. Indeed, with expansion the concept of needs may

outrun the resources available either for meeting needs or for heeding preferences. Then it will break down. Ironically, in certain connections it may outrun resources already and face breakdown well before any expansion is attempted. These breakdowns are my next topic.

DIALOGUE

CRITICAL READER: *Haven't you given more grounds for distrusting expansion than for embracing it?*

NOT-YET-REPENTANT AUTHOR: *I don't know. Perhaps it's impossible to assess the grounds on either side apart from discussing some particular candidate needs. There we would know just what points of expansion were contemplated and just how firmly the policy-making group was ready to agree on them. Only then could one decide whether the expansion was reasonable.*

READER: *Otherwise, you have mixed feelings?*

AUTHOR: *I do indeed. I fear having the heavy-handedness of the concept of needs carried forward to apply to matters best left to personal discretion—best left, even if currently no one wants to make any special use of the discretion. Not only that. I also fear that the trenchancy of the concept where it is morally more compelling, operating closer to the basic List and the Minimum Standards of Provision, will be blunted.*

READER: *Back to strict final priority?*

AUTHOR: *Yes. At least, the case for strict final priority becomes more and more compelling as we move back toward the basic List.*

READER: *You've allowed for that in your idea that the concept gives us a schema within which we may contract or expand its use according to the extent of consensus.*

259

AUTHOR: *Yes, but remember, to this contraction and expansion, which is bound to make the concept seem fluid, we have to add the variable provision for relaxation that comes with role-relative precautionary priority. I have misgivings, however, about the damage that may be done, assuming strict final priority, by contraction and expansion of the schema alone.*

READER: *Would you be good enough to tell us just what you have in mind?*

AUTHOR: *Too much expanded use—or too many attempts at expanded use—within the schema will weary people with the concept, won't it? It will seem more than it might seem continually vexed with dissension.*

READER: *Is that why distrust of the concept is so widespread among sophisticated people?*

AUTHOR: *Very likely—even now.*

READER: *And this before we've looked at the facts or prospects of real breakdowns?*

AUTHOR: *Alas! But on, to just that subject.*

E I G H T

THE CONCEPT OF NEEDS AT THREE POINTS OF BREAKDOWN

When and where the concept of needs is working well, I have argued, it does so in spite of complications about derivation, conventionality, and normativity; and when it is used most strictly it does so in accordance with the convergent demands of justice and of a surrogate for utilitarianism. It can also work usefully—though with some danger of straying from the path of justice—side-by-side with giving due attention, in accordance with the demands of liberty, to matters of preference only. It works well enough in its basic use guiding social policy to invite expanded uses of the sorts that I explored in the chapter just finished.

From the beginning, however, I have acknowledged that the concept of needs does not always work well. On some issues of social policy, far from working well, it is liable to break down. There it can no longer be relied on for coherent and convincing guidance. Plenty of other contexts exist in which such difficulties do not come up; they are the contexts assumed and illustrated in earlier chapters. There the concept deserves the reliance commonly placed upon it. On the other hand, contexts in which difficulties now to be discussed do come up are becoming increasingly familiar as scenes or prospective scenes for choosing social policies. The difficulties have become increasingly harder to ignore.

Even so, the first point of breakdown that I am going to treat is hypothetical and controversial rather than real and imminent. It is a point that we come upon after disposing,

261

as best we can, of the claim of addictions to the title of needs and the sanction of the Principle of Precedence. Suppose (what is not quite certain) we succeed in doing this. The very arguments on which this success depends show how vulnerable the normative use of the concept of needs is to any demonstration that human beings have, permanently and ineluctably, some needs that are morally embarrassing—ignoble, descending to outright pernicious. The best comfort that we can take on this point is to believe that the demonstration has not yet been forthcoming.

The other two points of breakdown to be treated do not wait on further demonstration. They are real already; or really imminent.

One has to do with the huge demands on resources that medical needs already make, now that it is possible through medical care to meet Minimum Standards of Provision for persons formerly outside the range of feasible standards. These demands will increase without limit, omnivorously, if the concept of needs is applied to endorse the indefinite and indiscriminate prolongation of human life.

But imminent, if not yet present demands restricted to much more modest ambitions respecting medical care (indeed restriction to Minimum Standards of Provision as they stood before the last half-century of developments in medical science) may fall upon us with omnivorous force if we grant that the proper application of the concept of needs is ultimately an application on the world scale, to the world population. This is the third point of breakdown (which I shall take up second). There seems to be no justifiable way of fixing on a smaller Reference Population; but a Reference Population identical with the world population may need—or may soon come to need—continually more than the affluent Selfgovlisets could supply, not to speak of needing more than they would be willing to supply.

All these difficulties have in common the fact that they impose limits to the convincing normative use of the concept of needs. One might say the same about the long-standing, occasional difficulty that sometimes resources do not suffice to meet all the needs of a given Reference Population, and thus needs conflict. When such a conflict appears, I have argued, one must appeal outside the concept of needs—certainly outside my account of the concept—for guidance. Now, conflicts between needs may appear hand-in-hand with the difficulties that I shall now treat, and aggravate them. However, appealing outside the Principle of Precedence to some basis for balancing between the needs in conflict or establishing an order of priority among them will not suffice to resolve these difficulties. That is to say, it is not just a question of there being some contexts in which the account will work only if some familiar supplementary principles are brought in to establish, temporarily, priorities among different needs. With these difficulties, the concept breaks down; it becomes ineligible for normative use. With embarrassing needs and longevity, the account works through to determinate results, but they are unacceptably anomalous; and there is no familiar principle outside the account to turn to for relief, permanent or temporary. On the extent of the Reference Population, the account works through to acceptable results only if some arbitrary, in the end unjustifiable, decision is made to fix it conveniently short of being extended to the whole population of the planet. The account itself is indeterminate on this point; and no supplementary principle is available that makes it determinate, free of anomaly.

Does shifting from strict final priority for needs to role-relative precautionary priority soften the impact of these difficulties? The relaxation of priority that goes with the second notion may be carried so far that in the end both the demands of needs and the demands of justice are to a large extent ignored. Effective priority vanishes at one extreme of role-relative precautionary priority. At the other extreme, answering more surely to the demands of justice (and of utilitarianism), lies priority strict enough even in the end, in the policies actually pursued, to satisfy strict final priority.

263

The breakdowns now at issue make so much priority ineligible even for a Selfgovliset prepared, with the List, Minimum Standards of Provision, and Criterion understood as in my account, to choose freely and unanimously to bring the priority about. Freedom to choose this is something that role-relative precautionary priority would otherwise permit. The breakdowns at issue shrink the scope of role-relative precautionary priority even further, however. They make strict final priority something that no one, in any role, not the most remote and punctilious planner, can without anomaly suggest for consideration. Role-relative precautionary priority thus loses any possible connection with strict final priority, and loses its capacity to figure as an approximation to that standard.

It may be suggested that these difficulties do not so much imply limitations of the concept of needs as defects in my account of it. Possibly. Certainly I cannot rule out, and do not wish to rule out, someone else's so far improving on my account as to eliminate the difficulties, and the indeterminacy of the account respecting conflicts between needs. However, there are historical reasons for believing that formerly the difficulties did not arise in practice. Thus the concept of needs did not have to be elaborated to deal with them. Its received character, which I hope to have captured in my account, is the character that the concept has had in the absence of such elaboration.

8.1* A Breakdown Merely Hypothetical? Needs That Are Embarrassments to Moral Dignity

What could be more paradoxical, and more intriguing, than the suggestion that some human needs, far from demanding any precedence in social policy, are so ignoble that we should disregard them, or perhaps even set at nought any attempt to meet them? But addictions may be brought forward as needs of just this sort; and behind them, fetched up from the lower depths of the human psyche, may come embarrassing needs more permanent and ineluctable than addictions.

8.11* Addictions

Addictions, to alcohol or to other things, are certainly inexorable enough to look like needs; and not gratifying them has the same consequences in deranged functioning—in deranging whatever functioning the addicts are still capable of. Indeed, the consequences may be more immediate and dramatic than that of any arguably more natural need.

People react to the spectacle of addiction in different ways. Some refuse to do anything to help. Far from being willing to contemplate providing what the addicts crave, even if the addiction is incurable, they would leave them to shift for themselves, within the limits of law and order, in the misery to which addiction has led them. "Serve them right." Others would try to cure the addiction, perhaps temporizing with the craving while the cure was going on. Such people might be ready, if the addiction proved incurable, to meet the craving for the rest of the addicts' lives, hoping to forestall the onset of addiction among younger people. This policy, too, is a form of temporization.

Thus at one extreme we would have people willing to use therapy and both forms of temporization. They can deal with an addictive need on the terms offered by the Principle of Precedence by extending the basic List to include, temporarily, the addictive need. People at the other extreme would reject any such extension. They would refuse to assimilate addiction, even temporarily, to needs on the basic List. However, such rejection and refusal do not undermine the Model and the Principle logically. They leave them standing, indeed logically protect their integrity and force. Unfortunately, looked at another way, the upshot may be a rigid moral idealism, which may turn out, overwhelmed by social turbulence, to be counterproductive; and rigid—rigorous—though such idealism might be, one may wonder how humanitarian it is.

Moreover, are the rejection and refusal well founded? It is too easy to think of addictions as willful personal aberrations. They may be needs with as cogent a derivation from social arrangements as any. To be accepted in certain circles, in certain societies—to have the minimum of social recognition expected in those societies—people may have to be heavy smokers or heavy drinkers. Other people in those circles will not be comfortable with them if they are not. One may object that all this shows is that the arrangements which make belonging to those circles so desirable are eminently pernicious and prime candidates for supersession. One may also object that in a complex, populous, modernized society, people have enough room for maneuver to find less addictive circles and thus to embrace existing arrangements for social recognition and companionship.

However, the case for treating addictions as derived needs returns in a subtler form. Some people, one may suppose, are more susceptible to addiction than others. Suppose further that they cannot know before they try using the drugs in question—drugs that (as seems to be typical) most people can use without addiction or serious damage. Trying the drugs is a danger for the susceptible people that can be prevented, let us assume, only by denying the drugs to everyone.

Experiments with prohibition show that this is exceedingly hard to do. Denying the drugs to everyone also provokes strong objections on grounds of unwarranted interference with the liberty of the nonsusceptible majority. But if the Selfgovliset licenses the production and the distribution of the drugs to please the majority, the addiction of some at least of the susceptible minority is a predictable consequence.

Moreover, by this route the addiction may get another claim to being a fully founded derived need; or if not that, something that in human sympathy, may command as much, or nearly as much, attention. The addiction is a need generated by the social arrangements that license the production and distribution of the drugs, taken together with a basic need or an arresting special need of the susceptible minority. Lurking behind their susceptibility, one may hypothesize, is either an extraordinarily high requirement as to the Minimum Standard of Provision for some need in the present List or a special need not in the List and not there because for most people it requires no attention. A need for an extraordinary amount of reassurance about one's capacity to go on functioning might fit the bill.

With all these considerations demanding that addictions be treated like derived needs, the program for dealing with them remains quite different from the program for dealing wth derived needs as such. Addictions are to be cured; prevented; at most, temporized with while measures for eliminating them go forward. If temporization shades off among some people into tolerance, that, one might say, is only an effect of relaxed vigilance in upholding the principle that sets most people in opposition to addiction. This principle has to do with something like self-sufficiency. It commonly accompanies a concern with needs, and shows up in the view that provisions for the Matters of Need in the basic List—not including addictions—should suffice as in some sense complete provisions.

It is a widely shared principle, to which Liberals as well as Marxists subscribe. Both Liberals and Marxists, by sharing the concept of needs, have in common some notion of normal nondependent functioning. For both it is a matter of principle and a condition on social policy that the people affected be enabled to function this way. It would be hyperbole to call this condition "self-sufficiency" outright, "self-reliance," or even "independence." One is not to suppose that it is a condition which enables those who meet it to dispense with the collaboration and companionship of other people, though in some societies a person's dependence on such relations may be significantly less than in others. The condition does not reach far enough to embrace happiness; and it does not guarantee moral integrity. Nevertheless, unless the condition is met, a foundation for human dignity or for the sorts of human achievements that Liberals and Marxists care about, will fail.

8.12* Ignoble Needs Claiming Permanence in the List

If this is the principle, connecting with human dignity, on which addictions are rejected—apart from temporization—from the list of accepted needs, basic or derived, however, the concept of needs will be all the more vulnerable to the suggestion that some ignoble and embarrassing needs have as much title as any to a permanent place in the basic List. Among these needs may be a need for aggression, alternating with a need for self-abasement; and a need to be deceived—more precisely, a need not to have illusions about human nature exposed so suddenly as to provoke useless rage or induce hopeless apathy. Can functioning dependent on needs like these comport with human dignity?

Marxists, of course, in their fundamental optimism about the possibilities of social transformation, believe that these needs come from the insecurities and invidious distinctions of a class-divided society. Marxists would argue, on lines touched on in the preceding chapter, that in a transformed society where only authentic needs were recognized, such needs would find no place. If it succeeded, this argument would remove the threat to the concept of needs. The suggestion that some embarrassing needs were permanent would be discredited by the demonstration that the needs in question were inauthentic.

Suppose, however, the suggestion persisted. What sort of reassurance could be found respecting the concept of needs if psychology and anthropology established the authenticity of some ignoble and embarrassing needs?

There would be at least one minor simplification of the issue. The people who though they adhered to the Principle of Precedence would refuse to temporize with ignoble needs, if these needs were assumed to represent curable, or at least preventable addictions, would be in a position too awkward to hold rationally when the needs turned out to be authentic (permanent, trans-culturally invariant). Those people could hardly undertake to give precedence to authentic needs and go on refusing to recognize ignoble ones. However, perhaps it is not quite clear what position they would move to. Would they agree to extend the List of needs, in accordance with the facts of life and the design of the universe? They might be so shaken in their expectations regarding human dignity that they would lose interest in the Principle of Precedence. So might we all, given ignoble needs of certain characters and dimensions.

8.13* Considerations Mitigating Impact on Moral Dignity

On the other hand, the prospects may be favorable to the Principle in several ways. For one thing, what by current standards are ignoble needs may come to be regarded differently in a suitably transformed future society. I do not quite know that Marcuse has in mind in foreseeing, or at least hoping for, "the reactivation of polymorphous sexuality" and its application to the "eroticisation of work"; and perhaps it is not a subject that inhibited minds like ours are fit to dwell upon. Clearly, however, Marcuse's own attitude toward polymorphous sexuality, considered as a complex need, illustrates the possibility of mitigating the problem about ignoble needs by changing one's view of them, from disgust to enthusiasm.

Such a result might be obtained by refining one or another of the ignoble needs that we have considered as examples. The need to triumph over others may mix good things with bad—a need to shine in the light of outstanding achievement, with a relish for other people's defeat and humiliation. If the need to triumph over others could be retuned so that the latter component tended to fade out while the other grew stronger, it would invite a different judgment, even if one were not ready to say that it was a different need.

269

Another measure of relief is offered by the possibility that the ignoble needs are not themselves to be regarded as items on the basic List, but only as implications of certain means—unfortunately indispensable means, perhaps, but only means—of meeting needs that are. The needs in question would not then be needs of individual persons. Instead, as necessary conditions for the success of social institutions, they would connect with the needs of individual persons only indirectly, through those institutions. Even if the form of words used suggests a need to be ascribed directly to persons, as when one says, with the Grand Inquisitor, "Men must be deceived"; or with Hobbes, "Men must be dominated," discussion may show that what is meant is that human beings have certain needs, which they cannot be sure of meeting without certain social institutions; and that these institutions cannot be carried on successfully except by a regime that practices deception or exercises unqualified sovereign power, manifested now and then in naked coercion. But the necessity of either of these conditions for institutional success might not itself have to be explained by reference to personal needs to be deceived and to be dominated. Without having on the basic List any such needs, taken as individual persons, people might act at cross-purposes with one another unless they were deceived or dominated. Maybe it is their envy or malice or rivalry in the pursuit of glory that has to be kept in check. But maybe not; with the best of good intentions toward one another, they may have to accept the dictation of some Sovereign in order to solve problems of coordination.

8.14* Ignoble Needs with Unmitigated Impact

What is to be made of ignoble needs that are authentic needs of individual human beings and that are going to remain ignoble in everyone's view? Liberals and Marxists will agree in being reluctant to admit them; and in being downcast in their hopes for human dignity, whether the dignity is to be achieved in our present society or in a transformed one, if that dignity must be compromised by the recognition of such needs. Yet their existence must be contemplated, partly because a good deal of impressive thought has already gone into contemplating them. Marx could be taken as the patron of the view that ignoble needs were inauthentic ones, which would disappear with the transformation of society. Freud may be taken as the patron of the opposed view that some ignoble needs are authentic, and will persist through whatever social transformations human beings and their institutions undergo.

In giving Freud this role, I may be relying as much on the shock that his pronouncements about the ubiquitous manifestations of the libido caused respectable people when those pronouncements were new, as upon any intrinsic features of his doctrines. However, it is an important ingredient of his doctrines that people are reluctant to recognize the energy and extent of their own sexual impulses, just because they regard being under the dominion of such impulses as ignoble. Freud also teaches (more uncompromisingly than Marcuse) that civilized social order maintains itself by denying or diverting those impulses in large part, with inevitable consequences in neurosis. The libido offers itself as a prototype of authentic yet ignoble need.

Somewhere in the literature of psychoanalysis, or in the writings of some rival school of depth psychology, cannot a footing be found for each of the ignoble needs that I have invoked as my chief examples?—a need to be deceived; a need to aggress against others and triumph over them; a need to abase oneself?

Freud himself can be invoked as an authority for the need to be deceived. People, because they will not and cannot face the facts of their own sexuality, create various illusions that mask the sexual impulses from consciousness. Without deception in such matters, and perhaps others as well (like the hope of immortality), people might become incapable of managing their lives. Perhaps without such deception they would find life too hard to bear and simply give up the struggle.

A need to be deceived, if it went no further, would not wreck the basic List or the Principle of Precedence, though it would no doubt be a source of chagrin to people with higher hopes for human dignity. We can substantially lower our notions of the degree to which human beings can be expected to be rational and still find their needs, taken en bloc, worth attending to. Something similar can be said respecting needs for aggression or for self-abasement, supposing that these could be shown to be authentic. Needs of those sorts would directly undermine our opinion of human decency or dignity more than a need to be deceived. Nevertheless, we could put up with a lowered notion of human decency and dignity and yet find human needs morally appealing. The needs for aggression or for self-abasement might be limited in scope and intermittent—matters of hygiene that could be taken care of discreetly by brief periodic visits to specialists in bondage and discipline; or perhaps, as regards a need for aggression—matters of sport in which like-minded people could be found for an occasional scrimmage.

To be content with the suggestion that ignoble needs, even if they are authentic, will not preoccupy (most) people most of the time, or require much in the way of resources, and hence (in both respects) will be easy to manage compatibly with giving most of our attention to the respectable matters on the List of needs, is too comfortable a solution to be fully trusted. It falls too tidily within the limits of a bourgeois conception of life. It also may be reproached, from the point of view of ethical theory, for neglecting the interpersonal complications of ignoble needs.

8.15* Degradation of Moral Community

The need to be deceived, if it is to be met, raises the complication that someone may have to do the deceiving. Now, it is bad enough that people should be deceived, though their being deceived will vary greatly in moral significance: Being deceived about the polymorphous energy of their libidos or about the prospects of immortal life might well not impair their own status as moral agents—at least there is no entailment that their status would be especially impaired. On the other hand, being deceived about their capacity to adopt life-plans for themselves, or to chose between right and wrong, would certainly render them very inferior sorts of moral agents. Suppose, however, that the moral significance of the deception on the side of the person deceived is not very great. Is it not still very objectionable that someone should practice the deception? Perhaps the objection can be escaped by letting people deceive themselves, and do so, according to Freudian doctrine, unconsciously. Yet will there not be observers who have detected this self-deception? Are they just to preserve a discreet silence? If they do, they are certainly failing to treat the people who are self-deceived as fully capable moral equals, almost as much as if they had contrived the deception in the first place. Thus the interpersonal complications of meeting a need to be deceived appear pretty sure to involve some people not only in specific moral delinquencies but also in general defection from the principles of mutual respect implied by a moral community.

The interpersonal complications are even more vivid and telling with the needs for aggression and for self-abasement; for here the complications involve interdependencies between the needs of different persons. (I did not assume, in the passage just finished, that anyone had a need to deceive; so deceivers and deceived were not necessarily linked by an interdependency of needs.)

The interdependencies might be simple or complex.

They are simple when one person, in meeting a need, meets the need of some other person or persons, though meeting the need or needs of those others is nothing that the first person has in mind. Thus someone, having a need

273

to aggress against other persons, might need to inflict pain on them, or humiliate them. She may well not seek, in causing pain, or humiliation, to meet the other persons' needs respecting physical or emotional security; that they need to be caused pain, or humiliated, may never occur to her.

The interdependencies are complex when meeting the need of one person entails, as a point of logic, meeting a need of someone else; then, meeting the other person's need is part of the objective in meeting one's own. For example, a person needing to abase himself may not be able to satisfy this need with just anybody; it may be important to find someone who needs to humiliate other people, perhaps (perfecting the complementarity) someone who needs to humiliate people who need to be humiliated.

Were the needs in question not needs involving pain or humiliation, but needs of the sorts initially represented on the list in my account, the meeting of which strengthens health and self-confidence, interdependencies simple or complex would be welcome. They would lay a foundation in mutual aid for social institutions. Perhaps a certain amount of interdependency respecting pain and humiliation could be tolerated alongside. Again, perhaps, most people could get along with trifling amounts of provision for the associated needs, and those who needed more could find one another often enough and pair off for mutual aid extempore. So complex is human psychology that the observable effects of these hygienic provisions might be, precisely, enhanced health and self-confidence.

However, if interdependent needs of these sorts were central and pervasive preoccupations of most people, and authentically so, persisting through all possible social transformations, the possibility of establishing a moral community among these people, or with them, would be deeply problematic. We might have to do with a set of sadists on the one hand, and a set of masochists on the other— masters and slaves. One set of people would not be respecting the moral integrity of people in the other set, and those would not be sufficiently self-respecting to stand up for themselves and check the abuses practiced on them.

Even if everyone was a sadist and masochist turn by turn, so that a basis for reciprocity and equity existed, the principles followed in either phase would run counter to the principles of a moral community as hitherto understood: People would sometimes be causing others as much pain or as much humiliation as the other could endure and sometimes be cooperating fully and enthusiastically—maybe, inventively—in their own pain and degradation. This is not a moral community, but the negative image of a moral community, parasitically presupposing, as the terms "humiliation" and "degradation" indicate, standards of evaluation that are followed without inversion in a community of another sort.

It is true, there might be intervals in the game, and during these intervals the players might meet and legislate regarding future rounds of play. If they treated each other with respect during a legislative interval and took the trouble, for example, to assign the parts in the next round of revels on a basis that all agreed was fair, something like a moral community would exist. Even the activities during the rounds of the game itself, if they are looked upon as falling under the legislation of a moral community, might be acceptable at least to the most broadminded among us, as a joint moral pursuit—a perverted way of seeking happiness, but a way nonetheless.

The assumption about legislative intervals, however, brings the needs in question back under a degree of moral control. It should not blind us to the significance of finding that interdependent needs for aggression and self-abasement, and maybe for being deceived, too, have the potentiality of extinguishing the moral content of the concept of needs as exhibited in the List, the Minimum Standards of Provision, the Criterion, and the Principle of Precedence. Even with the assumption about legislative intervals in place, adherents of received religions and ethical theories might turn their back on such practices in disgust, and reconsider whether human beings and their needs deserved attention after all. Human beings might appear to them, in their disillusionment, "the most pernicious race of little odious vermin that nature ever suffered to crawl upon the surface of the earth."

If cheerfulness breaks in at all in the face of this breakdown, it breaks in only with the reflection that the case for there being such needs remains controversial. One may therefore speculate that the breakdown in the concept of needs on this point is merely hypothetical—a breakdown that would occur if something turned out to be true, without there as yet being any good evidence that it is true.

8.2* A Breakdown Real and Imminent: The Claims of a Worldwide Reference Population

The consolation of being perhaps merely hypothetical cannot be had with the other two points of breakdown that I propose to treat. There are tendencies all too real moving toward both. One point, having to do with the need for medical care, has been reached already. Breakdown here aggravates trouble with the other point, which has to do with enlarging the Reference Population. The need for medical care may lead to breakdown even with a small Reference Population. Breakdown just comes earlier with larger ones. With larger Reference Populations, breakdown threatens whether or not the need for medical care is pressed. The Principle of Precedence, backing other needs, may impose an impossible task—or at least a task requiring moral heroism of a sort never yet displayed by human beings in a sustained way on a large scale. People in a given Selfgovliset may not deserve moral admiration if they confine their attention to a Reference Population whose needs can be met without undermining their own standard of living. But can they really be bound to sacrifice all the graces

of life—all the graces, not just luxurious clothes and jewelry—if meeting the needs of a larger Reference Population
requires the sacrifice? The best that can be had in the way of
comfort on this point is to maintain that the tendency
threatening to arrive at it has not yet gone all the way. The
tendency is real; breakdown is imminent; but there is still
time to check the tendency short of breakdown.

8.21* The Problem Set in a Fully General Framework

To treat the problem of variation in the extent of the Reference Population in all its dimensions, I shall open up possibilities that I have not so far allowed for in my account of
the concept of needs. Previously, I supposed that the Reference Population, the Minimum Standards of Provision,
and even the Matters of Need to be included in the basic
List, might vary from member to member of the Selfgovliset
in view. The Reference Population was to be fixed, ruling
out certain complications in the variations, by identifying
the member of the Selfgovliset with the shortest list and the
least generous Minimum Standards of Provision and discovering what Reference Population this member would
accept as demanding application of the Principle of Precedence. However—to open up the possibility of further
variations—may one not wonder whether even this least-
generous member of the Selfgovliset would not accept a
larger Reference Population than the one supposedly just
fixed, if the List in question were shorter, or the Minimum
Standards of Provision lower? And might not this member
go along with higher Minimum Standards of Provision, and
a longer List, if the Reference Population were smaller?

In other words, the Reference Population and the Minimum Standards of Provision (even the List of Matters of
Need and the Criterion) might vary relatively to one another, so that for every member of the Selfgovliset, not just
the least-generous member, we would expect to find a fam-

ily of combinations of List, Minimum Standards of Provision, Criterion, Principle of Precedence (in particular, that feature of the Principle specifying the Reference Population) mutually adjusted in each combination as to content, height, stringency, and reach. In the end this picture will have to be rejected; it is incompatible with certain unifying features present in the normative use of the concept of needs. However, one might note that the picture is not too complicated to be compatible with effective use of the concept of needs. The use of the concept, so depicted, would be neither chaotic nor unintelligible. Determinate answers as to what needs were to be met for which people would be forthcoming all along the line, though reached on a different basis, with possibly different least-generous members of the Selfgovliset identified to establish consensus for different Reference Populations.

8.22* Three Specially Significant Reference Populations

Assuming for the time being families of combinations, one might conceive of extracting from those families taken together two combinations with Reference Populations of special interest. These both differ from the one (P_g) that was fixed earlier by locating the member of the Selfgovliset least generous in defining Minimum Standards of Provision when a Reference Population was not in view and then identifying the most extensive Reference Population that this member would accept, given these Standards. The two combinations that I have in mind are those that involve, respectively,

P_{ext}, the most extensive Reference Population for which all the members of the Selfgovliset accept under the Principle of Precedence any List with Minimum Standards of Provision, however low.

P_{int}, the Reference Population to which all the members of the Selfgovliset are willing to give the most intensive attention, that is to say, the largest population for which they all accept the fullest List and highest Minimum Standards of Provision that they are willing to agree on for any population.

I shall argue later that there is a centripetal tendency for P_{ext} to coalesce with P_{int}. It will be convenient, for this argument, to assume that P_{int} is a subset of P_g and P_g a subset of P_{ext}. However, this assumption is not enough to capture fully the prior stages of the centripetal tendency. In those stages, members of the Selfgovliset may be supposed to be led to bring the List and the Minimum Standards of Provision for the whole of P_g—the membership of the Selfgovliset itself with some people in addition—up to the List and Standards that they began by accepting for smaller populations with which they identified more strongly. Those smaller populations would presumably differ from member to member of the Selfgovliset. Yet it is implausible to suppose that all the members of the Selfgovliset would agree on accepting the highest Minimum Standards of Provision for any population that is only a proper subset of the Selfgovliset itself. I shall therefore assume that P_{int}, besides being a subset of P_g, is identical with the Selfgovliset or includes it.

8.23* Dealing at Once with the Needs of All Three Populations

Could the Selfgovliset consistently abide by the different combinations of (mutually adjusted) List, Standards, Criterion, and Principle of Precedence answering to the three Reference Populations, P_{ext}, P_g, and P_{int}? There is no problem about fulfilling the requirements of all three combinations—i.e., heeding the Principle of Precedence in these various connections—so long as resources suffice. But suppose they do not: for example, suppose they have sharply diminished relatively to the populations in question.

Several procedures for approximating to fulfilling the requirements of all three combinations notwithstanding can be identified. Under one—Charity Begins at Home—one begins with P_{int} and provides for it as required by the version of the Principle applying to it; then, in order, one provides for the remainder of P_g according to the version applying to P_g, and, if there are any provisions left over, one gives them to what remains of P_{ext}, after P_g is subtracted from it. Under another—the World Citizen Approach—one furnishes provisions first to the whole of P_{ext} according to the version of the Principle applying to P_{ext}, then furnishes from what is left over the difference required to bring P_g up to the standards applying to P_g, and finally if there are any resources remaining use them up to bring P_{int} closer to the standards presupposed by the version of the Principle applying there. Both these procedures (in different degrees) confer some special favor upon P_{int}, which a sterner ethics would not allow, being unprepared to allow discrimination in the treatment of the different populations. It would say, if genuine needs are in question, P_{int} should do no better on the margin in meeting them than P_{ext} as a whole.

Neither our received moral notions nor standard received ethical theories seem to determine whether the Selfgovliset should follow the sterner ethics or, if it does not, whether it should practice Charity Begins at Home or the World Citizen Approach.

It may be objected that if received moral notions are taken in their proper context, one of reciprocal undertakings within an organized society, it is quite clear that they favor Charity Begins at Home. This objection does help explain how many people in the Selfgovliset will look upon the issue. It does not, however, seem to allow sufficiently for the possibility of criticizing organized societies and their working assumptions about reciprocal obligations.

Contractarian thinking sometimes suggests that everyone be brought into the community of reciprocal obligation who can contribute to its real income, through imports and otherwise. It sometimes suggests that everyone be brought in who is in a position to do harm if she is left out. Applied on the world scale, both these criteria would leave too many people out—arguably, from the North American point of view, whole countries full of people. How much harm could the Sri Lankans, left on their island, do to the United States?

Kant deals with the issue ambiguously. He holds, on the one hand, that the happiness or welfare of anyone sharing in our humanity imposes a duty on us to sacrifice our own welfare in part "without any hope of recompense" to meet that person's needs. On the other hand, in the very next breath, he says, "This duty is only a broad one; it has a latitude within which we may do more or less without being able to assign definite limits." Later, he maintains that the duty to be "beneficent, i.e., to be helpful to men in need according to one's means . . . without hoping for anything thereby" follows from its being impossible, given everyone's desire to be helped by others when he is in need, for anyone to universalize without contradiction "a maxim of not wanting to give assistance in turn to others." For who would help a person who announced such a maxim? Hoping for something in return seems to have crept back into beneficence with this argument. It does not seem to imply a duty to be beneficent to people abroad who are not, and who have no significant chance of being, in a position to help us.

Utilitarianism promises an answer that, at least so long as the three populations are distinct, it cannot deliver. In its Benthamite version, applying the felicific calculus, it would in principle choose between Charity Begins at Home and the World Citizen Approach by finding which led to the greatest sum of utility. In the absence of any way of carrying out the felicific calculus, however, there is no determinate way of reaching such a solution. Nor is much help to be gained from substituting for utilitarianism its traditional needs-based surrogate. This quasi-utilitarianism would proceed from making sure of the needs of some people to making sure of the needs of yet others. But it does so with the assumption that a fixed Reference Population is in view, with improvements to be made on the condition of groups belonging to it. Here it would beg the question between Charity Begins at Home and the World Citizen Approach (or among the three approaches, if the sterner ethics is counted) to choose either P_{ext} or P_{int} as the basis for applying the assumption. Furthermore, the choice of P_{ext} might lead, with straitened resources, to no one's having the means of a tolerable life. It is not obvious that this is better from a utilitarian point of view than making sure that at least some people have the means, in what may still be modest quantities. On the other hand, it does not follow from utilitarian doctrine that selecting them, even self-selecting them, will be just.

Utilitarianism has typically used a device to reduce the scope of obligations that in respect to this issue must seem an evasion. After proclaiming that in principle our concern should extend to all human beings (even to all sentient beings), it has allowed that in practice we may do most to promote universal happiness by accepting an assignment of tasks under which each of us concentrates upon people close to us. This is hardly a justification for Charity Begins at Home. It does not indicate how people closest to us are to be divided from people who are not, and hence does not support fixing P_{int} in any particular way. It cannot assure us that elsewhere the assignment of tasks will be adequately performed, so that what is P_{ext} for us (or even beyond) will be served properly. What resources will people have elsewhere? What skills? What kind of leadership? It does not say what minimal obligations remain to people who are not close to us, or in particular whether they are obligations that consort best with Charity Begins at Home, the World Citizen Approach, or the sterner ethics.

8.24* Arguments for Extending the Most Extensive of the Reference Populations

Utilitarianism is nevertheless clear about the scope of P_{ext}, ascribing maximum scope to it. There are in fact many arguments, in and out of utilitarianism, for increasing the scope of P_{ext} and hence increasing the weight of the claims that it makes on the concept of needs and the Principle of Precedence. Some of these arguments are suitable for special cases, some are perfectly general. The general ones conclude to accepting P_{ext} as embracing the whole world population of human beings. (One may, if one wishes, extend the embrace to the populations of other species, though I shall set this topic aside without prejudice, along with extensions to future generations.) Several of these arguments appeal poignantly to fundamental moral considerations like benevolence, due respect for human dignity, justice. However, they end up making such staggering demands that they rather tend to show how, except for some inconclusive misgivings and doubtful recommendations to the contrary, received moral views and standard ethical theories have ignored the issue. Repeating such arguments, as is commonly done in philosophical reflections on the increase in world population and the world food problem, all the while turning a blind eye to the moral heroism of the prescriptions emerging, risks reducing ethics itself to absurdity. In practice, as a result, less may be done to meet the needs of wider populations than more modest demands would have elicited.

I shall run rapidly through the arguments in question to convey a reasonably comprehensive view of their variety. What they amount to is in each case obvious enough, at least for my purposes, once the chief principle has been cited.

Some of the arguments are not moral ones.

To begin with, one might cite for any given group to be added to P_{ext} its capacity to make trouble for the Selfgovliset if its needs were not met—maybe military trouble, or at least terrorism. The weakness of this argument is that the group in question might not have any substantial capacity: It might not have the technology required to bring damage home to the Selfgovliset—either the technology of transportation or the weaponry. Could the group even so be used as pawns by a hostile power that did have the technology? But people in the group might (like Bushmen) be so distinctive in appearance that it would be idle for a hostile power to exploit their resentments in this way.

Another argument might be that people in every culture, however simple their technology, have something useful to contribute to the real income of the rest of the world, including the Selfgovliset. Perhaps the contribution consists in works of art, in literature, or simply, less readily exported, in the demonstration of various human possibilities, like the adaptation of the Bushmen to life in the desert. Many people take pleasure in the variety of nature and culture and for them such a demonstration—even the very existence of a different sort of people with a different way of life—would be something valuable. Unfortunately, many other people do not seem to care very much about this variety. Moreover, some, if they do care, may not in fact find anything interesting or gratifying in the spectacle, example, or other contributions that may be offered by a particular group being considered for addition to the Reference Population.

A nonmoral argument for extending P_{ext} at the margin to include some specific group might be made if the group in view had the capacity to cooperate in future endeavors of the Selfgovliset. A less self-interested argument would be possible if the group in view was specially congenial to members of the Selfgovliset by reason of a shared culture, perhaps, or a shared ancestry. I do not rank this as a genuinely moral argument, since it appeals to discriminatory feelings that readily lend themselves to abuse, sanctioning disregard, even contemptuous disregard, for the needs and aspirations of people who do not belong to the same race or religion. However, one can imagine that on occasion such an argument may lead, without ulterior effects of an untoward kind, to more generous policies on the part of the Selfgovliset.

Moreover, it is an argument often difficult—at least as regards the feelings to which it appeals—to disentangle from a genuinely moral argument that invokes the past history of a specific group, with its contributions to the culture or military success of the Selfgovliset, and declares that in just return for these contributions to meeting the needs of people in the Selfgovliset the people in the outside group deserve to be helped in meeting their needs. On the point of culture, many Americans and Canadians were moved by such an argument to assist the British during the Second World War; on the point of military contributions, perhaps the British might be moved by such an argument on behalf of the Nepalese, the source of the Gurkha regiments. The second example, of course, moves into the province of an argument that connects, under the concept of justice, the Selfgovliset with its colonies or former colonies, or indeed with any part of the world where people and institutions have been adapted to serve the interests of the Selfgovliset and have thereby become dependent to some extent on the Selfgovliset's following policies favorable to them.

A group outside the P_{ext} currently recognized might qualify under this argument simply by being next door to the Selfgovliset and trading with it, though less efficient economically. But being next door may give rise to another argument as well for inclusion on the margin: The activities of the Selfgovliset may directly interfere with the group's means of meeting its needs, for example, by diverting or polluting the group's water supply. Justice, demanding a rectification of this wrong, may be best assured by henceforth including the group in P_{ext}. In general, whenever a group outside, near or far, is in a plight caused by the practices of the Selfgovliset, it deserves attention on grounds of justice; and once given attention, it may remain visible enough in relation to needs to figure in P_{ext}.

Suppose the plight of people in unfortunate groups outside P_{ext} has not in any way been caused by the Selfgovliset. There is a powerful argument on grounds of justice even so for including them in P_{ext}; and the argument is so comprehensive that it embraces all the people in the world, insofar as they depend with the Selfgovliset on the same resources to meet their needs. The Selfgovliset may happen, perhaps just through geographical good fortune, to be in possession of a major share of the resources. Under resources here might be counted technology and capital equipment as well as farmland and minerals. However, leaving technology and capital equipment aside, the argument has a foundation sufficient for extending P_{ext} to embrace the whole population of the world if farmland and minerals (and access to fisheries, etc.) are so unevenly distributed that, apart from the Selfgovliset and some other countries, rich in varying degrees, people everywhere are destitute or running close to destitution, with no resources of their own reserved to meet their needs.

Dependency on the same resources does not by itself establish an obligation on the part of the Selfgovliset to do anything about it. The obligation comes in with the connection that can be made under justice between equal treatment and meeting needs and with the observation that possession by the Selfgovliset of an undue share of world resources prevents people in the poor countries from providing for their needs. We may consider that at the very least the Selfgovliset should retain no more than its due share of the current returns from the resources in its possession. But what would a due share be? I shall put aside the special complications of nonrenewable resources—where some provision, it is difficult to say what, should be made for future generations inside and outside the Selfgovliset, with the provision varying according to expectations about technological change. The basic questions arise for renewable resources like farmland, forests, and fisheries; and Locke's treatment of property gives some guidance as to what should be reckoned a due share of them.

Locke offers two criteria, both of which give better guidance during the acquisition of shares, before all the world's resources have been appropriated, than they do afterward,

286

when new grounds might arise from questioning the de facto shares. First, a due share is one that leaves "enough and as good" to every other man among those "yet unprovided." Second, a due share is one that does not exceed the capacity of the claimant to use it. The first criterion is the one that is taken over by Nozick in his "Lockean proviso." By itself, given the requisite abundance, the criterion would license appropriations far exceeding those licensed by the second criterion. On the other hand, if resources even at the beginning fell short of enabling everyone to appropriate up to the limits of the second criterion, even when so much weight is put upon "use" as to exclude frivolous, unneeded, applications, the first criterion would, as the second criterion, would not, give guidance inside those limits. It would prescribe, to wit, that people should appropriate no more than equal shares of the globally inadequate resources. (Would it be physically equal shares, or shares equally proportioned to needs? Locke does not say. I would guess that Locke probably meant physically equal shares, the simpler idea. The criterion, however, could be read either way, and I shall leave both options open.)

Does the proviso prescribe that people in the Selfgovliset should cut back to equal shares if appropriation ended some time ago, and it is now discovered that the possession of resources is so distributed that in the poorer countries people's needs cannot be met? Of course, if the appropriation contravened the criterion at the time of appropriation, an error occurred that now ought to be rectified. But this may not be the case. Due regard may have been given to the scarcity of resources and the derived rule about equal shares may have been observed. Since then, the whole world may have prospered for a time, but now have relapsed, unevenly, into a state of global scarcity. Or the derived rule about equal shares may not have had any occasion to be used, since there was abundance then, though scarcity now. What is to be done now?

The assumption is still that the plight of the people outside the P_{ext} currently accepted by the Selfgovliset is not something that the practices of the Selfgovliset have caused by direct interference. There are two cases even so. First, suppose that the plight of the people outside is clearly not of their making either. Fire and flood, the migration of fishes, or unfavorable changes in climate, have brought them low. Something ought to be done to help them. Even Nozick agrees; he would invoke the Lockean proviso to bring about a redistribution of resources or returns. But he does not say what pattern of redistribution. Equalization of resources per capita may be one answer, but it seems less congenial to the theory of entitlements than a proportional or progressive levy against the wealth of the Selfgovliset and similarly placed countries. How great a levy? A persuasive limit is supplied by the concept of needs. In effect, therefore, remedying the situation described amounts to extending the reach of the Principle of Precedence to embrace everyone in the world, if need be, in P_{ext}.

The second case allows that the worsened condition of people outside P_{ext} may be substantially of their own making. The conduct of the present generation of these people may have been careless, frivolous, improvident. People in the Selfgovliset may then, perhaps not unreasonably, think themselves excused in this connection from the prescriptions of distributive justice, especially if before the conduct in question resources outside would have sufficed, and more, to meet needs. It would be humanity, not justice, that would incline the Selfgovliset, if anything does, to offer help.

Yet even here, the improvident generation will have innocent children who suffer with them, and is it just to allow the children to suffer? Moreover, what are we to make of careless, frivolous, improvident conduct which many or most of the people in question are not personally responsible for? Defective political organizations beyond their control may have undertaken disastrous wars, and failed even in peacetime to adopt prudent policies. Again, are we to count unregulated increases in population as arising from a sort of irresponsible conduct that excuses members of the Selfgovliset from any duty under justice? There is every danger here of a failure of transcultural imagination, which prevents people in the Selfgovliset from understanding how those other people view procreation. There is also, again, an anomaly in allowing the suffering to fall upon the generation that succeeds the one whose irresponsibility, if it was irresponsibility, created the problem. And would it be morally or practically possible to help the children without helping the parents? Again justice calls for extending the Principle of Precedence so far that in effect the needs of everyone in the world population will be considered.

One might consider, however, that somewhere, early in these arguments for distributive justice given the undue share of resources possessed by the Selfgovliset, it has been assumed that people outside the P_{ext} hitherto recognized have a claim as human beings—as beings like enough to the people already embraced by the P_{ext}, indeed, like enough to the members of the Selfgovliset—to be treated on somewhat the same footing as candidates for justice. This argument converges with another one in which justice would not be mentioned, but which relied instead simply on respect for human dignity. One might embellish such an argument by pointing out the extent to which the dignity of members of the Selfgovliset would be compromised if beings so much like themselves were allowed to sink below the Minimum Standards of Provision for P_{ext}. The likeness, of course, could be particularized; and the particularization might emphasize such properties as the power to reason and the power to create. Could the members of the Selfgovliset claim to be worth much respect themselves if no care were taken to support the dignity of these others? A further embellishment might make the point that not only would the theoretical claims of members of the Selfgovliset be undermined by ignoring the needs, and hence the dignity, of the others; they might well be encouraging members of their own society to adopt a callous attitude that would be exhibited within the Selfgovliset.

This last thought appeals to self-interest; but not to self-interest alone, since the deterioration in moral community, with consequent adverse effects on the general happiness, is also at issue, and would be deplored by disinterested judgment backed by the sentiment of humanity. Resort to this sentiment may in the end be indispensable to motivating the acceptance of people outside as candidates for justice, at least if they are in no position to retaliate when their needs are disregarded. Why should one care about the likeness and dignity of other people, sufficiently to do something to meet their needs, or care at all to have their needs met, if one does not care directly about their having a happy condition and fate rather than an unhappy one? Even if the people outside were deemed to be markedly inferior as moral beings—like the birds and beasts, as most human beings have viewed them—they might have some claim to attention in fellow-feeling and humanity.

Is the task that the demands of humanity, and the demands of the other arguments for enlarging P_{ext}, bring forward under the Principle of Precedence no more than potentially overwhelming? There is probably still time, given the present demographic situation (including both population and trends) and present world resources, to make good modest Minimum Standards of Provision for a basic List of needs the world over, without requiring any Selfgovliset to make a substantial sacrifice of living standards. Moreover, insofar as those standards depend on an expanding technology using up a disproportionate share of world resources, they are not to be taken for granted, as they are in "Northern" abuses of the basic needs approach to international aid. It is bad faith to invoke a breakdown that has not yet come, even if it is imminent, as an excuse for not taking timely measures, including revisions in technological policy and social arrangements. Yet the shadow of breakdown in this connection already falls upon the concept of needs.

8.25* Coalescence Upwards of Minimum Standards of Provision

The shadow is denser because the arguments just run through are not alone in tending to give overwhelming weight to claims by the world population under the concept of needs. To speak still within the model of multiple families of combinations, one may say that there is a tendency for the combinations to coalesce upwards, with the List and Standards for P_{ext} rising to match those for P_{int}.

For it is anomalous to maintain openly, expressly, that people in P_{ext} outside P_{int} have fewer needs or need less ample provisions. Cultural differences may defer having to face such an issue; indeed, may for an indefinite period reduce the demands on resources arising from the needs of some members of P_{ext}. Those members may go on eating a simple vegetarian diet; and, assisted by a favorable climate, require little in clothing or in fuel. Yet cultural differences, like climates, may work the other way, too. A vegetarian diet may not suffice to meet the needs of people living in a polar climate; and those people could hardly forego the clothing and fuel deemed essential under the needs recognized for any P_{int} on the planet. Moreover, the cultural differences that make the needs of some people outside P_{int} easier and cheaper to meet are being steadily obliterated by the inexorable spread of Western technology and Western standards. Being outside P_{int} cannot itself be a ground for maintaining that a person has fewer needs or needs less ample provisions.

Whether people have certain needs must be treated as a question of fact rather than a question of policy. The longer List and ampler Standards for P_{int} cannot be defended simply as ingredients of a more comfortable policy. The more firmly established is the use of that List and those Standards for the needs of P_{int} the harder it is to refuse to generalize needs so conceived. Thus, counterbalancing the centrifugal tendencies, normative and descriptive, modelled by the idea of multiple combinations, there is a centripetal tendency operating in the use of the term "needs," which vindicates to a degree the simplified account based on one combination. The centripetal tendency magnifies the challenge posed by the arguments for extending the reach of the Principle of Precedence: Not only may it (by those arguments) reach uncomfortably far in the scope of P_{ext}; it is going to ask for uncomfortably much wherever it reaches.

Henry Shue, a notably forthright and effective philosophical champion of commitment to meeting the needs of the world population, has said, "It is concern about the strains of commitment that makes an advocate of significant redistribution like me so interested in establishing limits; I do not want groundless worries about 'bottomless pits' to make people resistant to major, but not endless, transfers." He has recommended in consequence, reasonably enough, that "we should at least try to find principles of justice that would gain sufficiently wide commitment, and voluntary compliance with the implementing taxation, that their enforcement upon the unconvinced will not require authoritarian government or bloody revolution."

Unfortunately, the worries about bottomless pits are not groundless. I agree that the grounds for them do not yet include facing a world problem become, irrevocably, so overwhelming that even resources mobilized under strict final priority would fall short of meeting needs. It may not even, as yet, be such a problem as to withstand being solved under some less exacting principles of justice, which obtain the commitment and compliance that Shue hopes for. On the other hand, such principles—the best of such principles—may even now be compatible with letting the world outside the affluent Selfgovlisets starve; and as the problem of meeting world needs worsens, the danger of any widely supported principles' falling short will continually increase.

8.3 A Breakdown Real and Current: The Bottomless Pit of Medical Care

Breakdown of the concept of needs in the face of the needs of the world population may be only imminent. The real tendency leading to the breakdown, one may believe, has not yet gone past the point at which it can be checked. Perhaps not much comfort can be taken from this possibility when one considers realistically the chances that the Self-govliset with the resources to do the checking will rise above their current practices and mobilize the effort required. Even this much comfort, however, for what it is worth, can hardly be found on the third of the points of breakdown that I have undertaken to treat. Already, the infirmities of some members of any ordinary Reference Population and the known provisions for dealing with the infirmities are so mismatched as to outrun the resources that any Selfgovliset has so far been willing to commit to medical care. The concept of needs, working through the Principle of Precedence, nevertheless calls for the commitment. It will go on calling for the commitment as the possibilities of using resources for this purpose multiply. They will multiply. They can be multiplied indefinitely by putting resources into medical research. All along the concept of needs, pressing ahead on the track laid down by its received use, will be calling for the prolongation of human lives regardless of the drain on resources. Not only does the concept of needs not help policy-making to find solutions to this problem; any social policy adopted to cope with it must struggle against the weight of the concept of needs and the Principle of Precedence. In that sense the concept of needs creates the problem.

8.31 Expectations Heightened by Scientific Medicine

In our century, prospects have sprung up with scientific medicine that utterly transform the background expectations with which the concept of needs was formerly used. These prospects arise, on the one hand, with the possibility of further reducing the mortality following upon accidents and infectious diseases. They arise, on the other hand, with the possibility of finding and using the means of replacing or substituting for bodily parts that inevitably decay with age. More speculatively (as a result of cracking the biological codes governing aging, perhaps) even the means of keeping them going without replacement may be discovered. One confronts in these connections people in dire straits, who may be expected to press their needs as far as any hope persists of meeting them. What could be more legitimate than invoking the concept of needs to support prolonging someone's life? What could be a more elementary use of the concept? Yet unchecked use of the concept of needs might in this connection soak up, in research and therapy, all resources available to any Selfgovliset and the Reference Population above bare subsistence—above the most rigorously conceived Minimum Standards of Provision for the other needs of the sick and any of the basic needs of the healthy. In effect, the members of the Selfgovliset at least would all be, so long as they were fit, entirely occupied in keeping themselves alive and contributing to the prolongation of life.

I speak of a breakdown in the concept of needs rather than of a breakdown in my account of it. I think my account gives an accurate explication of the concept in its received state, formed before the technological advances of the last couple of centuries and before the rise of the expectations that those advances have encouraged. It may be that scientific medicine is very far from being able to meet those expectations with any assurance: Almost all the spectacular increase in life expectancy that has occurred during the last couple of centuries is due, some authorities hold, to better nutrition and to measures of public sanitation; and what these things have mainly done is to reduce sharply the rate of mortality in infancy. The normal life span beyond infancy has increased less dramatically and, again, nutrition and sanitation rather than medical assistance may have played the major role. Nevertheless, there are widespread expectations now, which did not exist formerly, that scientific medicine has the potentiality of repeatedly bringing about significant increases in the life span, if the right discoveries are made from research that funding could start up or expand from this moment onward. Moreover, however modest in statistical effect the contribution of scientific medicine to prolonging life has been hitherto, it has developed devices, like machines for kidney dialysis, that do prolong lives at costs too high to permit under present policies their use wherever they are needed. The received concept of needs breaks down as visibly in the face of spending money to make such devices universally available as in the face of expectations of further advances.

Ultimately, the breakdown can be looked upon as a special case of needs conflicting—the need for medical care with other needs—because of a shortage of resources; but it is a case of peculiar interest because the shortage is one that may be expected to come from repeating again and again an apparently legitimate application of the concept. In the general case, external circumstances vary so that demands made under the concept can sometimes—more often than not—be met and other times not. Here the demands intensify while the circumstances remain the same.

8.32 The Backing for Medical Care in the Basic List

Just how is the need for medical care related to the needs in the basic List? The List may be supposed to imply, as straightforwardly as it implies anything, a need for sanitary precautions against infectious disease and a need for various measures of safety to protect life and limb on and off the job. Both needs could be derived by conceptual connection from the need for a life-supporting relation to the environment, taken together with the need to keep the body intact, and the need for food and water substantially free from contamination. Is the List to be understood as extending to a need for medical care of all the kinds that prolong life—repairing injuries; coping with infections; maintaining and replacing bodily parts?

There are reasons for regarding the need for medical care as secondary rather than primary, which helped persuade me against including it in the basic List to begin with. It may be nearly universal; something has to be done to meet it in almost everybody's case before the end of the normal life-span. Yet it is a need that arises before that time only when the other needs have gone unmet; medical care is called in to repair the damage done by omissions elsewhere, for example, in precautions against infection. Anticipating the troubles that will be generated by repeated invocation of the need for medical care, one might wish to seize on arguments for denying that, basic or derived, the need for medical care is a need like the others. Is it equally inevitable? Even as the end of life—the end of a normal life span—is approached, one might argue, it is not inevitable; if the other needs have been met all along, there is sooner or later nothing that medical care can do. It is death that is inevitable, not the need for medical care.

This will not work, however. Even if it had worked to argue this way in the past, it will not work now. People's organs fail, before the end of the normal life span, when there has been no omission in meeting other needs; and medical techniques have been introduced to remedy these failures, techniques that extend to replacing the organs. In just about every other case, too, within span or beyond span, we may suppose that death can be deferred, at least for a short time, if medical care is provided soon enough. Or else, in a fatal accident, the life span ends prematurely because of an inadequacy in meeting other needs. Now and then people drop dead suddenly; but then it was not known that the time for medical care had come beforehand.

The fact that the need for medical care becomes inevitable

for some people only at the end of life does not detract at all from its eligibility to being a course-of-life need—inevitably so—for everybody, any more than the need for sexual activity (or, at any rate, the derived need for a mate) is less of a course-of-life need because it does not have to be met in infancy or (in some cases) in very old age. The basic needs ascribed to the Reference Population are not needs all of which have to be met, on a rebuttably universal basis, for every member of the population at this moment, but course-of-life needs, which, rebuttably, every member will have to have met at least sometime in life.

On my basic account, one is prepared to generalize, anyway, over important differences, from the List as applied to people in the prime of life to the needs of people who are nearing its end. As I noted in introducing the Criterion of underanged functioning in a combination of basic social roles, the Criterion has to be relaxed for elderly people who are step by step retiring from the various tasks that fall under such roles (just as it has to be relaxed for children who are not yet called upon to take up all the tasks). However, to relax the Criterion in this way is not to detach it from the idea that the needs in the basic List are course-of-life needs. Some course-of-life needs have to be met in special ways—specially intensive ways, as with the need for companionship—in childhood, to prepare for adequate functioning in adult life; and others, nearer the end of life, in special ways that permit graceful retirement from the basic social roles. If one insists on the course-of-life conception, relaxing and generalizing the Criterion to include the elderly, the need for medical care as it exists for the elderly has a convincing claim here, too, to be included in Part One of the basic List.

Still, suppose someone has come to the end of what is agreed is a normal life span and has given up all the tasks of all four social roles. He is now struck by some malady that brings him to the point of death. Once he has died, is it not consistent with his dying to say that all the needs endorsed by the Criterion had been met for him for the whole of his life? But if this is so, it might seem that on the same evidence one could say beforehand that all his needs had been met, leaving no room for an unmet need for medical care. Similarly, it might be argued, so far as having needs attaches directly or indirectly to normal species functioning, the effects of normal aging would not give rise to a need.

This contention might go through if the point of death were undeferrable. The person's needs would have come to an end with the ending of his life. The issue, however, is what to make of opportunities to defer death. Presumably, in prolonging life, medical care might in addition lead to the person's taking up again at least the vestiges of social roles; but this consideration is not decisive. Given that needs on any convincing Criterion are going to be generalized to the elderly who are performing the tasks of all the social roles, and generalized beyond them to the elderly who gradually give up the tasks and the roles, the conclusion that people on the point of death whose lives can be prolonged by medical care need that care is irresistible.

8.33 No Way Out with Normal Life Span

Could we nevertheless use the notion of a normal life span to take precautions with the concept of needs against runaway demands from medical opportunities to prolong life? Might we not try, for example, to distinguish between cases in which the people involved, young or old, have yet to live out a normal life span (that is to say, the current median length of life for people of their sex and social circumstances who escape serious accidents and serious diseases) and cases in which the people involved have already lived out a normal life span so defined? Intuitively, we might think that it is more important to give medical care to the within-span cases than to the beyond-span ones. Is that not a distinction that would be effective if we had only enough resources to take care of the within-span cases?

Unfortunately, it will not serve the purpose here, where,

in general, we must take into account the possibility that there are enough resources left over to take care of some beyond-span cases, though maybe the resources will all be used up before one reaches an end of the beyond-span demands. The concept of needs in its normative use meets no barrier when it is brought to the point of shifting from the within-span cases to the beyond-span ones. Nor does it meet any barrier if we distinguish sub-classes of these cases. One might, for example, oppose within-span cases of accidents and infectious diseases that can be controlled short of destroying any vital organs with beyond-span cases in which bodily parts are finally failing. Could we not keep the first sub-class within the scope of the concept of needs in its normative use—within the scope of the Principle of Precedence—and set the second sub-class aside?

However, there are other sub-classes that form a natural bridge. There are beyond-span cases of accidents and infectious diseases. We do not in fact deny medical attention to such cases. We readily apply the concept of needs to the treatment of injuries and infectious diseases of people within the normal life span. We apply it no less readily to the treatment of such things in people beyond the normal span. Are not people in beyond-span cases of failure of bodily parts on a parallel footing with respect to within-span cases of failures of bodily parts? So far as the plight of the people involved goes, the concept of needs bridges between them, across the normal life span, on both these lines.

Will it be said that a difference between the cases can be found in the difference in the costs of dealing with them? I think, as things stand, cost does make a difference; as one ground among several, it may limit attention under the concept of needs to failures of bodily parts in within-span cases. However, if costs are allowed to have this sort of effect, and there are in fact resources still available being used to heed preferences in ways needs do not demand, current policies will in effect have not only abandoned strict final priority for needs; they will have abandoned it in cases where the concept of needs operates as vividly and poignantly as it ever does. Will there be any sense left in strict final priority, even as a preliminary consideration contemplated by the most conscientious planners? Will not citizens and consumers in effect be conspiring with planners to evade strict final priority for needs and the force of the Principle of Precedence at every juncture in the discussion of policy?

Yet had the Principle of Precedence been used hitherto only in application to within-span cases, or to within-span cases plus beyond-span cases of accidents and infectious diseases, the prospect of runaway demands for medical care might have been forestalled. Could we not at least roughly justify legislating such a condition on application for our present purposes? One should hardly expect concepts and principles developed for use in traditional contexts, where the normal life span was given by nature, to deal convincingly with choices in which extending that span becomes itself an issue. But why should we not, if it is expedient, carry forward, deliberately, the limitation of our concern to the normal life span? Hitherto, the beyond-span cases in which it has been feasible to replace bodily parts have not been very numerous, and the cases in which replacement has been feasible, yet on grounds of cost not carried out, have not been so visible as to impress on everyone the significance for the concept of needs of not there following the Principle of Precedence to the end. So we have in effect been thinking of needs in a way roughly consistent with adhering to a condition limiting our concern with needs to the normal life span.

As a minor drawback, such legislation has the imperfection of begging the question about what shall be taken as the normal life span. If it is adopted and heeded, it will tend to prevent the normal life span from being raised. To be sure, the normal life span might creep upward as an effect of measures taken apart from the Principle of Precedence to replace bodily parts. Maybe people will use their own savings to keep themselves going; or replacement will be carried out on other grounds; in the case of some bodily parts, replacement may become easy and cheap. It would still be a drawback to the presupposition that so far as it was effective it would be restricting the normal life span.

The major drawback, however, is, of course, once more the fact that the analogies and bridges supplied by the concept of needs run the other way. They would have the new situation dealt with in quite a different way from merely continuing to impose a limitation perforce that was never a limitation intended. In the end, there is no way out of acknowledging that nothing already present in the concept of needs saves the need for medical care from becoming a bottomless pit.

8.4 Yet Elsewhere, Lo! Continuing Work for the Concept of Needs

I have counterpoised three points of breakdown of the concept of needs against the account of the concept, on the whole vindicating its usefulness, that I was occupied with in the rest of the book. That vindication holds for uses of the concept limited to the connections and circumstances there assumed and illustrated. Apprehensions about the points of breakdown elsewhere should not persuade us that it is futile to go on using the concept in those connections. There is no alternative concept in sight that would elicit more agreement or more action. The concept of needs in fact discriminates better policies from worse ones and gets good things done that otherwise would not get done. That is not futility; it is the reverse of futility.

Perhaps I have exaggerated the breakdown at the three points that I discussed. It bears recalling that one point, embarrassing needs, is hypothetical rather than real. Another, dealing with needs on the scale of the world population, is very likely real only in tendency, with a chance still of being avoided. Even the one remaining, medical care and the prolongation of human life, is more imminent in aggravation than real in present impact, though decisions contrary to strict final priority for needs, even abandoning strict final priority as an ideal, are currently being made.

It might be said that the breakdowns, especially the latter two, are not so much breakdowns in the concept of needs as in our moral capacity. The concept tells us what to do; it is just that in these connections what it tells us to do is more than we can bring ourselves to do. I do not deny that real breakdowns will be moral disasters. I do not deny, that is to say, that in these connections we shall find ourselves—we maybe find ourselves already—making or consenting to unconscionable decisions, which flagrantly disregard needs on a grand scale. However, I do not think this is to be attributed to a breakdown in our moral capacity rather than in the concept of needs. The distinction between the two cannot be carried through. The concept of needs defines a limit of our moral capacity, in the sense that it represents a limit to which, in the past, people have been prepared to carry concern for populations substantially larger than their kith and kin. The presupposition has been that this limit fell, at least normally, well within the effective range of the resources that could be brought to bear in meeting it. Of course, there have been more often than not shameful shortfalls in actual policy. At two of the points of breakdown, however—the two that cannot be parried as hypothetical—the presupposition about resources is destroyed. Then the concept of needs can no longer be used with all the presuppositions and expectations that formerly attached to it as conditions of its acceptance and efficacy. But it was with those conditions in place that the concept of needs defined a limit—even an ideal limit—to what was expected in moral capacity.

The world has changed, or is about to change, so as to elude the grasp of our moral notions. Perhaps we can still forestall the change in the world population problem, that is to say, make sure that it does not escape the grasp of the concept of needs. We cannot do this with medical care and the prolongation of life. There we must be content at best with the thought that when we halt en route we can still have made sure of doing more to meet needs than was ever done before.

DIALOGUE

CRITICAL READER: *Was that an upbeat ending?*

NOT-YET-REPENTANT AUTHOR: *Not quite.*

READER: *Hasn't your case for the concept of needs faded away? It sounds pretty weak, in the face of the breakdowns that you've just surveyed, to say that the concept works well enough elsewhere.*

AUTHOR: *Reacting that way, if you'll excuse me for saying so, is fish-tank thinking, which philosophers seem to fall into as easily as anyone else. Tap a fish-tank and all the fish skitter to the opposite end. Either a concept works everywhere and we accept it with applause. Or we reject it, as if it were the same thing to be of no use sometimes as to be of no use ever.*

READER: *Is that the whole issue here? We might have counted on the concept of needs to help us precisely in the connections that you have surveyed. Then, when it's our only hope, it turns out to break down.*

AUTHOR: *But why should we expect it to solve problems that we might predict will overload it? At the points of breakdown we're putting the concept to use in regions beyond all past experience.*

READER: *Then it's obsolete.*

AUTHOR: *Not while there are other points at which it is useful, indeed, as things stand with the suggested alternatives, indispensable.*

READER: *Maybe it's too easily overloaded.*

AUTHOR: *The matters brought up in the earlier chapters of the book argue the contrary. We don't reject other things because they have limitations. Why should we reject the concept of needs because it can be overloaded? Here is a tractor that does admirably in a whole variety of tasks found in the countryside. But when we load a whole city, buildings, people, and all, onto a string of flatcars, the tractor won't budge it. Do we conclude that the tractor is badly designed?*

NOTES

Chapter One   Charges against Concept of Needs

The neglect by philosophers of the concept of needs amounts to giving it very little attention, compared to topics of comparable importance. It has not been complete neglect. In a number of his writings, Christian Bay has championed the concept; see, for example, his book *Strategies of Political Emancipation* (Notre Dame, Indiana: Notre Dame University Press, 1981), pp. 90–109. Following a pioneer effort by Paul Taylor, " 'Need' Statements," *Analysis*, vol. 19, no. 5 (April 1959), pp. 106–11, Kai Nielsen offered an analysis and defense of the concept in "On Human Needs and Moral Appraisals," *Inquiry*, vol. 6 (1963), pp. 170–83. See also Nielsen's "Morality and Needs," in J. J. MacIntosh and S. Coval, eds., *The Business of Reason* (London: Routledge, 1969), pp. 186–206. My own article, "Let Needs Diminish That Preferences May Prosper," in Nicholas Rescher, ed., *Studies in Moral Philosophy*, American Philosophical Quarterly Monograph Series, no. 1 (Oxford: Basil Blackwell, 1968), pp. 86-107, offered an analysis consistent overall with Nielsen's. (The view taken in the article of needs and preferences persists in the present book, though here I am concerned more with the role that the concept of needs properly plays than with questionable extensions of the role.)

Positions similar to mine (then and now), so far as they go, will also be found in T. M. Scanlon, "Preferences and Urgency," *The Journal of Philosophy*, vol. 72, no. 19 (6 November 1975), pp. 655–69, though Scanlon avoids the term "need" and aggregates and disaggregates topics in ways different from mine; in Knut Erik Tranøy, " 'Ought' Implies 'Can': A Bridge from Fact to Norm," *Ratio*, vol. 17, no. 2 (December 1975), pp. 147–75, especially in the passage pp. 149–55; in Thomas Schwartz, "Human Welfare: What It Is Not," contributed to Harlan B. Miller and William H. Williams, eds., *The Limits of Utilitarianism* (Minneapolis: University of Minnesota Press, 1982), pp. 195–206. (Schwartz, too, avoids the term "needs.") Most striking of all in degree of convergence with my position is the treatment of poverty and needs in Bernard Gendron's *Technology and the Human Condition* (New York: St. Martin's Press, 1977), pp. 210–28, which I came across after the features of my basic account had been established and so have taken as independent corroboration of my own views. After the present book was submitted for publication, Bernard Williams called my attention to David Wiggins's penetrating essay, "The Claims of Need," in Ted Honderich, ed., *Morality and Objectivity* (London: Routledge, 1985). Using an analytical apparatus interestingly different from mine, Wiggins identifies many of the complications that I treat and deals with them with something like the same results. Perhaps he makes too little of the opportunities for simplification that the subject affords; he jumps in my view too quickly from needs to rights; and he says too little about procedures for avoiding conflicts between needs or for escaping such conflicts once they have arisen.

In *The Needs of Strangers* (London: Chatto & Windus, 1984), Michael Ignatieff, with a conception of needs—or at least of the *problématique* of needs—not too different from mine, explores literary and religious questions that I leave pretty much untouched. My account and the account given in Raymond Plant, Harry Lesser, and Peter Taylor-Gooby, *Political Philosophy and Social Welfare: Essays on the Normative Basis of Welfare Provision* (London: Routledge, 1980) reflect exchanges of ideas between Plant and me, though some differences survive. There is a similar mixture of agreement and difference between my account and the positions taken by Richard Wollheim in "Needs, Desires and Moral Turpitude," in R. S. Peters, ed., *Nature and Conduct* (London: Macmillan, 1975), pp. 162–80. My differences on the subject of needs with H. J. McCloskey's "Human Needs, Rights and Political Values," *American Philosophical Quarterly*, vol. 13, no. 1 (January 1976), pp. 1–11, have to do with points of ordinary language analysis too minute to pursue here.

I shall pursue in the next chapter my very substantial difference with Alan White and his reliance in the analysis of the concept on a formula that makes every need relative to an end calling for justification; see White, *Modal Thinking* (Ithaca, N.Y.: Cornell University Press, 1975), chap. 8. Brian Barry, in the very brief discussion of needs offered in *Political Argument* (London: Routledge, 1965), pp. 47–49, relies on the same relational formula; but my difference with him is not so sharp, since his reliance is not unqualified. In *The Demands of Justice* (Notre Dame, Ind.: University of Notre Dame Press, 1980), James P. Sterba works with a conception of needs much like mine and connects it with justice in a way that my discussion in Chapter 4 of the present book can accommodate with little trouble. David Miller, in *Social Justice* (Oxford: The Clarendon Press, 1976), a book that I shall refer to several times, devotes a careful and subtle chapter to needs; but he, in my view, relativizes the concept too much in allowing it to vary with different life-plans. I shall be stressing instead the ways in which consensus about basic needs ascribes them to everyone, with variations in life-plans at most a secondary consideration. Nevertheless, our views are close enough for compromise to be easy: I do allow for variations in culture and in tasks, and in those ways for variations in life-plans; and we both resist the indiscriminate use of the relational formula.

The discussion of needs given by William Leiss, in *The Limits of Satisfaction: An Essay on the Problem of Needs and Commodities* (Toronto: University of Toronto Press, 1976), pp. 49–71, runs in directions contrary to mine. I nevertheless found the book stimulating, as I think anyone would. I have also learned from three other books treating needs that draw more on Marx's teachings than Leiss does: Agnes Heller, *The Theory of Need in Marx* (London: Allison & Busby, 1976); Patricia Springborg, *The Problem of Human Needs and the Critique of Civilization* (London: Allen & Unwin, 1981); and Kate Soper, *On Human Needs: Open and Closed Theories in a Marxist Perspective* (Brighton, Sussex: Harvester Press, 1981). Soper's book is especially thorough and searching. I have a project of someday writing a critique of it; but its intricacies would lead too far away from the themes of the present book to treat it here.

1.1 Explanatory Use of "Needs"

The citations from Mary Douglas are from the book that she coauthored with Baron Isherwood, *The World of Goods: Towards an Anthropology of Consumption* (London: Allen Lane, 1979) and in particular from pages 61, 74, 62, 74, 59, and 65, in that order.

1.2 Normative Use: Too Fluid

The citation from Robert R. Alford has to do with his *Health Care Politics* (Chicago: University of Chicago Press, 1975), p. 244.

I have translated Rosa's statement from an article in *L'Express* 8–11 June 1978, p. 172.

I have translated the passage of Fourastié from his book *Les 40,000 Heures* (Paris: Laffont-Gonthier, 1965), p. 182.

1.3 Too Easily Satisfied

The quotation from Lindblom comes from his book *Politics and Markets* (New York: Basic Books, 1977), p. 9, footnote (which in turn cites Paul Samuelson's elementary textbook). I have cast Lindblom (so far as I do) in the somewhat invidious role of belittling the concept of needs not just on the basis of this quotation but also from recollecting a number of conversations in which he vigorously pressed upon me the view of the concept characteristic of economists. An even more typical spokesman, however, is Lester Thurow. In "Toward a definition of economic justice," *The Public Interest*, no. 31 (Spring 1973), pp. 56–80, Thurow dismisses the concept of needs in one page (p. 66). Everything that he says there seems to me to have been said without due reflection, in ways characteristic of economists' views as I represent them. Lindblom's inclination to dismiss the concept of needs, I might note, does not sit comfortably with his defense elsewhere of ordinary knowledge against the pretensions of social science. See Charles E. Lindblom and David K. Cohen, *Usable Knowledge: Social Science and Social Problem Solving* (New Haven: Yale University Press, 1979).

The suggestion that abundance should be recognized by socialists to have been, historically, the normal case everywhere was made to me by Cornelius Castoriadis. He had in mind recent anthropological work like that of Marshall Sahlins, *Stone Age Economics* (Chicago: Aldine Atherton, 1972), see especially chap. 1, "The Original Affluent Society." Marx himself declaimed against needs as a limiting test in the Paris mss. See Marx, *Oeuvres*, ed. M. Rubel (Paris: Gallimard Pléiade, 1965, 1968), vol. 2, p. 77; p. 107. (I cite this edition of Marx's works not out of a perverse desire for a recherché reference but for its scholarly value, a point impressed upon me by Castoriadis in recommending it. The French version of *Das Kapital*, translated and corrected under Marx's personal supervision, has its own basic claim to attention among the classics of Marxism.)

For examples of widespread failure in the United States to meet the need for food, see Loretta Schwartz-Nobel, *Starving in the Shadow of Plenty* (New York: McGraw-Hill, 1981). The failure, in which Jürgen Habermas's thesis of "internal colonization" is vividly and poignantly illustrated, has more to do with the rigidities of bureaucratic procedure, of course, than with any lack of foodstocks. These rigidities, and their deeper political significance, have been studied by Frances Fox Piven and Richard A. Cloward in a number of works: *The Politics of Turmoil: Essays on Poverty, Race and the Urban Crisis* (New York: Pantheon Books, 1974); *Poor People's Movements: Why They Succeed, How They Fail* (New York: Pantheon Books, 1977); *Regulating the Poor: The Functions of Public Wel-*

fare (New York: Pantheon Books, 1971). For Habermas on internal colonization, see his *Theorie des kommunikativen Handelns* (Frankfurt am Main: Suhrkamp Verlag, 1981), vol. 2, chap. 8, sec. 2. (The first volume of this work has appeared in English translation by Thomas McCarthy under the title *The Theory of Communicative Action* (Boston: Beacon Press, 1983). Peter Morton, a Dalhousie student, first brought Piven's and Cloward's work to my attention.

1.4 Too Clumsy

In setting forth the third line of attack, which is the most sophisticated of the three, I begin with reporting the gist of some remarks made to me by an economist, Alan Williams, speaking somewhat in the role of a devil's advocate, and elaborate them to include a suggestion, put forward in the same spirit by a philosopher, L. W. Sumner, about preferences for the conditions of preferences. Not all the best objections to the concept of needs seem to have got into print. Sumner's have, however, in his book *Abortion and Moral Theory* (Princeton: Princeton University Press, 1981); see p. 181. In that book, Sumner himself objects to the imperialism of preference theorists, but on behalf of a moral theory that relies on experiences—"agreeable states of mind"—rather than on needs to identify people's interests.

1.5. Real Abuses

On the paternalism of professionals and bureaucracies, see William Gaylin, et al., *Doing Good: The Limits of Benevolence* (New York: Pantheon Books, 1978), which has much to say on this score in objection to the rhetoric of needs.

1.6 Prospects of Vindication

Two examples of the literature on social indicators are Raymond A. Bauer, ed., *Social Indicators* (Cambridge, Mass.: MIT Press, 1966); and *Towards a System of Social and Demographic Statistics* (New York: United Nations, 1975: ST/ESA/STAT/SER. F/18), prepared by Richard Stone, the Cambridge economist. Richard A. Musgrave discusses "merit wants" in his *The Theory of Public Finance: A Study in Public Economy* (New York: McGraw-Hill, 1959), pp. 13–14. The Basic Necessities Index was developed in 1980 at the National Center for Economic Alternatives, in Washington. G. Alperovitz and Jeff Faux explain it in "Controls and the Basic Necessities," *Challenge*, vol. 23, no. 2 (May/June 1980), pp. 21–29. See also the discussion in *Challenge*, vol. 23, no. 6 (Jan./Feb. 1981), pp. 44–52.

For a short guide to the extensive literature on the Basic Needs approach to international aid, see Graciela Chichilnisky, *Basic Needs and the North/South Debate* (World Order Models Project: Working Paper no. 21), New York: Institute for World Order, 1982. Chichilnisky gives a brief critical history of the approach, touching on the distortion introduced by Northern writers when they took up the approach, first formulated in Southern—developing—countries.

Dialogue between chapters 1 and 2

For a perceptive critique from outside economics of the approximations to utility that economists resort to, see K. S. Shrader-Frechette, *Science Policy, Ethics, and Economic Metholodogy* (Dordrecht: D. Reidel, 1984), chap. 5.

Chapter Two   Normative Use in Social Policy

2.1 The Relational Formula

I have already referred to the championship of the relational formula by Alan White and its more cautious endorsement by Brian Barry (see notes to Chapter 1). A champion more extreme and passionate than White has been Lewis A. Dexter, in private conversations with me. He thinks the relational formula exposes abuses of the concept so great and so inveterate, as are the abuses that the concept encourages in demands for social justice, that it is best suppressed entirely. Barry sees that the relational formula gives unilluminating results with basic needs; and it is this that makes him a less than whole-hearted champion of the relational formula.

2.2 Course-of-Life Needs

The lists of needs or social indicators are drawn, respectively, from Jan F. Drewnowski, "The Level of Living Index—New Version (A Revision of United Nations Research Institute for Social Development Report No. 4, Parts 1 and 2, September 1966)," in *Studies in the Measurement of Levels of Living and Welfare*, UNRISD report no. 73 (Geneva, 1970), p. 62; from Ernest Mandel, *Marxist Economic Theory*, tr. Brian Pearce, 2 vols. (London: Merlin Press, 1968), vol. 2, p. 660; Nestor E. Terleckyj, "Measuring Progress Towards Social Goals: Some Possibilities at National and Local Levels," *Management Science*, vol. 16, no. 12 (August 1970), pp. B-765–B-778; and *List of Social Concerns Common to Most OECD Countries*, (Paris: Organization for Economic Cooperation and Development, 1973), pp. 14–17. I am indebted to Dr. Terleckyj and to the Manager of OECD Publications for their help in completing this documentation. Cf. the similar list given by Claus Offe in "The Separation of Form and Content in Liberal Democratic Politics," *Studies in Political Economy*, no. 3 (Spring 1980), pp. 5–16.

Stress is not nervous tension, but a "non-specific" response in a "general adaptation syndrome" to specific external stimulation. Hans Selye, *The Stress of Life* (New York: McGraw-Hill, 1956), pp. 29–39. On stress as a new concept, see *ibid.*, pp. 37–43. Speaking of a need for some stress is reasonably well founded on what Selye says and matches his own usage on occasion. Selye, *Stress without Distress* (Philadelphia: J. B. Lippincott, 1974), pp. 32–33; p. 73; pp. 80–81; p. 85. Strictly speaking, however, it would accord best with his account to refer to a need for "A moderate level of stimulation, calling for the mobilization of adaptive energy"; that, too, seems to require a newly specialized term. For the terminology of "the *agon*," the need for struggle, held to be characteristic of Western culture, see Alvin W. Gouldner, *The Dialectic of Ideology and Technology* (New York: The Seabury Press, 1976), pp. 262–64.

2.3 Minimum Standards of Provision

Michael V. Tracey, writing on "Human Nutrition" in *The Encyclopedia of Ignorance*, ed. by Ronald Duncan and Miranda Weston-Smith (Oxford; New York: Pergamon Press, 1977) cites a study showing that in a sample of 900 healthy British children aged 1 to 18, every age group included a boy who consumed twice as much energy as another, and one 16-year-old boy was consuming less energy than one 1-year-old. No one knows why.

The point about interaction among the Minimum Standards of Provision was first suggested to me, I think, by Teddy Seidenfeld. It was pressed by David Gauthier in discussions that I had with him and Frank Cunningham at Toronto.

2.4 Criterion for Inclusion

It was C. G. Hempel who mentioned unrequited love to me.

The book on sleep is Ray Meddis, *The Sleep Instinct* (London: Routledge and Kegan Paul, 1977).

The example of solitary confinement as an inconclusive test of a need for companionship reflects a discussion with Lewis A. Dexter. My colleague Robert Martin objected to an earlier formulation of the Criterion that it might be taken to imply a need for a vacuum cleaner if a vacuum cleaner was indispensable to performing a certain task. I think the objection did not in fact go through given the context in which the formulation was offered; but it properly forced me to be more explicit.

On variations in life-plans I come some distance toward accommodating the view of David Miller, *op. cit.*, that needs are conditions for fulfilling life-plans; but I do not go all the way with him to including conditions that vary from one life-plan to another.

2.6 A Principle of Precedence

Harry G. Frankfurt, in "Necessity and Desire," *Philosophy and Phenomenological Research*, vol. 45, no. 1 (September 1984), pp. 1–13, holds that there is widespread acceptance of what he calls "the Principle of Precedence" for needs over desires. I, who have been using that name for the principle quite independently, during the years of gestating this book, take Frankfurt's observation about acceptance as some corroboration of my own position and his nomenclature as some confirmation of the propriety of mine. The Principle, without the name, can be found in a variety of places, some arcane, some vulgar: for example, in L. T. Hobhouse, *Elements of Social Justice* (London: Allen & Unwin, 1930), p. 132; p. 109; pp. 119–20; in newspaper cartoons, such as one about a father admonishing a boy about his pocket money, which my father sent me; in La Fontaine's fable "Le Milan et le Rossignol"; in Robert Frost's poem, "Two Tramps in Mud Time." In the epigraphs to the present book, I illustrate, in the one case, how the principle consorts with perfect mastery of the nuances of English; and, in the other, with the casual—but no less consequéntial—usages of a working politician. D. G. Long finds it in Bentham, as a condition to be met before diffusing wealth with the special object of promoting happiness: see Long, "Bentham on Property," in Anthony Parel and Thomas Flanagan, eds., *Theories of Property: Aristotle to the Present* (Waterloo, Ontario: Wilfrid Laurier University Press, 1979), pp. 221–54, at p. 246, citing Bentham manuscripts. In a review of the televised biography of Elvis Presley (*Newsweek* [12 February 1979, p. 97]), Harry F. Waters says, "Most inexplicably absent is Elvis the Stud. The superstar whose sexual liaisons reportedly numbered in the hundreds is never once shown straying from good wife Priscilla. So why, she plaintively inquires, isn't he home more? Nodding toward his retinue, Elvis solemnly explains, 'Baby, I have to look beyond *our* wants to *their* needs.' "

The neologism Selfgovliset is intended to meet Nuel Belnap's objection that the abbreviation SLS was not perspicuous.

314

Kate Soper, in *On Human Needs*, already cited, is one of the people who most strongly insists on the political nature of the concept of needs. My analysis of needs is very different from hers but I hope to do justice to the point.

Lexicographical priority is defined following Gerard Debreu, *The Theory of Value: An Axiomatic Analysis of Economic Equilibrium* (New Haven: Yale University Press, 1950).

Maslow's hierarchy of needs: See of Abraham Maslow's works, the following, among others: *Dominance, Self-Esteem, Self-Actualization: Germinal Papers of A.H. Maslow*, ed. by Richard J. Lowry (Monterey, Cal.: Brooks/Cole Pub., 1973); *New Knowledge in Human Values* (New York: Harper, 1959).

The economists who have been exploring the notion of lexicographical ordering with satiation limits include William Terrell (from whom I have learned most), in a number of papers read at economists' meetings; Richard H. Day and Stephen M. Robinson, "Economic Decisions with L** Utility," in James L. Cochrane and Milan Zeleny, eds., *Multiple Criteria Decision Making* (Columbia, S.C.: University of South Carolina Press, 1973), pp. 84-92; J. Encarnacíon, "A Note on Lexicographical Preferences," *Econometrica*, vol. 32, nos. 1-2 (January/April 1964), pp. 215-17; and, most fundamental of all, Nicholas Georgescu-Roegen, "Choice, Expectations, and Measurability," *Quarterly Journal of Economics*, vol. 69, no. 4 (November 1954), pp. 503-34, especially sections 4 and 5. Terrell cites, among nineteenth-century economists treating wants as falling into a hierarchy, Thomas Banfield and Karl Menger. For a more fully formalized treatment, reflecting this literature, of priority for needs, than anything that I set forth in the present book, see the contribution that the logician Peter K. Schotch joined me in making to the collection of essays edited by Norman E. Bowie, *Ethical Issues in Government* (Philadelphia: Temple University Press, 1981).

Chapter Three   Complications

3.1 Derived Needs

Coordinating schemes founded on mutual advantage without a system of sanctions are what David K. Lewis, following Hume, calls "conventions" in a narrow sense. See David K. Lewis, *Convention: A Philosophical Study* (Cambridge: Harvard University Press, 1969); cf. David Hume, "On the Origin of Justice and Property," *A Treatise of Human Nature*, ed. L. A. Selby-Bigge (Oxford: Clarendon Press, 1949; originally published 1739), part 2, book 3.

3.2 Conventional Determinants

For the difference in conventions about distance between people conversing with one another, see Edward T. Hall, *The Silent Language* (New York: Doubleday, 1959), chap. 10.

On the relation between derived needs and conventional features of Minimum Standards of Provision I am responding to some questions pressed upon me by J. T. Stevenson.

The quotation from Adam Smith is one that I owe to James S. Fishkin, who in his *Tyranny and Legitimacy: A Critique of Political Theories* (Baltimore: Johns Hopkins University Press, 1979), p. 36, cites for it *The Wealth of Nations* (1776), book 5, chap. 2.

Marx mentions shirts as necessities in *Capital* (*Oeuvres*, Pléaide edition), vol. 1, p. 853.

3.4 Further Aspects of Normativity

See John Sekora, *Luxury: The Concept in Western Thought* (Baltimore: Johns Hopkins University Press, 1977), on the traditional opposition of needs to luxuries and the dangers traditionally apprehended from luxurious living. On the will to power over "other bodies" as a need, see Friedrich Nietzsche, *Beyond Good and Evil*, tr. Walter Kaufmann, in *Basic Writings of Nietzsche* (New York: Modern Library, 1968), p. 393; and Hobbes, *Leviathan* (London: Crooke, 1651), chap. 11, at the beginning.

For Adler's theory of aggression, see Heinz L. Ansbacher and Rowena Ansbacher, eds. & translators, *The Individual Psychology of Alfred Adler* (London: Allen & Unwin, 1958), pp. 34–47.

Chapter Four   Reasoning about Justice

I distinguish "conception of justice" from "concept" as John Rawls does in *A Theory of Justice* (Cambridge: Harvard University Press, 1971), pp. 5–6.

4.1 Mutual Support

The quotation from Donagan is from *The Theory of Morality* (Chicago: University of Chicago Press, 1977), p. 85. By what I assume was a slip, the text reads "inasmuch" where I have put "insofar."

4.2 Justice via Rights

As current theorists of justice advocating rights regardless of needs I have in mind Nozick, his followers, and other self-styled "libertarians." See, for example, Robert Nozick, *Anarchy, State, and Utopia* (New York: Basic Books, 1974).

Henry Shue, in *Basic Rights: Subsistence, Affluence, and U.S. Foreign Policy* (Princeton: Princeton University Press, 1980), which offers a powerful argument for the relief of poverty abroad, treats basic needs as matters covered by rights. I am quite prepared to go along with the argument, if I am allowed to note that there is a step between recognizing the needs as something to be met under the Principle of Precedence and postulating rights as the most suitable means of getting them met. If they are, that is for me a contingent fact, just as it is a contingent fact—the same fact, in part—that the rhetoric of rights is more gripping than the rhetoric of needs.

The formulation of the difference principle comes from John Rawls, *A Theory of Justice* (Cambridge: Harvard University Press, 1971), p. 302.

On equality as an aspect of justice, see St. Thomas Aquinas, *Summa Theologiae* 2a2ae, Q. 58, art. 2 and art. 11; on benefits and burdens, Q. 59, art. 1.

4.3 Equality and Unmet Needs

Literal equality is equivalent to what Douglas Rae, Douglas Yates, Jennifer Hochschild, Joseph Morone, and Carol Fessler call "lot-regarding equality" in their book *Equalities* (Cambridge: Harvard University Press, 1981), p. 85ff.

The formula contrasting "treating people equally" with "treating them with equal respect" echoes Ronald Dworkin, in (among other places), "What Is Equality—Part 1: Equality of Welfare," *Philosophy & Public Affairs*, vol. 10, no. 3 (Summer 1981), pp. 185–246, at p. 185. Part 2 of this article appeared in the same journal, vol. 10, no. 4 (Fall 1981), pp. 283–345. The points that I make about Dworkin's views are points about views that he expresses in this article, though another striking instance of his overlooking equality-in-meeting-needs as a principle of distribution can be found in the essay, "Liberalism," chap. 8 of Dworkin's *A Matter of Principle* (Cambridge, Mass.: Harvard University Press, 1985), pp. 181–204, at the turn of pp. 192–93. (The essay in question was originally published in Stuart Hampshire, ed., *Public and Private Morality* [Cambridge: Cambridge University Press, 1978].)

The alternative interpretation of equality introduced at this point falls under what Rae et al. call "person-regarding equality" (*op. cit.*, p. 92ff.), of which they note the most compelling version is "needs-based person-regarding equality" (p. 99).

4.5 Equality-in-Meeting-Needs.

See Henry Sidgwick, *The Methods of Ethics* (London: Macmillan, 1962). Cf. with pp. 416–17, p. 447.

The quotations from Tawney are from the edition of 1964, R. H. Tawney, *Equality*, with a new introduction by Richard M. Titmuss (London: Allen & Unwin, 1964), the first quotation from pp. 49–50, the second from p. 113.

Jules Vuillemin told me that miners in France got a wartime ration of six liters of wine a day.

4.6 Practical Necessity and Equality

For T. H. Green's position that rights must be joined with genuine opportunities, see his lecture of 1880 on "Liberal Legislation and Freedom of Contract," cited by George H. Sabine, *A History of Political Theory*, 3rd ed. (New York: Holt, Rinehart and Winston, 1961), pp. 728–30.

Chapter Five   Utilitarianism Without Utility

5.1 Censuses of Needs

I treat the Census Notion more fully than I treat it here in my *Three Tests for Democracy* (New York: Random House, 1968) and even more fully in Chap. 8 (and the footnotes to this chapter) of the book that C. E. Lindblom and I wrote together, *A Strategy of Decision* (New York: The Free Press, 1963). In that book it figures in a discussion of incremental policy-making that involves the Revisionary Process among other features; but I failed to make it clear in either book that the power of the Census Notion cannot be fully appreciated if the availability of the Revisionary Process is ignored. Thus, even a sympathetic consideration of the Census Notion by Dan W. Brock in "Recent Work in Utilitarianism," *American Philosophical Quarterly*, vol. 10, no. 4 (October 1973), pp. 241–76, at p. 247, missed the implications of combining these ideas, and concluded that the Census Notion had only very limited possibilities of operation.

5.2 Revisionary Process

On the Revisionary Process as the way out of problems that may be raised for social choice by a given set of alternatives, see my "Policy Formation with Issue-Processing and Transformation of Issues" in Clifford Alan Hooker, et al., eds., *Foundations and Applications of Decision Theory* (Dordrecht: D. Reidel, 1978), vol. 2, pp. 1–15.

5.3 Defects of Utility

The current suggestion that any one person's scale can, given the similarity of human beings, be used to compare the utilities received by other people has been most prominently associated with John C. Harsanyi. See, for example, his essays on *Ethics, Social Behavior, and Scientific Explanation* (Dordrecht: Reidel, 1976), pp. 79–80; for his advocacy of von Neumann-Morgenstern utility functions, see pp. 48–49. The primary reference for the latter is John von Neumann and Oskar Morgenstern, *The Theory of Games and Economic Behavior* (Princeton: Princeton University Press, 1944, 2nd ed., 1947), pp. 17–30. Arrow's theorem is to be found in Kenneth J. Arrow, *Social Choice and Individual Values* (New York: John Wiley, 1951, 2nd ed., 1963), chap. 5.

For a demonstration of the difference that it makes to abandon Arrow's assumption—not an assumption necessary to his proof, but an assumption of his approach, common to rational decision theory, personal and social—that all alternatives open to choice are given, see the paper cited above in *Foundations and Applications of Decision Theory* (1978).

Ted Bond called my attention to the shift between treating utility as a property of means to pleasure or satisfaction and treating it as their equivalent.

See John Stuart Mill, *Utilitarianism* (1863) chap. 2, on higher pleasures.

On one view—the one that he explicitly supports—Marx treats "needs" as a wholly generalized term interchangeable with "wants" and either term as answering to anything that has "use value," having which is a condition of having "exchange value." See, for example, *Oeuvres* (Pléiade edition), vol. 1, p. 739: "Peu importe à la valeur le genre de valeur d'usage qui la soutient." Cf. vol. 1, p. 562, footnote: "Le désir implique le besoin." The other view, which is congruent with the one taken in the present book, shows up when Marx distinguishes, as he repeatedly does, "needs of primary necessity" or "primary needs" from others falling under the generalized concept. See, for example, vol. 1, p. 844, where he speaks of "besoins de première nécessité"; elsewhere he refers to "les vivres" or "les subsistances" of which the worker "a besoin pour son entretien et pour perpétuer sa race" (vol. 1, p. 168).

5.4 Liberalism Led Astray

For the Pareto welfare criterion, see Vilfredo Pareto, *Manuel d'économie politique*, 2nd ed. (Paris: Giard, 1927), pp. 617–18; or almost any intermediate textbook on microeconomic theory, for example, William S. Vickrey, *Microstatics* (New York: Harcourt, Brace, & World, 1964), p. 209 and *passim* thereafter.

Liberal support for making sure that people had the resources to exercise their rights was effectively established by the work of T. H. Green. See the previous note on Green's work.

On the incompatibility of the program of historical Liberalism with the Pareto welfare criterion, see Charles K. Rowley and Alan T. Peacock, *Welfare Economics: A Liberal Restatement* (London: Martin Robertson, 1975).

5.5 Utilitarianism, Liberalism Reunited

References to work by economists on social indicators and related matters will be found above in the notes to 1.6.

5.6 Provision for Preferences

In the case that I make out for consent to the inequalities by those worst off under them I am taking certain precautions inspired by G. A. Cohen's discussion, in manuscript, of a common error (which I am afraid I have elsewhere fallen into myself) in which the case for the Difference Principle in the original position is confused with the case that could be made for accepting functional inequalities in the status quo.

I found the quotation from Delacroix in the *Faber Book of Aphorisms*, ed. W. H. Auden and Louis Kronenberger (London: Faber, 1964; paperback edition, 1970), p. 251.

In the remarks on public goods I am relying on the standard discussion in John G. Head, *Public Goods and Public Welfare* (Durham, N.C.: Duke University Press, 1974). See especially chap. 3.

Jonathan Riley is an example of a writer who would object to restricting the operation of social choice by giving priority to meeting needs; and object, too, that devolving choices of private goods upon individual persons would not put those choices outside the field of social choice and the range of Sen's Paradox. For Sen's Paradox of Liberalism, see Amartya K. Sen, *Social Choice and Social Welfare* (San Francisco: Holden-Day, 1970); for Riley's position, see his *Liberal Utilitarianism: A Formal Theory of Liberal Democracy*, forthcoming from Cambridge University Press. I take a different view in "Can Democracy Be Combined With Federalism or With Liberalism?" in J. Roland Pennock and John W. Chapman, eds., *Liberal Democracy (Nomos XXV)* (New York: New York University Press, 1983), pp. 109–18. Riley has lately convinced me that our differences turn rather upon whether any matters can be given priority within the framework of social choice theory than on whether they deserve priority.

I owe the comparison of private charitable contributions with outlays on the Royal Navy to a remark by Calvin Woodard, an historian specially interested in the history of charity in nineteenth-century Britian.

Chapter Six   Needs and Preferences

6.1 Demands of Liberty

James S. Fishkin defines tyranny as deprivation that could be avoided in *Tyranny and Legitimacy: A Critique of Political Theories* (Baltimore: Johns Hopkins University Press, 1979), p. 18.

6.2 A Dead-End Path

See Miller, *Social Justice*, p. 134.

Jane Mansbridge in *Beyond Adversary Democracy* (New York: Basic Books, 1980), brings up as an objection to her own assimilation of interests to preferences the point about common interests disappearing when an alternative is added (p. 343, n. 9).

6.3 Precautionary Priority

See earlier references to literature on lexicographical ordering in notes to 2.6.

On satisficing and levels of aspiration, see Herbert A. Simon, *Models of Man* (New York: Wiley, 1961), p. 61; pp. 70–71; p. 253.

6.5 Erosion of Priority

Simulation of the market as means of planning: see J. C. Milleron, "Theory of Value with Public Goods: A Survey Article,"

Journal of Economic Theory, vol. 5, no. 3 (December 1972), pp. 419-77.

Many jurisdictions with different policies: See George J. Stigler, "The Tenable Range of Functions of Local Government," in *Federal Expenditure Policy for Economic Growth and Stability* (U.S. Congress, Joint Economic Committee, Washington, D.C., 1957), pp. 213-19.

Morton D. Davis, in *Game Theory* (New York: Harper, 1973), explains the notion of "core"—the set of joint payoffs none of them dominated by another payoff that attracts a stronger coalition (see pp. 145-57, on von Neumann's and Morgenstern's solution concept). James W. Friedman, *Game Theory with Applications to Economics* (New York: Oxford University Press, 1986), gives a more advanced treatment.

Chapter Seven   Expansion of Needs

7.1 List Unduly Narrow?

The need for work with "the challenge of growth-potential experience" is asserted in *Beyond Services and Beyond Jobs: People's Need to Grow* (National Council of Welfare, Ottawa, 1974), p. 8.

For Marx on the need for work, see Marx, *Critique of Gotha Program*; cf. the passage in the *Grundrisse* on "Labor as Sacrifice and Free Labor" (Pléiade edition, vol. 2, pp. 288-93); on the effects of automation, *ibid.* (pp. 305-306; 310-11).

It was Sharon Sutherland who came across the woman cleaning the latrine and came away indignant.

7.2 Advantages of Expansion

That needs unlike preferences are reliably parallel concerns is a point that reflects my reaction to reading, after being referred to it by Tom Sinclair-Faulkner, the review of Lindblom's *Politics and Markets* in *Religious Studies Review*, vol. 9, no. 3, July 1983, pp. 212-19, by Jon P. Gunnemann. Gunnemann makes the point that preferences set people at odds, hence a view of politics that takes preferences as basic is bound to underestimate the basis that might be found for a common policy. It is true that Lindblom gives more weight to "volitions," that is to say, considered preferences, than to preferences as such (see *Politics and Markets*, pp. 135-36). That may not be enough to escape Gunnemann's point; even if it is, the point is sound enough in itself.

For Hume's remarks on the circumstances that make justice idle, see his *Treatise of Human Nature*, ed. L. A. Selby-Bigge pp. 494–95; and his *Inquiry Concerning the Principles of Morals*, ed. Charles W. Hendel (New York: Liberal Arts Press, 1957), pp. 15–19.

7.3 Courses Expansion May Take

For Fourastié on the expansion of needs, see the citation in the notes for 1.2; for Marx, the early text quoted in 7.34. For Marx on the equivalence of having a use value and being an object of a need, see, for example, Pléiade edition, vol. 1, p. 300 (from *The Critique of Political Economy*), p. 621 (from *Capital*, book 1, chap. 2). I have benefitted, in thinking about Marx's views on needs, from an article by Nancy Holmstrom, "Free Will and a Marxist Concept of Natural Wants," *Philosophical Forum*, vol. 6, no. 4 (Summer 1975), pp. 423–46.

Fred Hirsch, who coined the term, discusses "positional goods" in his *Social Limits to Growth* (Cambridge, Mass.: Harvard University Press, 1976), pp. 27–31.

Marx explicitly condemns, in the *Critique of the Gotha Program*, a capitalism that pays its wage slaves enough to keep them in comfort. Marcuse is a Marxist writer with an inclination to favor austerity. See his *One-Dimensional Man* (Boston: Beacon Press, 1964), pp. 4–7. Marx himself has no hankering for it. See again the early text quoted in 7.34 on "the rich man . . . with rich human exigencies."

Kate Soper holds that for something to be a need a form of provision for it must be known. See *On Human Needs*, pp. 18–19, note 7. The point was first suggested to me by G. A. Cohen. The example of the dental vaccine is his; the caution about the microflora and microfauna is Professor Barbara Harsanyi's.

Maslow's conception of a fully developed personality might serve as well as any (see citations in notes to 2.6). I do not want, however, to be commited to all the details of his conception or confine my argument to the basis it might supply for a third part of the List.

What in my terms amounts to an expansion of needs embracing a third part of the List is implied by the recent discussions in Evan Simpson, "The Priority of Needs Over Wants," *Social Theory and Practice*, vol. 3, no. 1 (Spring 1982), pp. 95–112; and Mary Midgley, "Human Ideals and Human Needs," *Philosophy*, vol. 58, no. 223

(January 1983), pp. 89–94. Both these authors create some misgivings in my mind about expanding the concept too freely. Simpson maintains that anything that one has reason to fear losing induces a need for security of provision and makes this a central rational end. Midgley's chief examples of needs include "the need to be able to rely on other people" and "the need for a continuous central life that lasts through genuine, but passing, changes of mood."

On breakdown of middle-class prisoners in Nazi concentration camps see, for example, Bruno Bettelheim, *Surviving and Other Essays* (New York: Knopf, 1979), pp. 56–59; Bettelheim, *The Informed Heart: The Human Condition in Modern Mass Society* (London: Thames and Hudson, 1961). On Bettelheim's account, the breakdown had as much or more to do with the absence of strong political commitments as with the absence of middle-class comforts. Cf. Hannah Arendt, *The Burden of Our Time* (London: Secker and Warburg, 1951), pp. 421–28. At issue, nevertheless, for Bettelheim, is the personality structure of middle-class people, formed under expectations systematically denied in the concentration camps.

The early text by Marx is to be found in the Pléiade edition, vol. 2, p. 88. For Simmel's remarks on self-development through experience of multiple objects, see his essay, "Subjective Culture," in Donald N. Levine, ed., *Georg Simmel on Individuality and Social Forms* (Chicago: University of Chicago Press, 1971), pp. 227–34, p. 230 and p. 234 especially; p. 234 touches also on the difficulties of dealing with a great increase in the number and variety of objects.

Fourastié advances tranquility as a need created by modern technology in his *Les 40,000 Heures* (Paris: Laffon/Gonthier, 1965), p. 130. The quotation from Marx on labor as "life's prime want" comes from the *Critique of the Gotha Program*.

For the evidence of boredom etc., cited by the Canadian National Council of Welfare, see the pamphlet referred to in the notes to 7.1.

Citations bearing on the interest nineteenth-century economists took in hierarchies of needs will be found above in the notes to 2.6.

7.4 Risks of Expansion

Compare with the possibility of expanded needs' squeezing out attention to basic needs of others the "Northern" abuse of the basic needs approach to development in poor countries, which comes up in the next chapter. See 8.24, at the end.

In "Let Needs Diminish That Preferences May Prosper," I give an extended discussion of the ways in which needs may have an excessively restrictive impact upon preferences.

Chapter Eight   Three Points of Breakdown

8.1 Moral Dignity

The point that protecting a susceptible minority from addiction may interfere with the liberty of the nonsusceptible majority is one that was first put to me by Dan Wikler.

On moral nondependent functioning, see Mill, "On Liberty," and *Representative Government*, chap. 3; see Marx on self-development and free creative activity (Pléiade edition, vol. 2, pp. 63–64 from the mss. on economics and philosophy; pp. 209–210 from the *Grundrisse*).

The quotations from Marcuse come from *Eros and Civilization*, pp. 191–92; p. 197.

Hobbes's argument for the necessity of coercion by the Sovereign is, of course, to be found in *Leviathan*. For a current version, related to the game-theoretical problems of organizing society, see J. Howard Sobel, "The Need for Coercion," in J. Roland Pennock and John W. Chapman, eds., *Coercion (Nomos XIV)* (Chicago/New York: Aldine/Atherton, 1972), pp. 148–77.

For Freud on the need to be deceived, see primarily his discussions of repression as a defense mechanism, e.g., the article "Repression" in John Rickman, ed., *A General Selection from the Works of Sigmund Freud* (New York: Doubleday, 1957), pp. 87–97; but also his discussion of religion in *The Future of an Illusion*, tr. W. D. Robson-Scott, ed. James Strachey (London: The Hogarth Press, 1962). A search has failed to turn up actual evidence of a school of depth psychology firmly founded on a need for self-abasement. The techniques of abasement used in Synanon therapy consort with such a need, but do not strictly presuppose it. See Elliott L. Markoff, "Synanon," *International Encyclopedia of Psychiatry, Psychology, Psychoanalysis and Neurology*, Benjamin B. Wolman, ed. (New York: Van Nostrand Reinhold, 1977), vol. 2, pp. 63–67.

8.2 Worldwide Reference Population

For an argument, more explicit than anything that I give to this effect, showing that received morality neither contemplates nor sanctions the demands that may arise from the needs of the world population, see James S. Fishkin, *The Limits of Obligation* (New Haven: Yale University Press, 1982).

Kant, *The Metaphysical Principles of Virtue*, tr. J. Ellington (Indianapolis: Liberal Arts, 1964 [originally published 1797]), pp. 52, 117.

Nozick discusses the Lockean proviso in pp. 175–82 of *Anarchy, State, and Utopia* (New York: Basic Books, 1974). Locke's own discussion of his two criteria are to be found in chap. 5, the chapter on property, of his *Second Treatise of Government* (1690).

Graciela Chichilnisky attacks "Northern" abuses of the basic needs approach to international aid for economic development in her pamphlet *Basic Needs and the North/South Debate*, already cited.

Henry Shue is quoted from his paper, "The Burdens of Justice," *The Journal of Philosophy*, vol. 80, no. 10 (October 1983), pp. 600–608, at p. 606 and p. 608.

8.3 Medical Care

Hard evidence of current practice of triage in the allocation of scarce medical resources is not easy to come by, one conjectures for obvious reasons, but there is plenty of concern about its being practiced or about its being made inevitable by budgetary restrictions. See, for example, the discussion of hemodialysis and artificial hearts in Robert M. Veatch, *Case Studies in Medical Ethics* (Cambridge, Mass.: Harvard University Press, 1977), pp. 232–39; Louis R. M. Del Guercio, "Triage in cold blood," *Critical Care Medicine*, vol. 5, no. 4 (July–August, 1977), pp. 167–69; L. E. Morris, "Historical and Ethical Aspects of Intensive Care," in J. P. Prague and D. W. Hill, *Management of the Acutely Ill* (Stevenage: Peter Peregrinus, 1977) cited by V. A. Bishop, "A Nurse's View of Ethical Problems in Intensive Care and Clinical Research," *British Journal of Anaesthesia*, vol. 50, no. 5 (May 1978), pp. 515–18, at p. 516. I have been unable to check an article in *The Washington Post* (19 May 1978, A26): "Health Care Costs Spur Debate on Who Shall Live, Who Shall Die."

On the preponderant effects on the life span of improvements in nutrition and sanitation, see, for example, John E. Gordon,

"Ecologic Interplay of Man, Environment and Health," in *The American Journal of the Medical Sciences*, vol. 252, no. 3 (September 1966), pp. 121/341 to 136/356.

On dying without an unmet need for medical care, I am responding to a point advanced by Norman Daniels, in "Health-Care Needs and Distributive Justice," *Philosophy and Public Affairs*, vol. 10, no. 2 (Spring 1981), pp. 146–79, at p. 172.

ACKNOWLEDGMENTS

Work on this book began in the spring of 1977 with an invitation from the Institute of Society, Ethics, and the Life Sciences (Hastings Center) to spend two days there discoursing on the concept of needs. At that time I was prepared, to some extent, to explain how useful the concept was; I did not fully realize that it broke down, indeed aggravated problems, in just the connection—medical ethics—in which people at the Center most hoped for some light from it. My debt to the Hastings Center for starting me up was just the first of a series of debts that I have incurred to institutions. The Research and Development Fund for the Humanities and Social Sciences of the Faculty of Graduate Studies, Dalhousie University, enabled me to make a trip to England and France in the spring of 1978, during which I looked for philosophers who were thinking about needs— or who could be brought to think about them. The same Fund later paid for a number of expenditures on bibliographical research. In 1978–79, I held a Leave Fellowship from the Social Sciences and Humanities Research Council of Canada to work on the emerging book. During my tenure of this fellowship, I was able to visit England again, and this time Scotland as well; and to sojourn for weeks at a time at the universities of Pittsburgh, Toronto, and Wisconsin (Madison), discussing my work with all the philosophers there who would listen. Acadia University, Bowdoin College, Colby College, the University of Toronto, the University of Pittsburgh, the University of Wisconsin, the University of Glasgow, the University of Manchester, the University of Sussex, the University of East Anglia, Univer-

329

sity College, London, and the University of Cambridge have all in some guise or other sponsored lectures by me on various aspects of the concept of needs—in some cases, more than one lecture. The philosophy department at Dalhousie has had to hear from me on the subject again and again at its weekly colloquia; and that department has provided me, in the person of Margaret Eva Odell, with secretarial help sufficient to have the manuscript typed through thrice over. (Margaret, now my wife, has also kept me cheerful by providing continuous personal support.) Mary Gordon, a research assistant furnished me by the Government of Canada under a student summer employment scheme, helped me very substantially in filling in gaps in the notes; and Marlene McAdoo, secretary in the Dalhousie department of political science, put these into their final typed form. The staff of the college office at Wolfson College, Cambridge, has cheerfully undertaken several rounds of photocopying during the final (indeed, by my reckoning the postultimate) stage of revision; and Wolfson College has also favored work at this stage by assigning me during a sabbatical year a commodious apartment that includes a large study.

My debts to persons intersect with my debts to institutions, but go far beyond. I might not have found myself, as soon as I did, writing another book on any subject, had Sanford Thatcher not, by suggesting that Princeton University Press would welcome my submitting a book, incited me to look for a subject. I shall not name everybody else who counted substantially even if I try, but let me try, by the imperfect device of citing the names of the people whose help I now remember most vividly: at Hastings Center, Ruth Macklin, Arthur Cohen, and Michael Bayles; at Manchester, Raymond Plant, Hillel Steiner, Ian Steedman, and Ursula Vogel; at London, Jerry Cohen; at Sussex, Peter Burnett, Malcolm Dando, and Istvan Mészáros; at East Anglia, Martin Hollis, Tim O'Hagen, and David Miller; at the University of York, Tony Culyer, Albert Weale, and Alan Williams; in France, Cornelius Castoriadis, Louis Althusser, Jules Vuillemin, Gilles Granger, and the Michel Dupuy family, especially Corinne; at Pittsburgh, Annette Baier, Kurt Baier, Nuel Belnap, C. G. Hempel, Ned McClennen, Nick Rescher, and Teddy Seidenfeld; at Toronto, Frank Cunningham, David Gauthier, Karin Jasper, William Leiss, Francis Sparshott, Jack Stevenson, and Wayne Sumner; at Wisconsin, Andrew Levine, Mark Singer, and Dan Wikler. Ted Bond did me the great honor of attending faithfully four discussions of the concept of needs that I held at Cambridge in the fall of 1985, and showed me, among other things, how the case for needs illustrates the general thesis of the objective independence of value that he argues for in his book *Reason and Value* (Cambridge University Press, 1983). I had helpful conversations at other times and places with Francis Jacques, Virginia Held, Storrs McCall, Derek Parfit, David-Hillel Ruben, Bill Terrell, and Barbara Harsanyi; helpful memoranda from Bob Eden, my colleague in political science at Dalhousie, and from Carol Karamessines, the secretary who was working with me at the beginning of the project; and a helpful late exchange of letters on medical aspects of needs with Bob Levine of the Yale Medical School. Erwin Klein and Lars Osberg of the Dalhousie department of economics helped in several ways, Osberg chiefly by strongly reiterating the skepticism of economists about needs, which I first heard from C. E. Lindblom. Even more skeptical—indeed, the most impassioned opponent of the concept of needs that I have encountered—has been Lewis Anthony Dexter, with whom I have had several stimulating rounds of disputation on the subject. It was a friend of my son Nicholas's, Sheila McKeough, who suggested that one basic need was to have some of one's preferences heeded; my first wife Alice made a point to me, which I may not have dealt with adequately in any respect, about the difficulty of discovering one's needs.

Of my Dalhousie colleagues, Bob Martin, Peter Schotch, Sue Sherwin, and Rich Campbell have taken the most interest in the project (some of them by usefully resisting it). Campbell read, in an early draft, several chapters through and gave me some searching comments, as did my son-in-law Nick Portman. Albert Weale did the same for the whole draft at that stage (when the final chapters were no more than sketches). The fullest and most detailed comments that I got on the draft then came from Greg Kavka. I do not know whether it is to him or to Heidi Hurd that the reader and I owe the most gratitude of all. Heidi read a late draft in which I had (I thought) dealt with Greg's and others' earlier comments. Besides helping with the bibliography and writing a couple of essays on points raised in the chapters on justice and utilitarianism, she gave me, for each of the first six chapters, a bundle of comments, amounting to a preview of what a maximally enthusiastic and energetic reader would make of the book. It was a preview that sent me back to the typewriter for weeks, to make dozens of clarifications. I only regret that she was called away to recasting culture and community in Alberta before she had a chance to work through chapters 7 and 8. I was glad, after the manuscript was submitted, to have the support of the two readers for Princeton University Press (Daniel Hausman and Henry Shue) and the endorsement of Marshall Cohen and Sandy Thatcher. The two readers supplied some searching criticisms, which my most substantial postultimate revisions try to meet; and several suggestions that I have been glad to take up, for example, drawing upon Dworkin's work on equality (a suggestion of Hausman's) and (a suggestion of Shue's) giving some attention to the possibility of relaxing strict final priority only for needs introduced with expansive uses of the concept (see Chapter 7, at the end). In the course of preparing the manuscript for printing, I have accepted a number of further improvements from people working for the Press; I can name and thank in particular Marilyn Campbell, Senior Editor, and the copyeditor, Kathleen Hyde.

It is clear from the list of people that I have just set forth that I have had a chance to concentrate in this book a large part of the wisdom currently available in the world on the topics that I have discussed. Would that I had done so! I thank all those people—and those that I have not remembered to name, though I should have—for the chance; and if (as is, alas!, surely the case) I have not succeeded in making the most of it, I nevertheless hope that their help has borne some worm-free fruit.

Dalhousie University
Halifax, Nova Scotia
March 1985
Wolfson College
Cambridge
January 1986

INDEX

Library of Congress Cataloging-in-Publication Data

Braybrooke, David.
Meeting needs.

(Studies in moral, political, and legal philosophy)
Bibliography: p.   Includes index.
1. Justice. 2. Basic needs. 3. Policy sciences. I. Title. II. Series.
JC578.B67 1987   320'.01'1   86–43130
ISBN 0–691–07727–4 (alk. paper)
ISBN 0–691–02259–3 (pbk.)